The Political Economy of Labour Market Institutions

The Political Economy of Labour Market Institutions

GILLES SAINT-PAUL

OXFORD
UNIVERSITY PRESS

OXFORD
UNIVERSITY PRESS

Great Clarendon Street, Oxford OX2 6DP

Oxford University Press is a department of the University of Oxford.
It furthers the University's objective of excellence in research, scholarship,
and education by publishing worldwide in

Oxford New York

Athens Auckland Bangkok Bogotá Buenos Aires Calcutta
Cape Town Chennai Dar es Salaam Delhi Florence Hong Kong Istanbul
Karachi Kuala Lumpur Madrid Melbourne Mexico City Mumbai
Nairobi Paris São Paulo Shanghai Singapore Taipei Tokyo Toronto Warsaw

with associated companies in Berlin Ibadan

Oxford is a registered trade mark of Oxford University Press
in the UK and certain other countries

Published in the United States
by Oxford University Press Inc., New York

British Library Cataloguing in Publication Data

Data available

Library of Congress Cataloging in Publication Data

Data available

ISBN 0–19–829332–1

1 3 5 7 9 10 8 6 4 2

Typeset by the HK Typesetting Ltd.
Printed in Great Britain
on acid-free paper by
Biddles Ltd., Guildford & King's Lynn

Contents

Introduction

1. In several economies the functioning of the labour market is altered by a set of institutions that restrict the ability of private parties to freely set quantities and prices, along with a tax system that affects the value of working and of not working, often at the expense of the former. Key examples include employment protection legislation, which restricts the firm's ability to reduce their workforce; minimum wages that put a floor on the remuneration of labour; collective bargaining agreements that impose a rigid pay scale across skills, often compressing the distribution of wages; work rules that make it easier for incumbent employees to achieve higher wages and/or lower working hours; unemployment benefits that increase the reservation wage of incumbent employees; active labour market policies where the government directly acts as a substitute for private agents in search and recruiting, etc. Furthermore, many labour market institutions manifest together, so that we witness the coexistence of competing *social models* for organizing the labour market.

Standard economic analysis holds that such institutions are harmful for job creation and typically increase unemployment. This is why they are often called 'rigid', a term that we shall use to refer to any regulation that reduces job creation. Most orthodox recipes against structural unemployment involve a reduction or elimination of such arrangements. But, if they hurt everybody, they would not be observed in practice. Indeed, many orthodox reforms of the labour market have proved difficult to implement because of the reluctance of politicians or else because they faced fierce opposition from large or powerful sectors of society. Opposition is made worse by the recognition that the orthodox recipes ultimately call into question the social model as a whole, implying that unemployment can be cured only at the cost of a radical change.

For these reasons it is important to explain why we observe such regulations. This book studies the economic conditions under which we expect a given set of labour market institutions to arise and remain stable.

It provides theoretical guidelines about the gainers and losers from a given institution, which helps to identify the constituency that supports it. It derives predictions about how a reform can be made politically viable, depending on its design and on the initial conditions prevailing at the time of its implementation.

2. Our theory is articulated around several central concepts, the most important one being that of a *rent*. By rent we refer to the difference between the welfare of an employed worker and that of an unemployed one, or, more precisely, to the difference between what an employed worker can get from his employment relationship and his *outside option*, i.e. what his welfare would be outside that relationship. In general, the outside option is exactly the value of being unemployed, but in some cases one has to be specific. The rent can be expressed in terms of wages, in which case it is the difference between the employee's wage and his alternative wage, which is the one which, if paid forever, would make him indifferent to being in work or being unemployed. In that case we call it the *intratemporal rent* or simply the *rent*. It can also be expressed as the plain welfare difference between an employed and an unemployed worker—where welfare is defined as the present discounted value of income flows—in which case we call it the *intertemporal,* or *total* rent.

The rent is one of the most appropriate measures of imperfect competition in the labour market. It tells us how far wages are from market clearing or, equivalently, how remote the unemployed are from underbidding the employed successfully. As long as the rent is positive, involuntary unemployment must arise, because in a perfectly competitive labour market any worker looking for a job could find one instantaneously. In that case the welfare of the unemployed would be equal to that of the employed, and there would not be a rent.

3. Rents arise for two sets of reasons. First, they may arise because of microeconomic frictions that prevent wages from fully adjusting downwards in situations of involuntary unemployment. Such frictions include imperfect observability of effort at the firm level; turnover costs and specific investment in the employment relationship that create a situation of bilateral monopoly, allowing workers to extract part of the surplus generated by their job; costly search and recruiting, which is a special case of specific investment; the impossibility of writing a complete contingent wage contract, etc. Second, there exist labour market institutions whose effect is precisely to give rise to such rents. They often do so by

magnifying the microeconomic frictions: for example, a hiring restriction would increase the cost of replacing a worker by another one, thus making him more specific and increasing his ability to extract part of the surplus.

Why should we expect some economies to have a greater rent, hence to be more 'rigid', than others? First of all, there may be genuine differences in the severity of microeconomic frictions. For example, if workers are less likely to move it may be more costly for a firm to locate an appropriate worker, which in turn will increase the amount of resources spent on recruiting and therefore the surplus appropriable by the worker. Second, the rent may be high because society *chooses* a set of labour market institutions that generate a high rent. In such a case, the high rent arises as the outcome of political decisions. For this to be the case, it must be that those who benefit from the rent are numerous and/or powerful enough. This raises the following question: how does the rent affect the welfare of various workers?

The two main variables that determine a worker's welfare are wages and the fraction of time he or she expects to spend in unemployment. That fraction is smaller for the currently employed than for the currently unemployed. It depends on the two key transition rates that characterize the state of the labour market. These are the job loss rate, which we also call *exposure,* and the job finding rate, also called *labour market tightness.* When the rent increases, each individual worker asks for a higher wage. This reduces firms' incentives to hire. In general equilibrium, wages must be brought in line with productivity, which means that they cannot increase by the full amount of the rent. In order to bring wages down, the outside option, or alternative wage, must fall, meaning that the unemployed are necessarily worse off. Consequently, the unemployed will always be against an increase in the rent. In fact, we are able to show a more general result implying that under certain conditions the unemployed will generally favour free markets and oppose government interventions in the labour market.

4. Therefore, the support for rents must come from a subset of employed workers. Because the rent reduces employment, it typically reduces the job finding rate and may also increase the job loss rate. This effect harms employed workers, so that if some of them gain it must be that they have greater wages. Hence we conclude that labour market institutions are supported by a group of employed workers because this allows them to increase their wages. It is exactly as if these workers were organized

in a labour union that achieved monopoly power on labour supply and set wages above market clearing in the pursuit of its members' self-interest. Here, instead, workers vote for an economywide institution which alters the environment in which wages are set, in such a way that they expect wages to actually rise in equilibrium by enough to make them better off. We refer to that mechanism as the *political insider mechanism*.[1] Workers may be unable to coordinate in order to form a labour union, but by voting in favour of an institution that raises rents they are able to collectively achieve a higher wage level exactly as if they were organized in a union. Labour market rigidities allow insiders to monopolize the market at the economywide level even though their bargaining power may be quite reduced at the firm level.

Just as in the case of a labour union, there must exist a favourable enough trade-off between wages and employment for the political insider mechanism to give rise to enough support for the rent-raising institution. Under constant returns to scale to labour, such a trade-off does not exist as equilibrium wages are pinned down by the marginal product of labour, which is constant. In such a case there is no support for the rent. This suggests that there must be decreasing returns to labour in order for the mechanism to be effective—then, a reduction in employment will be associated with a rise in workers' marginal product and therefore wages.

5. Under what circumstances are there decreasing returns to labour at the aggregate level? Economic theory teaches us that there must be some fixed factor whose quantity does not adjust when the labour input changes. Otherwise the standard argument that one could replicate the existing production structure would automatically lead to the presumption of constant returns to scale. If there exists such a fixed factor, then by reducing the amount of complementary input, wage increases redistribute from such a fixed factor to labour, while at the same time reducing the return to the fixed factor. Hence, labour market institutions are a device to redistribute income between factors of production.

It is tempting to think that this fixed factor is capital; one would then be talking about the traditional 'class struggle' between labour and capital, and labour market institutions would be one weapon that labour could use, in a democracy, to resolve that conflict in its favour. However, in this book we take a different view, which, while more unusual, is more in line with orthodox economic theory and at the same time, I

---

[1] See the work of Lindbeck and Snower (1988), who have studied how microeconomic frictions increase incumbent employees' bargaining power.

believe, more in line with the realities of distributive conflict in modern societies.

The main characteristic of capital is that it is not fixed, but accumulable. Any change that reduces its remuneration, such as a decline in the complementary labour input, induces a fall in investment and a subsequent reduction in the capital stock, up to the point where the return to capital is restored to its desired level.[2] Conversely, wages must have fallen back to their equilibrium level. In other words, when one takes into account the adjustment of the capital stock, in the long run everything is as if there were constant returns to labour as capital adjusts one-for-one to changes in employment, thus leaving wages and rates of return unaffected.

For this reason we believe that the most relevant conflict that lies at the root of labour market rigidities in modern societies is that between more and less skilled workers. Any observer of European labour markets in the last thirty years of the twentieth century would agree that it is a good stylized description of these markets to think of the labour market for high-skill workers as in equilibrium, with wages that adjust to offset demand and supply imbalances, while the low-skill labour market is in disequilibrium, with involuntary unemployment and unresponsive real wages. We will henceforth assume that the labour force can be partitioned in two groups, that we label for simplicity skilled and unskilled, although by unskilled we mean a wider group than is usually referred to, i.e. the bulk of low and medium skilled workers who are most affected by minimum wages, employment protection and collective agreements.[3] Labour market rigidities impose binding constraints on unskilled labour but not on skilled labour, whose market remains in equilibrium, so that employment of skilled labour remains essentially unchanged in response to a fall in unskilled employment.[4] It is therefore reasonable to treat

[2] This is true in a variety of growth models. If there is perfect international capital mobility the rate of return, in the long run, cannot be different from the world rate of return, adjusted for country-specific factors representing risk, etc. In closed economy models such as the Ramsey model, the rate of return to capital cannot be different from the rate of time preference of consumers. In the Solow model, the national savings rate pins down the capital/output ratio in the long run, and thus wages. See Blanchard and Fischer (1989) and Romer (1996) for a discussion of growth models.

[3] At the bottom there may exist a 'secondary sector' of the labour market, which may be able to escape such regulations. Workers in this sector are essentially paid their outside option and for our purposes will support the same policies as the unemployed.

[4] This obviously depends on the supply elasticity, which it is reasonable to consider as small.

skilled labour as a fixed factor.[5] Consequently, labour market rigidities mostly redistribute between skilled and unskilled labour.

6. The above discussion suggests that the political support for labour market rigidities would come from unskilled workers—and not all of them, only those who are employed. Unemployed unskilled workers and skilled workers lose from them and thus oppose it.

If this was the end of the story, societies where labour rigidities are observed would be very conflictive: even though the group we label unskilled may be numerous or powerful enough to impose the institutions that suit it, we should observe constant political activity of the skilled group against such institutions. Yet this does not square with reality, and we believe that this is because of the *cohesion* effects that labour market rigidities exert upon the employed workforce.

Such cohesion effects exist because even without rigidities, redistributive conflict would arise between skilled and unskilled workers. To the extent that the latter are poorer than the former, they have an incentive to expropriate from them, i.e. to vote for any institution that results in a transfer being made to the unskilled by the skilled. They would indeed be able to impose such a transfer if they are more numerous, or more politically powerful, than the skilled—i.e. more generally, if the decisive voter is poorer than the mean.

Labour market institutions provide another way to achieve such redistribution, although to a well trained economist it is a far-fetched and inefficient way of redistributing income, since it forces part of the workforce to be idle and excludes the poorest, i.e. the unemployed, from that redistribution. But the key point is that rigidity is supported by a very different *coalition* than fiscal redistribution. By increasing the wage income of unskilled workers, rigidity reduces their shortfall from the skilled, thus lowering the incentive to expropriate from them. As a result, part of the skilled will *also* support rigidity, because they recognize that less rigid institutions would intensify the redistributive conflict between skilled and unskilled workers. That is, rigidity reduces their wages but

---

[5] It is interesting to study why the argument made about the adjustment of capital does not carry to the case of skilled labour. Obviously, its supply is not nearly as elastic, in the long run, as that of capital. But leaving that aside, let us consider a rise in the wages of unskilled labour, which triggers a fall in unskilled employment. Clearly, the skilled wage falls. But, at the same time, the job prospects of a worker who would enter the labour market as unskilled also fall because of the rise in unskilled unemployment. Consequently, the returns to skill need not fall, they may even rise. See Saint-Paul (1994a, 1996a) and Cahuc and Michel (1996).

also reduces the transfer that the unskilled extract from them, and if the latter effect is stronger than the former, they will indeed support the rigid institution.

One can show, as is done in Chapter 3, that if we consider an economy with a large number of worker types, rather than just two types, then the preceding argument carries through, in the sense that rigidity will typically be supported by a 'middle class' of employed workers with intermediate skill levels. It will be opposed by the unemployed, who are the great losers, by the most skilled, who would gain most from an increase in the employment of complementary labour inputs and would thus prefer to have greater wages even though they would pay more taxes, and by the poorest workers, whose wage income is so low that they would be better off with greater transfers.

Therefore, while rigidity, just as fiscal transfers, redistributes from skilled to unskilled workers, relative to fiscal transfers they actually increase the cohesion of the middle class. The losers from rigidity—the unemployed and the two extremes of the distribution of income—are likely to be less powerful politically than the losers from redistribution. For this reason we expect rigidity to arise even though it is an inefficient way to solve the distributive conflict between skilled and unskilled workers.

In some sense, cohesion among those who keep their jobs is increased because the poorest are excluded from the redistributive game. This alleviates the redistributive conflict, because those who remain in that game are made more homogenous. At the same time the total amount of resources that can be shared among the 'ins'— the employed—is larger because those who have been excluded are precisely those who contributed less to the total surplus. Here we clearly see that there are two redistributive conflicts going on. One is between the skilled and the unskilled workers; we call it *internal conflict*. The other is between the unemployed and the employed; we call it *external conflict*. A key insight is that external conflict is more likely to arise, the more intense the internal conflict, i.e. the greater inequality among employed workers. If all workers had the same marginal product, they would all contribute the same to total output, and excluding some of them would not affect output per capita for those who remain. By contrast, when inequality is greater, the poorest contribute much less to total output than the richest, and excluding the former substantially increases what can be redistributed to each remaining worker.

7. Whether or not we expect rents to be a stable political equilibrium depends on three underlying parameters that characterize the functioning of the labour market.

Exposure tells us how often workers expect to lose their jobs. It depends on technology, which determines the frequency at which firms want to destroy jobs, on people's preferences and other sociological factors, which determine how often they may want to quit their jobs, and on institutional factors such as home ownership or other labour regulations such as employment protection. The lower the exposure, the more the employed expect to keep their job for a long time. Exposure enters as the weight of the unemployed's welfare in the employed's welfare. When it is lower, this weight is lower because the event of becoming unemployed is more remote and thus more heavily discounted. Therefore, when exposure is lower, the employed care less about harming the unemployed and are more likely to support high rents or, more generally, institutions that reduce the job finding rate. This result tells us that we expect rent-creating institutions to prevail in societies which, for other reasons, have low labour turnover and low mobility.

Elasticity, which we define as the elasticity of labour demand for unskilled labour, tells us how big the scope for wage increases is when employment of unskilled workers is reduced. It is the standard parameter that intervenes in any analysis of a union's preferred wage or, more generally, of any monopolistic price-setting behaviour. The greater that elasticity, the less wages rise when employment of unskilled workers increases, and the lower the political support for employee rents. Elasticity is intimately linked to the degree of complementarity between skilled and unskilled workers. It is smaller, the more the two are complements in production. This tells us that rigidity is good at redistributing between groups of people who cooperate strongly in the market.

Inequality, i.e. the gap between the skilled and unskilled productivities, determines the intensity of internal conflict. As we have argued, it is because of that internal conflict that it pays the middle class coalition to opt for rigid labour market institutions. Therefore we expect that the support for rents will be greater, the greater the inequality. This is actually true over some range, if inequality is low enough. But past a certain threshold inequality reduces the support for rents, because at high inequality levels the cost of rigidity in terms of job loss is too big.

8. The existence of rents acts as a catalyst for other labour market rigidities, because they increase the employed's support for such rigidities.

The clearest example is that of employment protection legislation. When rents exist, losing one's job is associated with a welfare loss, precisely equal to the total rent. The employed therefore have an incentive to reduce the likelihood of job loss by means of an employment protection legislation that prevents firms from freely reducing their workforce in a downturn. That incentive is greater, the greater the rent, i.e. the less competitive the labour market. In a perfectly competitive labour market the rent would be equal to zero and being unemployed would be equivalent to being employed because anyone could find a job instantaneously at the going wage. Thus there would be no support for employment protection.

Therefore, rigidities that create rents are likely to lead to other rigidities that protect rents, which further deteriorates the competitive performance of the labour market. Furthermore, it is also true that employment protection itself increases the political support for high rents. This is because employment protection reduces exposure to unemployment, and because the employed's most desired rent is greater, as we have seen, the less exposed they are. The causality therefore goes both ways: rent-creating and rent-protecting institutions reinforce each other. We say that there is a *politico-economic complementarity* between the two types of institution because if one exists, support for the other is greater. Politico-economic complementarities explain why labour market institutions work together, i.e. why we observe consistent competing social models rather than menus of institutions that span the whole range of possibilities.

9. While our theory is successful at explaining why rigid wages coexist with employment protection, it is harder to understand why generous unemployment benefits are also typically part of the picture. That is, the case in favour of politico-economic complementarities between rents and unemployment benefits is much weaker than for employment protection. At face value, one would be tempted to claim that in the absence of rents, there is no involuntary unemployment, and thus no need for workers to insure themselves against the unemployment risk. Closer examination, however, suggests that this is a fallacy. For when unemployment is very low, so is the financial cost of benefits, so that insurance is cheaper even though it is less desired. Indeed, if workers were voting under a veil of ignorance—i.e. not taking into account whether they are initially employed or unemployed but instead assigning an objective probability to each event based on the actual unemployment rate—they would elect full insurance regardless of the unemployment rate.

If unemployment benefits are merely set to provide insurance against job loss, it is essentially incorrect to treat them as a 'rigidity' in the same way as minimum wages or employment protection. True, they increase unemployment, as these other institutions. But while 'rigidities' typically benefit the employed at the expense of the unemployed, unemployment benefits obviously redistribute in the other direction. While the political system is likely to deliver, as we show, too much of these other rigidities relative to the social planner's optimum, it is likely to deliver too little unemployment insurance. While a reduction in exposure increases the support for rents and also the support for employment protection (as is discussed in Chapter 4), it reduces the employed's most preferred unemployment benefit level, since they care less about becoming unemployed. Finally, the financial burden of benefits reduces the scope for complementarities with other institutions: if unemployment is greater, say because minimum wages are higher, the tax cost of benefits is larger which reduces the employed's support for unemployment insurance.

Things are different, however, if unemployment benefits, which increase the worker's outside option in the wage formation process, are used by incumbent employees to achieve higher wages in equilibrium. They will be used as an instrument to achieve higher wages if other institutions cannot be perfectly manipulated in order to target the employed's most preferred wage level, say if there exists some ceiling on minimum wages or on the degree of wage compression that collective agreements may specify, or some constitutional limits on work rules that can be imposed on employers. In such a case the logic of the political insider mechanism applies to unemployment benefits as well, and they vary in a similar way to other rigidities. The unemployed will then want less insurance (at the margin) than the employed; the political system will deliver too generous benefits relative to the social optimum; and lower exposure will increase the employed's most desired benefit level. Furthermore, it may well be that benefits are more efficient at boosting wages when the rent is higher, which may generate a politico-economic complementarity between unemployment insurance and other institutions that allow insiders to achieve greater wages.

10. If, in a given country, the underlying economic conditions are such that a set of 'rigid' institutions provides a political equilibrium, it would be foolish for an economist or an international body to recommend that

they make their labour market more 'flexible'.[6] A government attempting such a reform would necessarily face political opposition, and could be forced to withdraw its reform to maintain itself in power. Even if the reform was made politically viable by some clever design to compensate losers (which is possible, as we discuss in Chapter 8), the resulting situation would be unstable and people would soon vote for a return to the previous arrangement. The reform would only have brought turbulence and policy uncertainty, and thus may have eliminated any of its positive employment effects.[7]

On the other hand, it may be that changes in underlying parameters make society less willing to keep its rigid institutions. This would happen, for example, if faster technological change increased exposure; if biases in that change increased inequality in the zone where it reduces the support for rigidity; if greater international capital mobility increased elasticity; or if some innovation increased substitutability between unskilled workers and some other factor, perhaps capital, again increasing elasticity. In such a case the support for rigidity would automatically be reduced, not least because it is more costly in terms of jobs.[8] If the change is strong enough then society would eventually shift from rigid to flexible institutions, even without any recommendation by economists.

The problem of reform, however, becomes more interesting if several stable outcomes may coexist. For example, underlying parameters may change in such a way that an economy which is originally flexible would not want to become rigid, but that an economy which is originally rigid would remain so, despite the fact that the support for the status quo would be lower than without the change in underlying parameters. That is, the support for rigidity is greater if it is originally the status quo than if it is not, i.e. there is *status quo bias*.

Status quo bias implies that an economy in a stable political equilibrium with reform imposed on it by a dictator would end up in another situation that would also be stable, i.e. once the dictator was gone there would not be sufficient political support to revert to the old ways. The problem of reform becomes meaningful if there is status quo bias be-

---

[6] Unless, obviously, the political support for rigidity arises from ignorance about its adverse economic effects. In that case, however, policy recommendations are not really needed: dissemination of economic theory and evidence should be enough.

[7] For a convincing example, see Bertola and Ichino (1995).

[8] See Krugman (1995) for an argument that skill-biased technical change has increased unemployment in Europe in the 1970's because relative wages have failed to adjust, although Card *et al.* (1995) find a much more mixed picture.

cause the economy may be locked into an 'undesirable' situation (from the viewpoint of some social welfare measure that differs from the decisive voter's objective) and could be led, by some properly designed reform, to a more desirable, equally stable, equilibrium. Status quo bias also implies that institutions are persistent, and that different social models may be observed across two economies with similar underlying characteristics because one of them experienced some specific shocks in the past, which led to institutions that survived into the present even though the shock has finally died out.[9] Complementarities are likely to increase the status quo bias, particularly if a comprehensive reform of the labour market cannot be written on the political agenda.

11. Status quo bias arises when a given set of institutions typically create their own constituency. The existence of high rents is a powerful source of status quo bias. Any reform implies some labour reallocation, and those who expect to lose their jobs are likely to oppose the reform. Clearly, the greater the rent, the more these people expect to lose, and the greater their opposition to the reform. When rents are large, institutions may create their own constituency by maintaining a fraction of the workforce in activities that exist precisely because of that institution. This is what we call the *constituency effect*. The strength of the status quo bias generated by the constituency effect is greater, as we saw, the greater the rent (without rents job loss does not make the worker unhappy); it is also greater, the lower the political weight of the unemployed. The unemployed are those whose job finding prospects are improved by change, so they provide a counterweight to the constituency of job losers; the lower their political power, the smaller that counterweight. Finally, the constituency effect generates a stronger status quo bias, the more sluggish the job creation process, because those who expect to find jobs because of the reform again provide less of a counterweight to those who expect to lose their jobs.

The constituency effect is particularly prominent when one considers institutions such as employment protection. Employment protection prevents firms from getting rid of their workers when hit by a shock that should make them obsolete. Consequently, there exists a mass of workers whose jobs would be instantaneously destroyed if that regula-

---

[9] In Saint-Paul (1997a), I speculated that the tight labour markets that Europe experienced in the post-war period subsequently allowed insiders to get high rents, which eventually led to a set of rigid institutions that persisted beyond the period of tight labour markets.

tion were slashed, who provide a powerful constituency in favour of the status quo. Clearly, these workers would not exist if the economy did not have employment protection, for any job which becomes obsolete would then be instantaneously destroyed.

Workers' uncertainty about whether they will end up in the pool of losers or gainers from the reform is also likely to strengthen the status quo bias by virtue of a mechanism which we call the *identifiability effect*. People know for sure their situation under the status quo, but may be uncertain about where they will end up after a reform. If the decisive voter is employed, then an increase in uncertainty typically increases his likelihood to end up unemployed as the outcome of the reform, which, as long as rents are positive, reduces his support for the reform. If the losers from the reform were perfectly identified, to the extent that they are a minority, the decisive voter would typically expect to keep his job, and would support the reform. It is because it redistributes losses from nondecisive to decisive voters that uncertainty increases status quo bias. In a world where the decisive voter is employed and where losers are job losers, this condition is likely to be satisfied.

12. How can reform, other than implemented by a dictator, overcome the status quo bias and lift the economy from an undesirable, stable political equilibrium to a more desirable one? This is a vast topic which we only deal with in part and for specific cases. Two general principles emerge, that are illustrated by the examples studied in the second part of this book.

First, reform should be designed so as to redistribute gains from nondecisive to decisive voters. For example, in Chapter 8 we study how reform can be made viable by means of a two-tier system that preserves the privileges of the originally employed workers while the new legislation applies only to future hires. It is shown that the financial burden of such reform falls upon the firms that employ the incumbent workers. Firms have zero political weight in our analysis, so that the reform design clearly redistributes gains from nondecisive agents to decisive ones. If these firms could vote, they would not accept the reform. Another example is that of a reform which specifies that the redundancies that take place during a certain period around the date of the legislative change should proceed according to some ranking of employees by seniority. Such a clause would overcome the identifiability effect by guaranteeing the decisive employed voter that he will not lose his job because of the reform.

Second, one can take advantage of initial conditions such that the support for the status quo is small. For example, in the case of employment protection, an economic boom reduces the share of old, obsolete jobs in total employment, and therefore the constituency against reform. Or, the support for reduction in wages may be greater at the start of a recession when the employed are more exposed to unemployment.

With this discussion of reform we conclude the general presentation of the theory. It is now time to go into the details. The book is divided in two parts: the first part, Chapters 1–5, discusses the political support for labour market institutions. The second part, Chapters 6–9, analyses the obstacles to reform and draws conclusions about how it should be designed.

Appendix. Some notes on the literature

This book is not meant to be a survey or a textbook but aims to bring together my research results over the last seven years and articulate them into a coherent theory of labour market institutions. The reader can refer to my articles and working papers cited in the bibliography, although the present book contains a large number of new results and new interpretations of previous results.

There are, however, several strands of literature connected with this work, which we discuss here.

First, there is the vast literature on the effect of labour market rigidities on employment performance, which is often cast in the European context. For surveys, the reader can refer to Layard *et al.* (1991) for a thorough exposition of the modern theory of equilibrium unemployment, as well as Bean (1994a, b), Blanchard (1996), and Siebert (1997) for more policy-oriented views. All these surveys more or less support the 'orthodox' view that labour rigidities are the key responsible for high unemployment, a view shared by the OECD (1995), while Alogoskoufis *et al.* (1995) are more balanced, and Manning (1995) challenges the orthodox view. Finally, Bertola (1998) provides a detailed survey on the impact of microeconomic rigidities on aggregate employment, while Phelps (1994) develops a general equilibrium theory of economic activity where labour rigidities play a central role. This literature inevitably leads to a derivative one which discusses the impact of policies to cure unemployment; a good panorama can be found in de la Dehesa *et al.* (1997), while Calmfors (1994) focuses on active labour market policy.

Second, the present work is related to the traditional, but still active, literature on political economy and endogenous policy determination. The existence of a redistributive system of taxes and transfers plays a key role in determining the political support for labour market institutions, as we argue in Chapter 3, and this has been studied in a voting context by Meltzer and Richard (1981) which forms the basis of the fiscal model of Chapter 3. Along with that there exists a vast literature on the political economy of fiscal policy, see e.g. Alesina (1994) and Persson *et al.* (1997).

One difficulty with the political economy approach is that there is no canonical model of how collective decisions are made; in this book we follow the tradition of the median voter theory, which states that policy is determined by the preferences of some decisive voter, which is often the median of the relevant distribution of tastes, and will, importantly, be considered as employed. But we take it more as a useful metaphor than as an exact description of the complex process of political decision making. Alternative approaches could be considered where competing interest groups devote resources to lobbying activities, as in Krueger (1974), Becker (1983, 1985), Bernheim and Winston (1986), and Grossman and Helpman (1994).

Third, various works, other than mine, have studied the political economy of specific labour market institutions from a political economy perspective. These include both works on the determinants of specific institutions, as well as works more specifically concerned with reform. Here one has to mention the important literature on corporatism, which studied the impact on macroeconomic performance of economy-wide wage setting arrangement by centralized unions and employer organizations, in a context where government policy was sometimes treated endogenously. See, for example, Calmfors and Driffill (1988), Calmfors and Horn (1985), Burda (1997), Teulings (1997), Driffill and Van Der Ploeg (1993), and Newell and Symons (1987) for recent developments. Olson's well known work (1982) should also be mentioned. It approaches rigidities from a very different angle from this book, based on the view that there is a tendency for rigidities to rise over time because interest groups tend to become more powerful in stable environments.

Among the recent papers that bear some connection with the present work we should mention Acemoglu and Robinson (1998), who develop a theory of how inefficient redistribution may arise; Robinson (1998), who studies the political support for worker bargaining power in an over-lapping generations model, and shows that policy cycles may emerge;

Grüner (1999), who shows the impossibility of using transfers to make a labour market reform viable whenever there is incomplete information; Hassler *et al.* (1998) who, following Wright (1986), study some aspects of unemployment benefits that are complementary to the ones studied in Chapter 5; Frederiksson (1997), who went further in the analysis of the political support for active labour market policy; and Krusell and Rios-Rull (1996), who do not study labour market institutions but whose analysis of the political economy of stagnation is related to our discussion of employment protection in Chapter 4.

Empirical work is inevitably fragile and complicated, and we have preferred to leave these aspects aside in this book, whose focus is theoretical. In Saint-Paul (1996c, 1999a) I have found some empirical evidence consistent with the theory elaborated here, but it is subject to many different interpretations. One should also mention the work by Gray (1998, 1995), on the determinants of French assistance programmes, and Di Tella and McCulloch (1995), on the determinants of unemployment benefits. There exists also an empirical literature in the American tradition on congressional voting records, that has studied the determinants of preferences for things such as unemployment benefits and minimum wage rates: see Blais *et al.* (1989), Lipford and Yandle (1987), Silbermann and Durden (1976), and Uri and Mixon (1980). Lastly, Rodrik (1999) has found that democracies pay higher wages than nondemocracies, in accordance with the view that the decisive voter is likely to be an employed worker.

Finally, one should mention that there exists a strand of literature which approaches labour market institutions from a very different perspective, seeing them as the proper response of a benevolent policymaker to labour market imperfections. Such a view can be found in the works, for example, of Agell (1999) and Agell and Lommerund (1992), who insist on the role of rigidities as social insurance; of Guesnerie and Roberts (1987), who argue that if taxes are too distortionary minimum wages are an optimal second best redistribution tool; and of Acemoglu (1996), who makes a case in favour of employment protection in search markets, because there can be too little investment in human capital. While the present book mostly takes a positive perspective, at various points we will also look at the social optimum. Our results generally support the conclusion that if the decisive voter is employed, there will be too much rigidity relative to the social optimum, but that the social optimum may well involve a positive level of labour market regulation. It is unlikely, however, that the rigidities that are observed in practice are the most adequate policy instruments in order to cure labour market failures. For a discussion in the case of employment protection, see Chapter 4.

Part I

The support for labour market regulations

1
The no-rent society

We start by describing the functioning of a perfect, or almost perfect, labour market. It bears little relationship to the real world, but is a useful starting point in order to discuss where the incentives to alter the functioning of the market come from, and will help us to introduce some key concepts and notations.

In our utopia, like in the real world, workers are assigned to jobs and sometimes they lose their jobs. However, having a job does not give the holder of the job any special advantage relative to other workers. The employer can instantaneously locate another worker in the labour market, perhaps an unemployed one, and replace his employee with that new one. The incumbent employee is in no situation to ask for a wage that would make him strictly better off than some other equivalent participant in the labour market, for if he tried his employer would instantaneously fire him and replace him with that other participant.

This is a *no-rent* society: holding a job does not make you any happier than any alternative situation. The employed cannot increase their welfare beyond that of the unemployed, in other words they do not have a rent. In the rest of the book we define the rent as the difference in welfare between an employed worker and an unemployed one.

In such a world there cannot be any involuntary unemployment; an unemployed worker who would be strictly better off if he or she held some job would instantaneously be able to underbid the holder of that job and replace him. Unemployment is either voluntary, in the sense that the unemployed are actually indifferent between their situation and having a job, or there can be full employment. Full employment does not mean that unemployment never occurs. Rather, those who lose their jobs stay unemployed for a negligible amount of time and find a job moments after. Because the contribution of their unemployment spell to their lifetime welfare is negligible, they are indeed as happy as an employed worker.

In such a society, would people support an institution or policy that alters the functioning of the labour market? In order to answer that question, we need to be able to compute how such institutions affect individual welfare.

1.1 Basic notions

At this stage, it is useful to introduce some formulas. Assume that an individual's welfare, or 'utility', within any given period only depends on his income. If that person is employed his welfare is equal to W, where W is the wage, which we take as fixed for the time being, while if he is not it is equal to B, where B is whatever income flow accrues to the unemployed. If the person does not know whether he is going to be employed or unemployed in period t his expected utility is $U_t = p_t W + (1 - p_t)B$, where p_t is the probability that he is employed in period t.

In this book we will take a dynamic perspective, because we are interested in the consequences of individual mobility between various situations (essentially being employed or being unemployed). For this reason, we must be able to compute somebody's intertemporal welfare, which is the discounted sum of his entire flow of utility from now to the end of his life. Thus our individuals live several periods, and their utility is the present discounted value of their expected income flow:

$$V_t = \sum_{s=t}^{T} U_s \frac{1}{(1 + R)^{s-t}},$$

where R is the discount rate and V_t the individual's utility as of t. In that formula U_s is the expected income flow at s from the point of view of period t, that is to say p_s is the probability of being employed at s conditional on the information available at t.

It is possible to rewrite this formula recursively, that is to say to define today's welfare as a function of tomorrow's welfare:

$$V_t = U_t + \frac{E_t V_{t+1}}{1 + R}, \tag{1.1}$$

where E_t denotes the expectation conditional on the information available at date t. This formula holds at any date except the last one, and it will be convenient to let T become very large, that is to assume that people forever live.

We assume that at t people know for sure whether they are going to be employed or not at t, and that they have a probability S of losing their job between t and $t + 1$, so that their probability of being employed at $t + 1$ is $1 - S$. It is then useful to make a distinction between the welfare of an employed worker and the welfare of an unemployed worker. Let us call them V_{et} and V_{ut}. One can then rewrite (1.1) the following way:

$$V_{et} = W + \frac{1}{1 + R} \left[(1 - S)V_{et+1} + SV_{ut+1} \right]. \qquad (1.2)$$

This formula tells us the following. The welfare of an employed worker today is equal to the sum of his wage today and the discount factor times his expected welfare tomorrow. His expected welfare tomorrow is equal to the probability that he is employed tomorrow times the welfare of an employed tomorrow, plus the probability that he is unemployed tomorrow times the welfare of an unemployed tomorrow.

Similarly we assume that an unemployed worker finds a job between t and $t + 1$ with probability A, while he or she remains unemployed with probability $1 - A$. An equivalent formula can then be written for the unemployed:

$$V_{ut} = B + \frac{1}{1 + R} \left[(1 - A)V_{ut+1} + AV_{et+1} \right]. \qquad (1.3)$$

In the formulation above, time is 'discrete': it is represented as a succession of dates or 'periods'. But, we actually prefer to use a continuous time representation. It is not difficult to extend our formulas to a continuous time framework. This amounts to assuming that there is a very small time interval dt between period t and period $t + 1$, neglecting second-order terms in dt, and expressing variables in a flow fashion, i.e. per unit of time. Given that the time interval is very small, the corresponding wage, discount rate, and probabilities of changing situation must also be very small (one earns very little during a second, has a very small chance of losing one's job next second, and will lend at very low interest rate if reimbursed next second). These quantities are therefore infinitesimal and it is their equivalent per unit of time that is finite. Thus the wage paid during the small time interval dt is $W = w\,dt$, where w is the wage rate per unit of time. Similarly we have $B = b\,dt$, $R = r\,dt$, with r and b the discount rate and the unemployed's income per unit of time. Finally, the probability per unit of time (or flow probability) of losing one's job is $s = S/dt$, and the flow probability of finding a job is $a = A/dt$. Unlike probabilities that are between zero and one, flow probabilities can be arbitrarily large. They express the fact that the probability of changing situation during an infinitesimal time interval is infinitesimal (thus automatically lower than one), but can be quite large per unit of time, i.e. relative to the length of the interval.

Substituting these definitions into the above formulae and neglecting second-order terms we get their continuous time equivalent. The welfare of the employed now evolves according to

$$rV_e = w + \dot{V}_e + s(V_u - V_e). \tag{1.4}$$

Here r is the real rate of interest, w the real wage, s the probability per unit of time that the worker loses his or her job, and the dot denotes time derivative: $\dot{V}_e = dV_e/dt$. Similarly, the welfare of an unemployed worker is

$$rV_u = b + \dot{V}_u + a(V_u - V_e). \tag{1.5}$$

These equations are the limits of (1.2) and (1.3) in the continuous time case. Written in this form they are analogous to an arbitrage equation for the price of an asset. For example, the left-hand side of (1.4) is the rate of return r times the value V_e of an asset which is 'being employed'. (1.4) then tells us that this must be equal to a dividend, which is the flow of income to an employed, i.e. the wage, plus expected capital gains, which is the sum of the deterministic rate of appreciation of the asset $\dot{V}_e$ plus the probability that the person loses his or her job a times the capital loss associated with that event, which is simply the difference $V_u - V_e$ between the value of being unemployed and the value of being employed. A similar interpretation can be made of (1.5). This analogy is useful because it allows us to write directly equations such as (1.4) and (1.5) without undertaking all the steps required by their recursive interpretations.

Two crucial variables are a and s, the job finding and job separation rates. a describes the state of the labour market. The higher a, the tighter the labour market. If a is equal to zero then the unemployed never find a job. If it is equal to infinity then they find a job instantaneously. Average unemployment duration is equal to $1/a$. s is the probability per unit of time that an employed worker loses his job. The higher s, the more the employed are exposed to unemployment.

The variables a and s determine the unemployment rate in steady state. A fraction a of the unemployed find a job per unit of time. A fraction s of the employed lose their job per unit of time. If N denotes the total labour force and L total employment, the instantaneous change in employment at any point in time is given by the difference between the outflow from unemployment and the inflow into unemployment:

$$\dot{L} = a(N - L) - sL, \tag{1.6}$$

or equivalently

$$\dot{u} = s(1 - u) - au, \tag{1.7}$$

where $u = (N - L)/N$ is the unemployment rate.

In steady state, unemployment is constant, so that the outflow from unemployment is equal to the inflow into unemployment. Therefore, in steady state:

$$u = \frac{s}{s + a}. \tag{1.8}$$

So far there are only two types of worker, employed and unemployed. Thus the inflow rate into unemployment is exactly equal to the probability that an employed worker loses his job. We also want to allow for new entrants into the labour market; this will give us an extra degree of freedom which allows us to disentangle the inflow into unemployment from the employed's probability of losing a job. To do so we just assume that a fraction p per unit of time of the whole labour force retires, and that retirement yields a zero discounted utility $V_r = 0$. This outflow from the labour force is compensated by an inflow of p people per unit of time. We naturally assume that all new entrants start being unemployed: to find a job, one must first look for one, which by definition means being unemployed.

It is easy to extend (1.4) and (1.5) to take this new source of mobility into account if one sticks to the asset market interpretation. The only thing one has to do is to add to the right-hand sides of (1.4) and (1.5) the capital gains associated with the event of retiring from the workforce. This capital gain is $V_r - V_e = -V_e$ for the employed and $-V_u$ for the unemployed. Consequently, (1.4) and (1.5) now become

$$rV_e = w + \dot{V}_e + s(V_u - V_e) - pV_e \tag{1.9}$$

$$rV_u = b + \dot{V}_u + a(V_u - V_e) - pV_u. \tag{1.10}$$

The computation of the unemployment rate is also changed. In equation (1.6) we have to add the employment outflow due to new entrants:

$$\dot{L} = a(N - L) - (s + p)L.$$

From there it is easy to see that in steady state the unemployment rate is now given by

$$u = \frac{s + p}{a + s + p}. \tag{1.11}$$

Given the transition rates s, p, and a, and given the income of the employed w and of the unemployed b, the above analysis allows us to compute the evolution of unemployment, its steady state level, and the welfare of the employed and the unemployed. But not all these variables are exogenous. More specifically, we are going to assume that b, s, and p are exogenous, and a and w are endogenous. Equilibrium in the labour market is therefore characterized by a certain wage and a certain degree of labour market tightness. These two variables are then determined by firms' labour demand behaviour, and by the process of wage formation, which itself depends on how intensively the unemployed compete for jobs.

In our utopian society, this competition is strong enough to eliminate any welfare difference between the employed and the unemployed. If the employed were strictly better off than the unemployed these would be pleased to offer their services for lower wages and firms would instantaneously fire their employees to replace them with unemployed applicants. Therefore, the welfare of the employed cannot be different from that of the unemployed:

$$V_e = V_u. \tag{1.12}$$

Taking differences between (1.9) and (1.10) we get that

$$(r + s + a + p)(V_e - V_u) = w - b + \frac{\mathrm{d}}{\mathrm{d}t}(V_e - V_u). \tag{1.13}$$

At face value this is hard to reconcile with the no-rent hypothesis (1.12), unless unemployment benefits are precisely equal to the wage: $w = b$. In that case people are clearly indifferent between being employed and unemployed, regardless of the job finding rate a. However, there does exist a solution for $w > b$. It is given by $a = \infty$. If at the same time $V_e = V_u$, the left-hand side of (1.13) is then indeterminate and that equation is satisfied in a general sense. This simply means that if the employed have a greater income than the unemployed, the only way for the unemployed to have the same welfare as the employed is through full employment or, equivalently, instantaneous job finding. In our economy everybody is employed all his life. Those who lose their jobs find another one the minute after.

How, then, is the wage w determined? Assume that being employed means producing a certain amount of 'cookies' per unit of time and that these cookies are given to the worker. Then w is simply equal to how many cookies one produces. This assumption means that the marginal product of labour is constant.[1] It will hold if there are constant returns to scale in the production function, if there is no fixed factor other than labour, and if workers are paid their marginal product. In that case the wage is entirely determined by technology: w is a fixed technological parameter.

Is everybody in this utopian world as happy as possible? Clearly, as long as $w > b$ the best one can do is to produce all the time, which is what happens in our full employment equilibrium.

In such a world people would unanimously oppose any labour market institution of any sort.

1.2 Introducing rents

Conversely, if such an institution exists in the first place, they would unanimously support its removal (provided it is the only rigidity). To see this, it is useful to consider the impact of an institution that generates a *rent* for employed workers, i.e. that enables them to set wages so as to end up strictly better off than the unemployed. That would be the case of any hiring or firing rule that would make it more costly for the employer to get rid of the worker and replace it with an outsider in the process of bargaining, or in case of misconduct. To use a popular but vague definition, we shall refer throughout the book to institutions of this type as 'rigidities'. We will not take rigidity as a well defined concept of our theory but rather as a shortcut to refer to any institution that reduces the job finding rate a.

A simple way to represent such a rent is to assume that the employed must be paid enough so as to be better off than the unemployed by a fixed amount equal to Q (in intertemporal terms). Thus the no-rent condition

---

[1] Provided also that firms are wage takers.

(1.12) must be replaced with

$$V_e = V_u + Q. \tag{1.14}$$

Equation (1.14) tells us that wages are set in such a way that the welfare of an employed worker, in present discounted terms, must exceed the welfare of an unemployed worker by an amount Q. V_u intervenes because it is the worker's *outside option,* that is, what the worker would get outside the employment relationship. Q is the (total) *rent*; the greater the rent, the greater the welfare that the employed can get relative to their outside option. Q measures how far the labour market is from a competitive one, or how rigid real wages are. It is taken as fixed for convenience; in fact it is likely to depend on many variables, as discussed in the appendix. Throughout the book we shall use (1.14) whenever the effect that we are dealing with can be exposed under the assumption of a fixed total rent Q, but we will depart from it when the effects that we are considering rest on the dependence of the total rent on some characteristic of the economy.

One may be surprised at the fact that wages do not enter explicitly into (1.14), which is supposed to determine them. However, it is not difficult to express it in terms of wages. For that, we just have to eliminate V_e between (1.14) and (1.9), assuming for simplicity that we are in steady state ($\dot{V}_e = \dot{V}_u = 0$). We get

$$w = (r + p)V_u + (r + s)Q. \tag{1.15}$$

This equation tells us that the wage is the sum of two terms. The first term $(r + p)V_u$ is the annuity value of being unemployed, i.e. the *alternative* wage that would make the worker just indifferent between working and not working. The second term is the annuity value of the rent, i.e. the extra flow of income that must be paid to the worker in order for his intertemporal welfare to exceed that of an unemployed by Q. This formula has the convenient property that a tighter labour market increases wages. The reason is that a tighter labour market increases the unemployed's probability of finding a job and therefore V_u. For (1.14) to still hold, V_e must rise accordingly, so that wages have to go up, as (1.15) makes clear.

Equation (1.14) also tells us that rents necessarily generate a positive level of involuntary unemployment. The unemployed must be strictly worse off than the employed—so any unemployment must be involuntary—and at full employment an unemployed worker would find a job instantaneously (i.e. $a = +\infty$ in (1.10) and (1.5)). But then the welfare of the unemployed would be equal to that of the employed, which contradicts (1.14).

Equation (1.14) may represent a variety of mechanisms. Economists have developed models where rents must be paid to workers to deter them from misconduct (the *efficiency wage* model), or because it is costly for the firm to replace incumbent employees with outsiders, which enables them to extract surplus from the firm and end up better off than the unemployed (the *insider–outsider* model).

In general the rent will be affected by many factors, including other parameters of the model such as r or s, but for the time being it is sufficient to consider it as exogenous, even though this is not the most reasonable assumption. In the appendix to this chapter we discuss a variety of versions of the efficiency wage and insider-outsider models that have different implications for the determination of the rent Q. We further discuss the dependence of Q on the model's parameters in Chapter 4, when it becomes relevant.

Under both the 'efficiency wage' and the 'insider–outsider' interpretation it is not difficult to see that a wide array of labour market institutions affect the rent. This includes unfair dismissal legislation, hiring rules that make it costly to find an outsider, and more generally any institution that either directly affects wages such as minimum wages and collective bargaining or that affects the firm's ability to replace insiders with outsiders. Even in a completely unregulated labour market the microeconomic frictions pointed out by these models will persist, so that Q cannot fall to zero. However, to make our point most clearly we shall assume that people can actually choose any level of the rent Q between zero and infinity. Despite that the rent is only indirectly affected by institutions we consider what happens if people directly vote on it.

Equation (1.13) allows us to compute the steady-state value of labour market tightness. Substituting (1.14) we get that

$$a = \frac{w - b}{Q} - (r + s + p). \tag{1.16}$$

Equation (1.16) tells us that, given the rent, there exists a positive relationship between a, the degree of labour market tightness, and w, the wage. This relationship represents the wage formation mechanism. The tighter the labour market, the more easily the unemployed find a job, and the larger the wage that the employed can get.

The corresponding unemployment rate can be obtained by substituting (1.16) into (1.9):

$$u = \frac{(s + p)Q}{(w - b) - rQ}. \tag{1.17}$$

The larger the rent Q, the less tight the labour market: unemployment and unemployment duration are longer. Since it is not possible to do better than producing cookies all the time, the way the rent is enforced, in equilibrium, is not by increasing the welfare of the employed but by maintaining the unemployed out of jobs longer. That way they are strictly worse-off than the employed because they expect to earn b rather than w for a longer fraction of their lifetime than the employed, contrary to the previous case where they expected to find a job right away. The rent makes its way into lower employment through the following economic mechanism. Starting from full employment an increase in the rent from zero to Q creates an incipient increase in the wage required by workers. Job creation falls and unemployment start rising. The rise in unemployment lowers the welfare of the unemployed and consequently the wage required by the employed in order to be better off than the unemployed by Q. This process continues until (1.14) is matched with the fixed equilibrium wage w. Therefore it is the labour market tightness parameter a rather than the wage w that adjusts to restore equilibrium. Unemployment acts as a discipline device to prevent wages from rising above the level guaranteed by the economy's productive ability.[2]

The mechanism is represented in Figure 1.1 in the (a, w) plane. The upward sloping curve WS represents the wage formation process, summarized by equation (1.16). The horizontal line MP is the labour demand, or marginal product, schedule, which tells us that wages are technologically determined. An increase in the rent shifts WS upwards to WS'. At the same unemployment rate (or tightness) the economy would move from E to F, which is above MP: employees would have to be paid a wage higher than productivity. Firms then stop hiring, unemployment rises, and the economy ends up at the new equilibrium point E'. (Alternatively, we could draw the same diagram with employment rather than labour market tightness on the horizontal axis.)

That people uniformly dislike rents can be seen by solving for V_e and V_u. Substituting (1.14) into (1.9) and (1.10) in steady state we get:

$$V_e = \frac{w - sQ}{r + p} \tag{1.18}$$

[2] Under the efficiency wage interpretation of (1.14) it is in a literal sense that unemployment acts as a discipline device: its threat prevents workers from cheating.

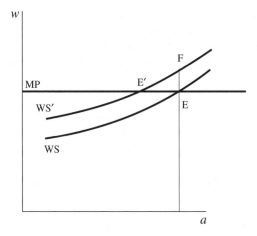

Figure 1.1. Wage and tightness determination: impact of an increase in the rent

$$V_u = \frac{w - (r + p + s)Q}{r + p}. \tag{1.19}$$

A unit increase in Q lowers the employed's welfare by $s/(r+p)$, and the unemployed's welfare by $(r + p + s)/(r + p)$, which is larger. The unemployed, therefore, suffer more from the rent than the employed. But both agree that it should be dismantled, or set as low as possible. So far there is no conflict of interest between the employed and the unemployed, despite the fact that Q determines the difference between the welfare of the former and that of the latter.

So, workers dislike rents. What about capitalists? Here, profits are constantly equal to zero because of perfect competition among firms; wages are equal to productivity. So whoever owns a firm is constantly indifferent about Q. Competition ensures that all losses and gains from policy changes are passed on to workers.[3]

What about a social planner? Its objective is the present discounted value of output, which here is simply given by

$$\Omega_t = N \int_t^{+\infty} ((1 - u_v)w_v + u_v b)e^{-r(v-t)} \, dv.$$

---

[3] This will change when we consider turnover costs, as established firms may make capital gains or losses when there is a policy shift, even though their expected present discounted value was equal to zero when they entered the market.

Note that b is counted as output since we have assumed it is 'manna from heaven' rather than a transfer. Social welfare can equivalently be computed as the sum of all individuals' utilities and all firms' present discounted profits. Since the latter are always zero, we have

$$\Omega_t = N(u_t V_{ut} + (1 - u_t)V_{et}). \qquad (1.20)$$

If, as will happen in Chapter 4, there existed firms with a nonzero value, one would have to add the value of these firms to (1.20). Here, however, maximizing the present discounted value of output is like maximizing the sum of the employed's and the unemployed's utility. One can thus check that if both the employed and the unemployed gain from a policy shift, Ω_t unambiguously increases.[4] Therefore, not surprisingly, the social planner will also elect the lowest possible value of the rent Q.

Another labour market institution that enters the analysis is b, the unemployment benefit level. Conceptually, b affects labour market outcomes differently from the rent Q. While Q affects the welfare of the employed differently from that of the unemployed, b affects them by the same amount. This is because it affects the employed's welfare through their 'outside value' (or 'outside option'), that is, through their welfare should their employment relationship be terminated, which is defined by V_u. That outside value affects wage determination in most models of wage formation, including the one we are dealing with here. In principle, an increase in b makes unemployment less unbearable and increases the workers' outside option and consequently their wage. Under our assumption of a fixed rent, the employed's change in welfare

---

[4] For simplicity we have not discussed how the economy adjusts to a change in parameters. One may either consider u as a state variable, in which case a policy change has no impact effect on u, or allow for massive job creation and job destruction, in which case u can jump. In that latter case, u_t can be considered as the pre-reform unemployment level in (1.20), but V_e and V_u can no longer be taken as their steady state levels defined in (1.18) and (1.19). That is, in (1.20) one should replace V_e and V_u by $V_{et}^* = (1-p)V_e + pV_u$ and $V_{ut}^* = (1 - q)V_u + qV_e$, where V_e and V_u are still defined by (1.18) and (1.19), while p_t (resp. q_t) is the probability than an employed (resp. unemployed) worker finds himself unemployed (resp. employed) immediately after the reform.

If one defines u_t^* as the post-reform unemployment rate, one must have $u_t^* = p(1 - u_t) + (1 - q)u_t$, implying

$$\begin{aligned}\Omega_t &= u_t V_{ut}^* + (1 - u_t)V_{et}^* \\ &= u_t^* V_u + (1 - u_t^*)V_e.\end{aligned}$$

So, one can alternatively compute social welfare using the post-reform unemployment rates and the steady state values of V_e and V_u.

is by construction equal to that of the unemployed's: the relationship $V_e = V_u + Q$ must hold. An institution that works its way through the outside option always generates unanimity between the employed and the unemployed, unlike institutions that increase the rent. (This property has important consequences for the political viability of some reforms—see Chapter 8.) This is so, unless the outside option of the employed is different from the value of being unemployed, which may be the case if one makes a distinction between the short-term unemployed and the long-term unemployed (as in Chapter 5). For the time being, however, in our simple world where people can only be employed or unemployed, the employed's outside value is the unemployed's welfare.

Now, do people care any more about unemployment benefits than about Q? While they may in principle increase V_u and thus V_e, in equilibrium this is not the case. In the no-rent, full-employment case, this is obvious: unemployment benefits are immaterial, since everybody is always employed. But (1.18) and (1.19) tell us that even for $Q > 0$, in equilibrium b has no impact on the welfare of either group. Inspection of (1.16) reveals that this is due to the fact that the fall in the job finding probability (the increase in unemployment duration) exactly offsets the direct impact of an increase in b. The mechanism is essentially the same as for an increase in Q: the incipient rise in V_u pushes wages up, which reduces job creation and labour market tightness, until wages are back to their equilibrium level.

While this suggests that people are indifferent with respect to b, this result ignores the tax cost of financing unemployment benefits. They are treated as manna from heaven; that is, when we let b increase while not changing the rest of the model we are actually increasing the total resources available to that economy. Even in that case, these extra resources turn out to be exactly dissipated, in equilibrium, by the increase in unemployment. If one were to take into account the resource cost of increasing b, it would have to be subtracted from w in (1.18) and (1.19), and one would get the result that unemployment benefits reduce welfare (since we just saw that without such a resource cost welfare would be unchanged).[5]

---

[5] Note that utility is linear here, meaning either that people are risk-neutral or that they have access to perfect financial markets (which implies access to privately provided unemployment benefits). If they were risk-averse there would clearly be a social demand for unemployment insurance, and economists have developed good arguments for why only the government may be able to provide such insurance. These themes are developed in Chapter 5.

1.3 A more general result about the support for free markets

The above discussion suggests that in that society there will be strong support for free market institutions. In fact, we can go further and prove that people will be in favour of letting firms unilaterally set any characteristic of the employment relationship. We will do this as a corollary of a more general result, which tells us that in some sense the unemployed are in favour of free markets.

To prove it, we need to introduce firms into the analysis. Up to now, they were only a veil which, because of perfect competition, ensured that each worker was getting exactly what he or she produced. The only decision they were making was how many people to hire, but because of constant returns and competition we could ignore that decision problem and directly postulate an exogenous wage w. But we can no longer ignore the firm's decision problem if it is setting some other variables.

The starting point is to write down the evolution equation for the firm's value, i.e. the expected present discounted value of its profit flow. It is simplest to assume that each firm only hires one worker.[6] Therefore the value of the firm is also the value of the job to the employer. We call m the productivity of that worker, and J the value of the job. We can write an equation analogous to (1.4) or (1.5) for J:

$$rJ = m - w + s(-J) + \dot{J}. \tag{1.21}$$

It is easy to apply our asset value interpretation to (1.21). The term $m - w$ is simply profit, which is the dividend. Capital gains include a deterministic appreciation term $\dot{J}$ and the expected capital loss made when the job is destroyed. As what is then lost is the value of the job J, and this happens with a flow probability s, the contribution of that event to expected capital gains is $-sJ$.

In steady state we have $\dot{J} = 0$, implying

$$J = \frac{m - w}{r + s}. \tag{1.22}$$

The value of the firm is equal to profits divided by the appropriate discount rate, which reflects the death rate of jobs in addition to the rate of time preference. Now, under perfect competition, there is free entry of firms. Entry will stop when the value of a job is zero. Thus in

---

[6] Under constant returns this assumption is immaterial.

equilibrium we must have $J = 0$, or equivalently $w = m$. Free entry drives wages up to the point where they are equal to productivity; each worker gets what he or she produces, which is what we have assumed throughout. From the viewpoint of individual firms, however, m is not necessarily equal to w. w is the wage that they must pay their workers, which must obey (1.15). Substituting (1.15) into (1.22) it is possible to express J, the value of a job, as a function of V_u and of the exogenous parameters m, r, s, and p. The variable V_u is taken as given by the firm and it characterizes labour market conditions, which influence the wage that it must pay. The parameters m and s, productivity and the job destruction rate, have been treated so far as parameters of the economy only because we have assumed that they were the same for everybody. More fundamentally, they characterize a job/worker pair.

Hence we can, in general, write the value of the firm as

$$J = J(V_u, x), \tag{1.23}$$

where x represents some characteristic of the employment relationship that is variable. In our current setting, a job is characterized by its destruction rate s and its productivity m; these two quantities may vary. For example, in Chapter 4 we consider what happens when there is a trade-off between job duration and productivity depending on the degree of employment protection granted to the worker. x would then be employment protection. More generally, one may also consider the role of working conditions, working hours, etc. The bottom line is that x is a characteristic of a job which may be set at different levels and that affects the firm's profits. As wages rise with the worker's outside option we must have $\partial J / \partial V_u < 0$.

We ask the following question: will people prefer to let firms unilaterally set x, or would they prefer it to be set directly by regulation? To answer that question, we need to sort out how x affects the welfare of workers. Let us start with the unemployed.

In general equilibrium the variable x influences all equilibrium variables, such as unemployment, the job finding rate, and the utility of the employed and unemployed workers. Consequently, we can write a reduced form for the value of being unemployed:

$$V_u = V_u(x).$$

This equation relates the value of V_u which arises in equilibrium to the value of x. The unemployed's preferred level of x is determined, provided the right concavity assumptions hold, by

$$dV_u/dx = 0,$$

where, one must insist, the total derivative means that one is looking at the marginal change in V_u across two different equilibria. People internalize all the general equilibrium effects of x when voting on that variable. If, instead of being voted on, x is determined by firms, they will set x by maximizing (1.23) while taking V_u as *given*. Thus, the first-order condition is

$$\partial J(V_u, x)/\partial x = 0, \tag{1.24}$$

where the partial derivative means that one considers an individual firm's incentives to change x *given* the equilibrium. Such a firm rightly considers that its own decision has no influence on the economy's aggregate behaviour, and hence on V_u. The key mechanism that establishes a link between the market-determined value of x and the one preferred by the unemployed is free entry of firms. The free entry condition is

$$J(V_u, x) = 0.$$

In any equilibrium V_u and x must be related to match that condition. Therefore, when x changes the equilibrium value of V_u must also change to maintain the free entry condition. Consequently, the derivative of V_u with respect to x is given by

$$\frac{dV_u}{dx} = -\frac{\frac{\partial J}{\partial x}}{\frac{\partial J}{\partial V_u}}.$$

Since $\partial J(V_u, x)/\partial x = 0$ for the market-determined value of x, it follows that one also has $dV_u/dx = 0$ at that point. The unemployed would vote for the value of x that the market would spontaneously provide. [7]

Thus, we have just established that the market will adopt the value of x that maximizes the utility of the *unemployed*. The two conditions for this result to hold are (1) free entry at no cost (or at a constant cost), and (2) that x is unilaterally set by firms rather than bargained between firms

---

[7] It is useful to note why one could not reproduce the same reasoning by replacing V_u with V_e. V_e is endogenously determined within the firm/worker match and therefore not considered exogenous by the firm. Consequently (1.23) would not hold with V_u replaced with V_e.

and workers. The free entry mechanism is crucial. It means that firms compete for hiring workers, so that any incipient increase in a firm's profits is eventually passed on to workers in the form of higher wages and a higher probability of finding a job. The wage formation mechanism ensures that the outside option V_u adjusts to offset any increase in profits, so that maximizing profits given V_u is equivalent to maximizing V_u in general equilibrium.

Hence, the unemployed support free markets. What about the employed? Whether they agree with the unemployed in general depends on the wage formation mechanism. Clearly, in the no-rent society we have $V_e = V_u$, so that the employed will also want to leave the choice of x to the market. Even if wage formation is given by (1.14) with Q fixed, maximizing V_e is like maximizing V_u, so that the employed will also support free markets. But, if the total rent Q depends on x directly or via some endogenous variable, as in some of the models we discuss in the appendix, the employed will want a value of x different from the one preferred by the unemployed; that is, they will not want to leave it to the market. This is likely to arise in some situations, as in the case of employment protection that we discuss in Chapter 4.

1.4 Conclusion

The main message of this chapter is that in our ideal society neither the employed nor the unemployed have any taste for European-style labour market rigidities. Both will unanimously oppose an institution that rises the rent Q or the benefit b. A perfectly functioning labour market guarantees that each individual gets his or her maximum attainable income for the maximum fraction of the time. Therefore, people could only lose by altering the functioning of the labour market.

This is not to say, however, that people would not want a rent for themselves. If a given individual could get a higher value of Q while not affecting the rest of the economy, the equilibrium value of V_u would be unchanged (because this individual is too small to affect the job finding probability of the unemployed), and the individual would indeed improve his situation. However, when it comes to voting on institutions that affect everybody, people would want such institutions to generate a rent as low as possible. Therefore, for a rent-generating institution to have political support, it must be the case that it does not affect everybody, at least to the same extent. That is, it must provide some way for some agents to increase their welfare at the expense of other agents. This principle is a crucial theme that is recurrent throughout this book. We start dealing with it in the next chapter.

Appendix. Models of wage formation

Economists have developed a battery of models of wage formation which deliver equations similar to (1.14). These models are useful because they have the potential of explaining the existence of rents and therefore of involuntary unemployment, because they can establish a link between wages and labour market tightness, and relate wage pressure to labour market frictions and unemployment. We briefly present them here, referring the reader to Layard *et al.* (1991) for a thorough exposition.

Perhaps the most canonical one is the 'insider–outsider' model (see Lindbeck and Snower 1988), where the existence of turnover costs create a positive, specific surplus associated with each job/worker match, and where part of this surplus is appropriated by the employee.

The value of a job J to the firm is defined as the expected present discounted value of output minus wages. We assume that if the job were vacant its value to the firm would be equal to zero. This is the firm's 'outside option'. The net value of a job to the firm, which we define as the difference between what it gets by employing the worker and what it would get by not employing the worker, is therefore equal to $J - 0 = J$. Similarly, the net value to the worker is the difference between what he gets by being employed in that firm and what he would get by not being employed, i.e. $V_e - V_u$. Here the worker's outside option is the value of being unemployed V_u.

The total surplus of the match is the sum of the firm's and the worker's net value:

$$M = J + V_e - V_u.$$

The 'Nash bargaining solution' assumes that the worker and the firm bargain over wages in such a way that a fraction φ of the total surplus goes to the worker and a fraction $1 - \varphi$ goes to the firm. This implies that

$$V_e = V_u + \varphi M$$
$$J = 0 + (1 - \varphi)M.$$

In the absence of any turnover costs free entry of firms implies that the value of a job, in equilibrium, must be equal to zero. This in turn implies that $M = 0$ and therefore $V_e = V_u$. We are back to the no-rent case examined in the text.

If there is a cost C of creating a job, free entry implies that the value of a job is equal to the entry cost C. In equilibrium $J = C$, so that $M = C/(1 - \varphi)$, and

$$V_e = V_u + \frac{\varphi C}{1 - \varphi}.$$

The model implies an equation like (1.14), with a fixed rent $Q = \varphi C/(1 - \varphi)$, which is increasing in the hiring cost C and in the worker's weight in bargaining φ.

One can also consider the role of dismissal costs. If the firm considers that it would have to pay the dismissal cost F should it decide not to employ the worker, then its outside option is no longer zero, but $-F$. The total surplus of the match is then

$$M = J + F + V_e - V_u,$$

and the sharing rule implies

$$V_e = V_u + \varphi M$$
$$J = -F + (1 - \varphi)M.$$

One then has, under free entry, $M = (C + F)/(1 - \varphi)$, and the rent is now equal to

$$Q = \frac{\varphi}{1 - \varphi}(C + F).$$

It is therefore the sum of the hiring and the firing costs that determine the rent. It is, however, debatable whether F should be included in the wage formation process. First, if wages are negotiated for the whole duration of the employment relationship after C has been incurred, but prior to the signing of a formal contract, the firm's outside option remains equal to zero. Second, the notion of a firm's outside option refers to what the firm would get outside the relationship, making no difference between a firm-initiated separation and a worker-initiated one. Essentially, there is no economic difference between a quit and a layoff in bargaining models. But dismissal costs are a tax on firm-initiated separations only, so the model provides no guideline as to whether or not they should be included in the firm's outside option.

It is important to stress that in the above model, each individual bargains directly with his employer over his own wage. Another class of insider–outsider models assume instead that workers of a given firm are organized into a labour union, which negotiates over wages on behalf of all employees. The union maximizes some utility function which is often the sum of the utilities of its individual members. Different assumptions may be made regarding how wages are set:

1. In the *monopoly union* model, the union sets wages unilaterally and the firm then freely sets employment. It faces a downward sloping labour demand relationship which tells by how much employment must be reduced in order to increase wages by a given amount.

2. In the *right to manage* model, the firm and the union bargain over wages and then the firm sets employment taking wages as given. The monopoly union model is a special case of the right to manage one, where all the bargaining power accrues to the union.

3. In the *efficient bargaining* model, firms and workers jointly bargain on employment and wages. Employment is then set efficiently, with the marginal product of labour being equal to the workers' opportunity cost.

The other important model of wage formation is the 'efficiency–wage' one, where firms must pay a rent to workers in order to avoid misconduct or 'shirking'. Following Shapiro and Stiglitz (1984), let us assume that the worker's flow of utility is $w - e$, where w is the wage and e is effort. The worker, however, may choose to 'shirk', in which case he is not exerting any effort and his flow of utility is w. Shirking is only imperfectly detected by firms, with probability q per unit of time. Furthermore, the maximum penalty that can be imposed if shirking is detected is dismissal. Firms set wages at the minimum level that deters shirking.

Using our asset value equations we can write the value of not shirking to any individual worker:

$$rV_e^N = w - e + s(V_u - V_e^N) + p(-V_e^N) + \dot{V}_e^N. \qquad (A1.1)$$

Similarly, the value of shirking is

$$rV_e^S = w + s(V_u - V_e^S) + p(-V_e^S) + \dot{V}_e^S + q(V_u - V_e^S).$$

The last term, $q(V_u - V_e^S)$, represents the capital loss made when the worker is caught shirking, which happens with probability q, per unit of time, in which case he is fired and becomes unemployed.

Firms will set the wage at the lowest possible level that deters shirking, implying $V_e^N = V_e^S = V_e$. Substituting that condition into the above equations we see that this is equivalent to

$$V_e = V_u + e/q. \tag{A1.2}$$

The model tells us that a fixed rent must be paid to workers, which is equal to $Q = e/q$. It is increasing in effort and decreasing in the probability of detecting a shirker. In the extreme cases where $e = 0$ (no disutility of labour) or $q = \infty$ (shirking instantaneously detected), the rent falls to zero and one is back to the full employment case.

Both the efficiency wage model and the insider–outsider model boil down to a fixed total rent. The only difference is that in one case, this rent depends on turnover costs, and, in the other, it depends on informational problems in monitoring the worker.

These models can be extended in various directions, which allow us to move away from a fixed total rent and introduce other determinants.

First, in the insider–outsider case, the hiring cost C can be made endogenous. In particular, it is reasonable to assume that it is higher, the tighter the labour market. Thus, in the context of our notation one would have $C = C(a)$, $C'(.) > 0$. Such a dependence is found in *matching* models (see Pissarides 1990), where in order to hire somebody a firm must post a vacancy and incur a fixed cost per unit of time of maintaining the vacancy idle. Workers apply to the vacant job at a rate which depends on the total number of vacancies and of unemployed workers. The higher the number of vacancies relative to the stock of unemployed workers, the tighter the labour market, the longer it takes to fill a vacancy, and the higher the cost incurred to fill a position.

Second, an important shortcoming of the above models for our purposes is that the rent does not depend on the expected remaining duration of the job. Thus a worker whose employment spell is about to end must be paid a wage which is virtually infinite in order that his welfare exceeds that of an unemployed by Q—or the firm must make a credible commitment to give a fixed severance payment Q to the worker upon separation. It would be equally reasonable to assume that the worker can get a fixed rent *per unit* of time he expects to remain within the firm, or at least that Q is an increasing function of the worker's expected tenure.

In order to put this in the context of the efficiency–wage model, it is necessary that the gain from shirking (which is e) is increasing with the job's expected duration. One example of this is as follows. Assume that there is no effort, but that the worker can try to get access to a technology that allows him to steal a quantity h per unit of time from his employer without being detected. He can, however, be detected when trying to access that technology, which happens with probability q per unit of time, in which case he is fired. Finally, while trying he is successful with probability λ per unit of time.

The utility of trying is thus given by

$$r V_e^T = w + s(V_u - V_e^T) + p(-V_e^T) + \dot{V}_e^T + q(V_u - V_e^T) + \lambda(V_e^{ST} - V_e^T).$$

This equation is identical to the one defining the utility of shirking above, apart from the addition of the last term, which represents the capital gain made if the worker is successful in accessing the stealing technology. V_e^{ST} is the utility of stealing, which evolves as follows:

$$r V_e^{ST} = w + h + s(V_u - V_e^{ST}) + p(-V_e^{ST}) + \dot{V}_e^{ST}. \qquad (A1.3)$$

Finally, the utility of not trying to steal is

$$r V_e^N = w + s(V_u - V_e^N) + p(-V_e^N) + \dot{V}_e^N. \qquad (A1.4)$$

Again, wages are set so as to deter trying. In equilibrium we have $V_e^N = V_e^T = V_e$. The no-trying condition is

$$V_e = V_u + \frac{\lambda}{q}(V_e^{ST} - V_e^T).$$

In steady state, (A1.3) and (A1.4) imply that $V_e^{ST} - V_e^T = h/(r + s + p)$. Consequently, we have

$$V_e = V_u + \frac{\lambda h}{q(r + s + p)}.$$

In this model, the rent is now equal to $Q = \frac{\lambda h}{q(r+s+p)}$. What do these complications bring us relative to the simpler shirking model described above? If the job separation rate is held fixed, nothing. But if it is allowed to vary, this makes quite a difference.

In the shirking model, using (A1.2) and (A1.1) allows us to express wages as a function of the value of being unemployed. We get, in steady state,

$$w = e + (r + p)V_u + (r + p + s)\frac{e}{q}. \qquad (A1.5)$$

The first term, $e + (r + p)V_u$, is the opportunity cost of labour, or 'alternative wage', i.e. the wage such that people are indifferent between being unemployed or earning that wage forever. The second term, $(r + p + s)\frac{e}{q}$, is the 'intratemporal' rent, i.e. the rent that must be paid per unit of time over the alternative wage. This rent increases almost proportionately with the job separation rate s, meaning that wages must become higher and higher when the worker is more and more exposed to unemployment.

In the 'trying' model, we can get the counterpart to (A1.5) by simply replacing e/q with $\frac{\lambda h}{q(r+s+p)}$ in (A1.5), leading to

$$w = e + (r + p)V_u + \frac{\lambda h}{q}. \qquad (A1.6)$$

The key difference from (A1.5) is that the intratemporal rent is now independent of the job separation rate s.

2

A less perfect world: market rents and redistributive conflict

2.1 Two dimensions of redistributive conflict

The previous chapter described a positive utopia, a land of opportunity where each individual could work and reap the return of his or her work without affecting the welfare of others. One important aspect of that ideal world is that people were producing their own output; each additional worker was increasing output by a fixed amount—in other words there were constant returns to scale.

Let us consider another world where instead of producing coconuts, people are fishing in the same pond. This pond produces a fixed supply of fish and if N people are fishing each of them is getting a fraction $1/N$ of the output. An additional worker does not increase output but instead reduces the income of the others. (In the language of the previous chapter's model that would mean that the wage w, is no longer fixed but is equal to Y/L, where L is total employment and Y the total output that should be divided among people.) Fishermen then have an interest in preventing outsiders from accessing the pond. By doing so they get more for themselves and are (implicitly) redistributing fish from outsiders to themselves. This is the first dimension of redistributive conflict, between the 'ins' and the 'outs'. For the sake of brevity we shall refer to that sort of conflict as 'external'. In our context it will refer to conflict of interest between the employed and the unemployed.

External conflict is more likely to arise, the closer we are to a pond economy—the more remote from a coconut economy—that is, when there are decreasing returns to scale so that Y/L is a decreasing function of L.

The 'ins' also have an incentive to steal fish from each other by using coercive means or to adopt a collective transfer scheme that achieves a similar outcome. This is the second, more direct, dimension of redistributive conflict, among the 'ins'. We will call it 'internal' conflict.

However, if our fishermen are identical, say if they all have caught the same quantity of fish and if they own the same asset, their redistributive conflict cannot be mediated by an institution. Institutions are anonymous and treat identical people equally. It is impossible to write down in the law a sentence like 'Mr Smith will write a check to Mrs Jones'. Therefore, institutions can only mediate redistributive conflicts between groups of individuals that differ by their economic characteristics (we ignore institutions that discriminate according to race, sex, etc. and that do not typically prevail in modern democracies).

Consequently, internal conflict is more likely to arise, the greater the observable economic differences across employed workers—i.e. the greater the inequality. In the context of our analysis internal conflict will refer to redistributive conflict among employed people of different skill or income levels.

Let us consider again an economy such as the one described in the previous chapter but assume now there are two groups in society; call them A and B. These two groups interact with each other in the market place and also jointly decide, by some political mechanism that we do not actually need to specify, on common policies and institutions. Assume that group A is more powerful than group B, so that its members can design institutions in the way that suits them best—to put it another way, the 'decisive voter' is a member of group A. There are many ways that group A can increase its welfare by manipulating institutions, but one possibility is simply to introduce a regulation that alters the functioning of the labour market in such a way that in equilibrium group A will be better off. Since in the absence of market failures such as externalities, imperfect competition, or increasing returns the market would lead to an efficient outcome, it must be that group B is worse off. Therefore, such regulation indirectly redistributes from group B to group A.

We thus see how the existence of redistributive conflict between the two groups opens the possibility of the emergence of a constituency in favour of labour market rigidities.

How efficient institutions are at redistributing from group B to group A depends on the extent to which both groups interact in the market. If groups A and B live in autarkies on separate islands, a labour market institution cannot improve group A's welfare, for group A is again in the no-rent situation described in the previous chapter: its income only comes from its own autarkic activity, i.e. from the quantity of goods that its individuals are able to produce.

Groups A and B may interact either through the exchange of goods or because they constitute different factors of production that cooperate in the production process. The two cases are not that different, and given that this book deals with labour market institutions, we shall assume that they cooperate in the production of a single good. We could interpret group A as 'labour' and group B as 'capital', but we can equally think of group A as 'unskilled labour' and group B as 'skilled labour'.[1] Indeed, as argued in the Introduction the latter interpretation is more correct because capital is not in fixed supply and adjusts in the long run.

Instead of having each individual producing a fixed amount of good, as in the previous chapter, the total amount of good is now a function of the input of each factor:

$$Y = F(L_A, L_B).$$

The key difference from the previous chapter is that instead of being fixed, the quantity of goods produced by a (marginal) member of group A now depends, in general, on how many members of each group are employed in the production process. (The special case where each group produces its own output without interacting with the other would be represented by a linear production function $F(L_A, L_B) = \alpha L_A + \beta L_B$.) More specifically, if F is a standard, neoclassical production function, with constant returns to scale, and if there is perfect competition among firms for the hiring of factor services, each factor will be paid its marginal product. Therefore, the wage of each group is given by

$$w_A = F_1'(L_A, L_B) = f(L_A/L_B), f' < 0$$
$$w_B = F_2'(L_A, L_B) = g(L_A/L_B), g' > 0,$$

with $f(x) = F_1'(x, 1)$ and $g(x) = F_2'(1, 1/x)$.

Thus we see that, as illustrated in Figure 2.1, group A can increase its wage by reducing the equilibrium ratio between L_A and L_B. One will already have recognized a standard argument about a union acting as a monopoly: this diagram could be about a single firm, with the members of group A (the insiders) organized into a labour union and increasing their wage by restricting hirings. But here the members of group A

---

[1] The fact that capital hires labour does not make a difference, as argued in the Introduction, as what matters is that each factor is paid its marginal product.

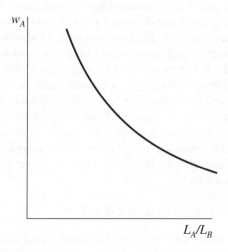

Figure 2.1. Group A's trade-off between employment and wages

do not have monopoly power over the firms in which they are working. Rather, they vote on institutions that they know will increase their
equilibrium wage. By making such institutions available on the policy
agenda, the political system therefore provides the members of group A
with a *coordination device* that helps them achieve monopoly power at
the *economywide* level. This is doable because factor A is cooperating in
production with factor B, which allows an artificial increase of A's wage
above the market clearing level by rendering factor A artificially scarce
relative to factor B.

The mechanism is different from the wage-setting behaviour of a
union that has a monopoly over recruitment. Rather than directly setting
wages, here the decision is about an institution that indirectly affects the
ability to achieve higher wages (although if that institution is a minimum
wage the mechanism is quite direct). But the economics is essentially
the same as in the standard insider model where wages are directly fixed
at the firm level. For that reason we shall sometimes refer to this as
the 'political insider' effect. The important thing to keep in mind is
that monopoly power is achieved through the political system, so that

the degree of monopoly power depends on the political system. For example, if unemployment benefits are determined by a corporatist body representing unions and employers, the outcome will be different than if the whole population, including the unemployed, the retirees, etc., were determining it. In the former case the employed have a larger political weight than in the latter, and may be more effective at bidding up wages using that institution.

In order to study what is the nature and the level of regulation preferred by group A, we shall import this simple production structure into the model described in the previous chapter. It can be extended very easily to capture the phenomena discussed here. Instead of thinking about that model as a model of the whole labour market, let us assume it is a model of the market for group A. Group B's labour is in fixed supply L_B and we assume that the market is unregulated, that is, group B will be fully employed. It is not obvious how group A can design an institution that affects its wage outcomes but not group B's wage. However, at this level of abstraction we will assume that it is possible.

Given our assumption that L_B is fixed, everything boils down to the fact that group A faces a downward sloping demand curve for its labour at the aggregate level. That is, we can simply reuse the previous chapter's model, but assume now that there is a negative relationship between the wage w and employment l, where these variables now refer to group A only. The wage schedule is $w(l) = f(l/L_B)$. This relationship is the inverse of the labour demand curve, which determines employment as a function of wages.

2.2 The structure of regulation: rents vs. outside options

Group A's employed workers can use a variety of institutions in order to affect their wages. The question we deal with in this section is: which type of institution are they more likely to use? We make a distinction between regulations that increase the rent Q, and those that increase b, the unemployed's income level. The former may benefit the employed by increasing the difference between their welfare and that of the unemployed. The latter may benefit them by making the unemployed better off, which in turn raises the employed's outside option in the wage formation process.

Suppose now that the employed of group A have to vote on a labour market institution, and that this institution increases the rent Q. In the previous chapter we have seen that in the utopian society this would be rejected. This arose from the fact that the employed's utility was given by

$$V_e = (w - sQ)/(r + p) \qquad (2.1)$$

and that w could not be different from the fixed number of cookies or coconuts produced by an individual. However, this is no longer the case now. There is scope for the employed of group A to increase their wage by reducing their supply relative to group B, by virtue of the monopoly mechanism we just discussed. Thus an increase in Q will not only entail costs, captured by the sQ term, but also benefits, captured by the fact that w increases with Q. This opens the possibility of a positive political support for a rent-generating institution. Again, the support comes from the fact that the institution indirectly redistributes income from B to A.

What happens, next, if instead of raising Q the employed can increase b, the payments to the unemployed? We are able to show that raising the rent is always more efficient, from the point of view of the employed of group A, than raising b.

To establish that result we need to reintroduce the resource cost of unemployment benefits into the picture. The rent is a set of regulatory provisions which in equilibrium ends up compelling employers to pay employees more than their outside option by an amount Q. It is therefore automatically financed as wage costs, i.e. out of the employee's output. By contrast b is a transfer to a person who does not produce; we thus have to specify who eventually pays for it. Let us assume that it is financed by a lump-sum tax, and, without loss of generality, that both the employed and the unemployed pay the tax. It is important to note that we assume this tax is only paid by the members of group A and not by the members of group B. That is, each group has its own, break-even unemployment benefit scheme. The reason why we assume this is that unemployment benefits for members of group A financed by a tax on members of group B is very much like a direct transfer from group B to group A, which we study below. Here we focus on indirect redistribution through labour market institutions that have no component of direct redistribution in the way they are financed.

Thus the tax paid by any member of group A must be equal to bu, where u is the unemployment rate. The net income of an employed is thus $w(l) - bu$, and the net income of an unemployed is $b(1 - u)$. It can be checked that taking the tax into account does not affect the formulae (1.11) and (1.16) that determine a and u. (1.18), which gives the value of being employed, must be rewritten using net income instead of wages:

$$V_e = \frac{w(l) - bu - sQ}{r + p}.$$

In order to be able to compute V_e we clearly need to know the equilibrium level of employment. This was already computed in the previous chapter, where we showed that

$$1 - l = u = \frac{(s + p)Q}{(w(l) - b) - rQ}. \tag{2.2}$$

This equation now determines l implicitly, as $w(l)$ appears on the right-hand side as well.

Consider now a change in Q and b such that total employment (and thus the gross wage) is *unchanged*. That is, we are substituting one instrument for the other, at the margin, so as to reach the same point on the wage/employment trade-off. Using (2.2) we find that this implies the following relationship between the change in b and the change in Q:

$$dQ = \frac{-u.db}{s + p + ru}.$$

The effect of the change on the value of being employed is then equal to

$$dV_e = -\frac{u.db + sdQ}{r + p}$$
$$= \frac{p + ru}{r + p} dQ.$$

This is positive if $dQ > 0$. Consequently, as long as there is room for reducing b and substituting an increase in Q that achieves the same gross wage instead, the employed will be willing to do it. Thus, they always prefer to boost their wages through the rent than through the outside option (here, unemployment benefits). This is not difficult to understand. Increasing the outside option redistributes income from group B to all members of group A, whether employed or unemployed, equally. This is because in equilibrium both the employed's and the unemployed's welfare increase by the same amount when the outside option improves, as an outcome of the wage formation process. By contrast, increasing the rent redistributes from group B to only the employed of group A; the unemployed are excluded from such redistribution, so the employed gain more, per unit redistributed.

This result is a useful benchmark, which tells us that the employed will typically favour rent-creating institutions over those that enhance their outside option. In the context of the present model, it would imply that they will choose a zero level of unemployment benefits, and a strictly positive level of the rent. This extreme result will be qualified in Chapter 5, where we analyse the role of unemployment benefits, in particular their role in providing insurance. For the time being let us note that we have ruled out any resource cost of enforcing the rent (for example costly litigation procedures); if such a cost was reintroduced the employed of group A may want to use both Q and b as instruments.

2.3 Heterogeneity and the support for minimum wages

The employed of group A want to reduce the supply of group A workers in order to bid up wages. Whether they use the rent or the outside option, they do so at the expense of making themselves more costly, which reduces their job prospects and therefore their utility when unemployed.

In the above framework, minimum wages fall into the category of institutions that raise the rent Q. For any rent Q, the equilibrium is identical to what would arise if workers were unable to achieve any rent in wage formation but if instead there was a minimum wage precisely equal to the equilibrium wage for group A.

However, when agents of group A are heterogeneous, the minimum wage is a much more powerful tool for the decisive insiders of group A than other institutions that uniformly increase the rent.

When agents of group A are heterogeneous, it is actually possible to target which members of group A one wants to exclude from the labour market, that is, to reduce the supply of group A's workers without making oneself more costly to employ. Minimum wages make sure that the least skilled among group A's agents are barred from employment. This allows an increase in the wages of the most skilled among group A's workers without lowering their job prospects, because such an increase is now achieved by a rise in the *demand* for these categories rather than an increase in their ability to set wages. That is, minimum wages increase the demand for the decisive workers of group A by reducing the availability of substitute labour—the least skilled.

Let us see what happens when members of group A differ by their productivities. Assume any member of group A is characterized by a number $i \in [0, 1]$ representing his or her labour endowment. If they are distributed over that interval with a density given by $f(i)$, total labour input from group A is given by

$$l_A = \int_0^1 l(i) f(i) i \, di,$$

where $l(i)$ is the number of agents of type i who are actually employed.

There is a separate labour market for each type i. For simplicity we assume that workers are not able to achieve a rent: $Q = 0$. Therefore, without minimum wages there would be full employment for all types. If w denotes the marginal product of l_A, then the wage of type i must be given by

$$w_i = iw. \tag{2.3}$$

Assume there is a minimum wage equal to $\bar{w}$. Then it becomes unprofitable to hire workers of a skill lower than $i^* = \bar{w}/w$. The minimum wage excludes those workers from employment ($l(i) = 0$), thus reducing l_A and increasing w, i.e. increasing wage for all other group A workers who remain employed (for these workers $l(i)$ remains equal to 1).

The logic is described in Figure 2.2. The upper right quadrant describes the linear equilibrium relationship WW (2.3) between i and $w(i)$, and determines i^*, the least productive type employed, as the intersection between that line and a horizontal line at the minimum wage $\bar{w}$. The lower right quadrant describes the relationship between l_A and i^*, i.e. $l_A = \int_{i^*}^1 f(i) i \, di$. The lower left quadrant is the marginal product (or labour demand) schedule for group A labour: it tells us how the wage of the highest type w depends negatively on the aggregate supply of group A l_A. w must be consistent with the position of the WW locus, which is checked on the upper left quadrant by means of the 45° line.

An increase in the minimum wage is depicted in Figure 2.3. As aggregate supply is reduced, w rises (the WW schedule rotates upwards to WW′), and those who remain employed are better off.

If the rent Q was strictly positive, then each type i would have a probability of finding a job determined by (1.16), i.e.

$$a_i = \frac{iw - b}{Q} - (r + s + p).$$

By raising w for these workers, minimum wages would actually increase both their wage and their employability.

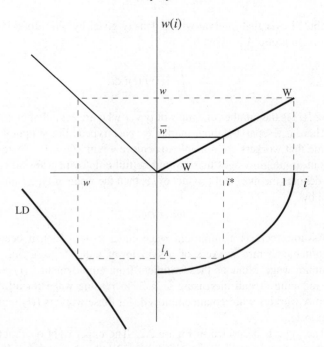

Figure 2.2. Equilibrium effect of the minimum wage

So, for those who remain employed the minimum wage entails only benefits, no costs. At what level, then, do we expect the minimum wage to be set? Workers with productivity less than i^* oppose any increase in the minimum wage, as do type B workers, whose marginal product falls with l_A. As long as there is a majority of type A workers above i^*, the minimum wage will increase. This process will stop when there is exactly 50 per cent of the workers who are employed and of type A. In that case workers of type i^* are pivotal voters. They oppose an increase in the minimum wage because they would lose their jobs, and they oppose a reduction in the minimum wage because their wage would fall.

2.4 Determinants of the rent: exposure and elasticity

Let us now return to the case where workers of group A are homogeneous. We want to analyse how the rent elected by the employed will

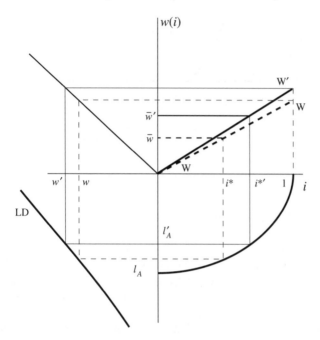

Figure 2.3. Increase in the minimum wage

depend on the underlying parameters of the economy. They will simply set the rent that will maximize their utility, that is $V_e = (w - sQ)/(r+p)$. The first-order condition is consequently

$$w'(l).\frac{\mathrm{d}l}{\mathrm{d}Q} = s.$$

The left-hand side is the marginal gain from increasing the rent: by reducing the ability of outsiders to compete, the rent allows the employed to move the economy along the labour demand schedule, thus increasing wages and reducing employment. The marginal cost comes from the lower utility associated with the status of being unemployed; this lower utility comes from the fact that the unemployed's job finding probability falls when the rent is higher, but the formula shows that it is precisely equal to the frequency of job loss. Every time the employed loses his job, he loses the rent. If job loss is very infrequent, then the cost to the insiders of increasing the rent is lower. Equilibrium determination

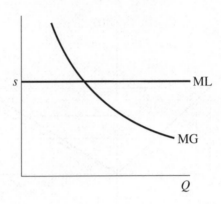

Figure 2.4. Determination of the rent

is illustrated in Figure 2.4. The curve MG represents the marginal gain in terms of increased wages. It must be downward sloping for the first-order condition to capture an optimum. The horizontal line ML is the job loss frequency.

These arguments suggest that the employed's incentives to support labour market rigidity will be greater, the more responsive wages are to employment (i.e. the lower the wage elasticity of labour demand), and the lower the frequency of job loss—the less the employed are exposed to unemployment. An increase in the rate of job loss shifts ML upwards, while a lower elasticity of labour demand means that a given reduction in employment achieves a higher wage increase. In other words, w' is greater, so that MG typically shifts upwards. The responsiveness of labour demand to wages plays the same role as in the traditional monopoly union model, which is not surprising since, as we argued above, labour market institutions are used by insiders to collectively achieve monopoly power. More interestingly, the elasticity also captures the degree of 'market interaction' between group A and group B and therefore the amount of redistribution achieved by market regulation. A low elasticity of labour demand (i.e. a higher elasticity of $w(l)$) means that group A and group B are quite complementary in the production process,[2] i.e. that altering the functioning of the labour

---

[2] For example, if the production function is CES (Constant Elasticity of Substitution), $Y = \left[L_A^\rho + L_B^\rho\right]^{1/\rho}$, one has $w(l) = \left[l^\rho + L_B^\rho\right]^{1/\rho-1} l^{\rho-1}$, and one can check that the elasticity of w with respect to l is equal, in absolute value, to $(1-\rho)(1-s_A)$, where s_A

market achieves a substantial transfer from group A to group B. At high elasticities the production function becomes closer to a linear one, $F(L_A, L_B) = \alpha L_A + \beta L_B$, where in effect the two groups do not interact at all in the production process. Each group produces its own cookies and aggregate output is the sum of the output of the two groups. The economy is like an aggregate of two Robinson Crusoe economies, and altering the functioning of the market does not achieve any transfer from B to A.

The importance of the exposure parameter s comes from both the dynamic and the institutional aspect of the problem. Here the employed are not negotiating their own wages for the next three years, say, but setting an institution that affects wages economywide and for a long time. Thus they take into account the fact that it will also affect their future wages and the duration of their future unemployment spells.[3] Their exposure to unemployment is therefore a relevant parameter to take into account when they decide on their preferred level of the rent. If wages were set by a monopoly union this effect would be absent or much weaker. It would be nonexistent if unions negotiated at the firm level, since such unions have no impact on their employees' wages and job prospects elsewhere. If unions were bargaining at a more central level, the effect would remain much weaker than here, since they would just set wages for a short period of time, and consider that the current wage contract has little impact on the employed's job prospects in the future.

Let us now make our argument about elasticity and exposure more precise by considering a specific example. We assume a constant elasticity of wages with respect to *unemployment.* That is, we assume

$$w(l) = (1 - l)^{\eta}\omega. \tag{2.4}$$

This formula does not make much sense at full employment, since wages are assumed to be equal at zero there, but we shall not use it in the neighbourhood of full employment and it is otherwise quite convenient. The parameter η then captures the responsiveness of wages to employment. The parameter ω allows us to adjust the level of the marginal product of labour. Furthermore, we assume no unemployment benefits, $b = 0$, and

---

is the share of group A labour in value added. Therefore, it is larger, the smaller ρ, i.e. the greater the complementarity between the two types of labour.

[3] The merit of our formulation is that all these effects are subsumed in the simple term $-sQ$ in the numerator of (1.18).

a zero interest rate: $r = 0$. Equation (2.2) then gives us a simple formula to compute unemployment:

$$u = 1 - l = \left(\frac{zQ}{\omega}\right)^{\frac{1}{1+\eta}},$$

where $z = p + s$ denotes the total inflow rate into unemployment. This simple formula makes it very easy to compute the marginal wage gain from an increase in the rent. It is given by

$$w'(l)\frac{dl}{dQ} = \frac{\eta\omega^{\frac{1}{1+\eta}}}{1+\eta} z^{\frac{\eta}{1+\eta}} Q^{-\frac{1}{1+\eta}} = \frac{\eta z}{(1+\eta)(1-l)}.$$

The equilibrium value of the rent is then simply obtained by equating that to the marginal cost s, implying

$$Q = \left(\frac{\eta}{1+\eta}\right)^{1+\eta} \omega z^\eta s^{-(1+\eta)}. \tag{2.5}$$

One can check algebraically that Q is increasing in η:[4] a lower elasticity of labour demand (a higher η) increases the rent. Note that this effect prevails *despite* the fact that the increase in η also reduces the marginal product of labour at any employment level according to (2.4). That is, η is not a pure elasticity parameter but also affects the average level of the marginal product of labour. Indeed, a more sensible experiment would be to increase η while also adjust ω so as to offset the negative impact of η on the marginal product of labour, in which case the increase in Q would be even higher as (2.5) implies that Q is increasing in ω.

The exposure parameter s affects Q both through s and z. It plays a twin role, entering both an employed worker's subjective probability of being laid off and the inflow into unemployment. Controlling for the latter, i.e. maintaining z constant, an increase in s unambiguously reduces the rent. Now, the rent depends positively on z, which increases by an amount $dz = ds$. But it is straightforward to check that the net effect of s on the rent remains negative.

That the rent is increasing in z is not an uninteresting phenomenon. It implies that an increase in p, the inflow rate of new entrants into the labour market, tends to increase the support for labour market rigidity.

---

[4] To see this, note that $(z/s)^\eta$ is increasing in η because $z > s$, while it is also true that $\left(\frac{\eta}{1+\eta}\right)^{1+\eta}$ is increasing in η, which can be checked by differentiating.

This is because, as (2.2) makes clear, the employment-limiting effect of the rent, which makes it possible for wages to rise, is increasing in the inflow into unemployment. Insiders achieve their Malthusian goal of limiting employment by the following mechanism. A higher rent increases the wage they can attain, which in turn reduces labour demand and labour market tightness. But labour market tightness affects employment less when inflows are lower. In the limit case of a zero inflow full employment cannot be avoided in the long run.

To put it another way, a greater value of p makes it more likely that a given reduction in employment falls upon new entrants rather than the currently employed, increasing the gains to these employed of a higher rent.

One can also look at the equilibrium unemployment rate associated with that rent. We get

$$u = \frac{\eta z}{s(1 + \eta)}. \tag{2.6}$$

A higher value of η therefore unambiguously increases unemployment, because of the induced increase in Q. This effect is not due to the negative impact of η on the marginal product of labour as unemployment does not depend on ω. The elasticity of the marginal product matters for unemployment but not its level. A uniform increase in the marginal product schedule generates a proportional increase in the employed's preferred rent, and unemployment is unaffected.

Note also that unemployment turns out to be *falling* with the exposure parameter s. This is quite a paradoxical result. Given the rent, an increase in exposure increases the inflow into unemployment (mechanically), and reduces labour market tightness (here, because workers must be paid higher wages in order to be compensated for lower tenure). So, unemployment unambiguously increases, as evidenced by (2.2). However, there is an additional effect that exposure makes insiders more reluctant to vote for high rents. Under our specification, the fall in the rent turns out to more than offset the direct effect of s on unemployment, so that unemployment actually falls. Obviously, this dominance could well be reversed under alternative specifications.

The above analysis has considered the preferred level of the rent for a worker who is sure to keep his job, despite the fact that increasing the rent, since it reduces labour demand, may lead to his dismissal. The validity of that assumption depends on how the reduction in employment associated with a hike in labour costs takes place. In Chapter 7, these aspects are discussed in greater detail.

2.5   Labour market regulation vs. the fiscal system

We have just analysed how redistributive conflict between the two groups can be mediated by labour market institutions. Now, is that not a strange way to transfer money from group B to group A? If group A is powerful enough to establish rigidities from which it benefits, why can't they just pass a law requiring that group B pays a tax, whose proceeds are paid to group A? If it can do so why would they ever want to top up such a transfer scheme with rigidities that reduce the efficiency of the market?

An economist's a priori answer to that question is that it is always more efficient to redistribute money by using transfers than by distorting the price system. That is, if we want to redistribute some money from group B to group A, it is better to tax group B and give the proceeds to group A rather than raise the wage of group A. Such an increase can only be achieved by a reduction in the L_A/L_B ratio, which, if we preclude imposing slavery on group B, must imply that some members of group A must be unemployed. This is a clear waste of resources which would be avoided by taxing group B instead and letting group A be fully employed. This is obvious at least in the case where taxes are 'lump-sum', i.e. not distortionary.

Even in the case where taxes are distortionary, labour market regulation is unlikely to be an efficient way of redistributing income. It is in fact equivalent to a very peculiar tax system that is unlikely to be optimal. Figure 2.5 illustrates this point. We are assuming an elastic supply of labour by the members of group A. Assume institutions allow an increase in the wage of group A to w', above its market clearing level w. Employment is then lower than at equilibrium, and there is a level of involuntary unemployment equal to U among A's people. The marginal worker would be willing to work for a wage $w'' < w < w'$ but does not find work. The gain from the higher wage to group A, in terms of welfare, is given by the difference between the rectangular area X (the gain to the employed of having a higher wage) and the triangular Y (the loss of the unemployed that would otherwise be employed at wage w). If w' is not too different from w then Y is small relative to X and group A gains as a whole.

Assume now that instead of that institution we impose a tax on group A's labour precisely equal to $w' - w''$ and that we give all the tax proceeds to group A. Then the outcome would be exactly the same: the buyer's price of group A's labour would be w', the seller price w'', employment would be the same, and the tax transfers would give the members of

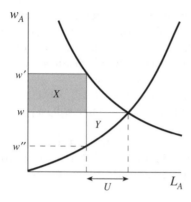

Figure 2.5. Effect of wage rigidity on group A's welfare

group A exactly as much income as their wages under a wage floor equal
to w'. Thus our institution acts exactly in the same way as a transfer to
group A financed by a tax on group A's employment. But, if one wants to
give money to somebody, it is quite strange to finance that transfer with
a tax on that precise person's activity. Certainly it is not optimal—in fact
the optimal (Ramsey) tax structure is independent of the use being made
of the money and involves taxing a wide array of goods to minimize its
distortionary burden.

Do we conclude, then, that labour market institutions cannot be explained by redistributive motives? We would indeed conclude so if the
motive for redistribution from group B to group A was the existence
of a central planner that cares about 'equality' (assuming group A is
poorer) or if group A behaved as a large family or tribe that maximizes
its aggregate welfare and then shares it among the members of the tribe
according to some internal rule unrelated to how it obtains its income.
However, this is not the case; we are dealing with selfish individuals who
support redistribution between groups not because they care about group
income *per se* but because they may individually benefit as a member
of the favoured group. This gives us a hint as to why redistributive
conflict may be mediated by labour market rigidities even though it is
economically inefficient. Fiscal redistribution maintains *all* members
of group A in employment, and therefore redistributes identically to
all members of group A. Redistribution through regulation creates a
difference between those members of group A who keep a job and those

who become unemployed. That is, it artificially splits group A into two economically identifiable groups, that end up being treated differently even though they have the same economic characteristics. It reduces the size of the group that benefits from redistribution, thus increasing each individual's share of the total transfer.

If that effect is strong enough it will outweigh the negative contribution of the deadweight loss, and there will be political support for the regulatory form of redistribution.

Therefore the question we now need to answer is whether society will elect to redistribute from group B to group A using regulation, or whether it will prefer direct redistribution (the fiscal option).

2.5.1 Group A's preferences

We continue to assume that the decisive group is the employed of group A. For simplicity we first assume that $s = 0$, i.e. that people keep their jobs forever. We will then briefly discuss how exposure s will affect the choice between the two regimes. If $s = 0$ the employed of group A will compare the two options by simply looking at their *individual* income. We shall rewrite the production function as $F(l, L_B) = L_B h(l/L_B)$. Therefore the wage of a member of group A is $w(l) = h'(l/L_B)$, while the wage of a member of group B is $w_B = h(l/L_B) - l/L_B \cdot h'(l/L_B)$.

There is an extreme case where under the fiscal option group A could entirely expropriate group B. Normalizing group A's labour force to one, a member of group A's income would then simply be equal to GDP, i.e. $L_B h(1/l_B)$. However, this is an extreme case, if anything because taxes are distortionary and because we do not expect fiscal redistribution to make the payers ex-post worse off than the recipients. If, for example, group B is richer than group A without redistribution, they could always throw away part of their income to mimic group A's situation and benefit from the transfer instead of paying taxes. So we assume that there is a maximum share θ of group B's income that group A can appropriate. Ideally θ should be endogenous, depending on the structure of the tax system and on its distortions, but for our discussion it is enough to assume that it is exogenous.

Under the fiscal option the post-transfer income of any member of group A is thus equal to

$$
\begin{aligned}
y_f &= h'(1/L_B) + \theta L_B w_B \\
    &= \theta L_B h(1/L_B) + (1 - \theta)h'(1/L_B).
\end{aligned}
$$

This is a linear combination of the wage and GDP per member of group A. Under the regulatory option their income is simply $y_r = h'(l/L_B)$, where l is the corresponding level of employment, which is lower than 1.

The regulatory option will be preferred by the insiders of group A if $y_r > y_f$.[5]

The condition that the regulatory option is preferred is equivalent to

$$h'(l/L_B) - h'(1/L_B) > \theta[L_B h(1/L_B) - h'(1/L_B)].$$

The left-hand side is the wage gain obtained by moving along the negatively-sloped marginal product schedule. The right-hand side is the rent that can be extracted from group B under the fiscal option.

The most transparent way to rewrite that condition is as follows:

$$\bar{\eta}(1 - l) > \frac{\theta s_B}{1 - s_B}, \tag{2.7}$$

where

$$s_B = 1 - h'(1/L_B)/(L_B h(1/L_B))$$

is the income share of group B in the fiscal regime, and

$$\bar{\eta} = \frac{h'(l/L_B) - h'(1/L_B)}{1 - l} \frac{L_B}{h'(1/L_B)}$$

is the elasticity of wages with respect to employment when one moves from the fiscal to the regulatory regime.

Equation (2.7) implies that the regulatory regime is more likely to prevail when

1. θ is lower, i.e. the scope for fiscal redistribution is more limited. This is almost by construction and requires no further comments, beyond noting that nothing precludes that (2.7) be satisfied even for $\theta = 1$.

2. l is lower, i.e. regulation manages to exclude a lot of people from redistribution, thus reducing the number of people who share the cake. However, too low a value of l also reduces the political influence of group A's employed workers, an aspect we have ignored in our analysis.

[5] Again, note that in the regulatory case there are *fewer* employed workers of group A than in the fiscal one. Thus we assume that those who end up being unemployed as a result of the regulatory choice have no political influence. This is a complex issue associated with the identifiability of the losers from the reform, to which we return in Chapter 7.

3. $\bar{\eta}$ is higher, i.e. a given reduction in the number of employed workers in group A achieves a higher increase in wages. This means that the relationship between l and y is more concave, or alternatively that there is more complementarity between the two groups in the production process. A high $\bar{\eta}$ means a low wage elasticity of labour demand. We already saw that this increases the equilibrium level of regulation. The preceding formula tells us that it is also true that regulation is more likely to arise.

4. s_B is lower, i.e. group B earns a low fraction of national income. Otherwise, large income increases can be achieved for each member of group A by simply redistributing from B to A. Equation (2.5) thus tells us that small groups (in terms of income share) will prefer to get transfers (although if they are smaller they are also less likely to be politically decisive), while large groups are more likely to favour regulation.

Let us now move away from the assumption that $s = 0$ and examine how exposure to unemployment affects the trade-off between the two options. Under the fiscal option the labour market clears. As we saw in Chapter 1, a worker who loses his job finds another one instantaneously at the same wage. Exposure s is irrelevant and the welfare of a member of group A is just equal to its discounted income $w_A/(r + p)$. On the other hand, (1.18) clearly implies that the welfare of an employed in the regulatory regime is a decreasing function of his exposure to unemployment s.[6] Rent creation is less attractive when one expects to lose the rent more frequently. Consequently, a greater exposure to unemployment always reduces the likelihood that the regulatory option is preferred to the fiscal one.

Therefore, the factors that tend to increase the equilibrium level of the rent in the regulated economy also increase the likelihood that regulation is preferred to the fiscal option. This is not too surprising since it means that the gain from increasing the rent is higher.

2.5.2 Group B's preferences: a theorem

Throughout we have assumed that institutions were unilaterally determined by the employed of group A and that the unemployed and the

---

[6] The envelope theorem implies that as Q is determined optimally, the net effect of s on V_e is simply equal to $\partial V_e/\partial s = -Q/(r + s) < 0$.

members of group B had no influence whatsoever over political outcomes. This is a useful shortcut, but it oversimplifies the political arbitrages that prevail in reality. Clearly, how institutions affect other groups will also have an impact on whether these institutions are adopted or not. Even if a group is not able to impose its preferences, it can have an influence by, for example, blocking a given reform.

Clearly, to deal with that question one needs a mechanism that tells us how the preferences of all members in society are aggregated into a collective decision. None of the available approaches is without problem, however. For the time being we limit ourselves to the insights that can be obtained by looking at each group's preferences.

Here we focus on group B, the 'skilled' workers who work in a market without rigidities and are fully employed. We could do the same analysis as previously but instead we are going to tackle the problem from a different angle. We ask the following question: what is the amount of money that the members of group B would have to pay in order to convince the insiders of group A to eliminate the rigidity? And, are they willing to pay that amount?

It is useful to distinguish two polar cases. Suppose first that the money can be paid to these insiders but not to the unemployed who would get a job as a result of the reform. This would happen if it was possible to transfer money to the incumbent employees of group A but not to the unemployed despite the fact that both end up in identical situations after the move. Group B would then have to transfer to each employed of group A an amount equal to his wage loss from liberalization. This amount is equal to

$$w(l) - w(1) = h'(l/L_B) - h'(1/L_B),$$

and it has to be paid to l workers. Let us denote the wage of group B in the flexible world by w_{Bf}. The net income of a member of group B after he has paid that transfer is therefore equal to

$$
\begin{aligned}
y_{Bf} &= w_{Bf} - l(h'(l/L_B) - h'(1/L_B))/L_B \\
&= h(1/L_B) - h'(1/L_B)/L_B - lh'(l/L_B)/L_B + lh'(1/L_B)/L_B.
\end{aligned}
$$

They will agree to pay if that net income is greater than their wage in the rigid economy, which is equal to $w_{Br} = h(l/L_B) - lh'(l/L_B)/L_B$. The condition $y_{Bf} > w_{Br}$ is equivalent to

$$L_B(h(1/L_B) - h(l/L_B)) > (1 - l)h'(1/L_B). \tag{2.8}$$

The left-hand side is simply the output gain from shifting from one economy to the other. The right-hand side is the product of the unemployment rate in the rigid economy and the wage of the flexible economy. This condition tells us that if the output gain pays for more than the wages of the people who find jobs, shifting from rigidity to flexibility generates a surplus which can be split between the incumbent employees of group A and the members of group B in order to make them all better off.

Condition (2.8) is *always* satisfied. Concavity of h implies that its slope at $1/L_B$, $h'(1/L_B)$ is always smaller than its coefficient of variation between l/L_B and $1/L_B$, $L_B(h(1/L_B) - h(l/L_B))/(1 - l)$. That this always holds is not surprising; we are in a world where we allow individuals in identical situations to be paid different transfers. In such a world any market distortion can be removed because such a removal increases aggregate output, and the extra output can be distributed among individuals in any arbitrary way, so that it is always possible to make everybody better off. (In other words the economy reaches a Pareto-efficient allocation.) This is exactly what (2.8) tells us is taking place. One could even consider transfers from the formerly unemployed to the former insiders as the unemployed's income jumps upwards from 0 to $h'(1/L_B)$ as a result of the reform. As we have ruled that out, a quantity $(1 - l)h'(1/L_B)$ must accrue to them out of the extra output, but there is always some surplus left which allows group B and the insiders of group A to agree on the reform.

However, a fiscal institution, in practice, cannot treat identical people differently. Therefore we now consider what happens when the transfer must be paid to *all* members of group A regardless of whether they were employed or not in the rigid world. The transfer that compensates insiders for their wage loss must now also be paid to outsiders, even though these are already quite happy because of having found a job. Consequently the total cost to group B of the transfer policy is now $1 \cdot (h'(l/L_B) - h'(1/L_B))$ instead of $l \cdot (h'(l/L_B) - h'(1/L_B))$, and their net income is now

$$
\begin{aligned}
y_{Bf} &= w_{Bf} - (h'(l/L_B) - h'(1/L_B))/L_B \\
&= h(1/L_B) - h'(l/L_B)/L_B.
\end{aligned}
$$

Flexibility will be preferred by the members of group B if $y_{Bf} > w_{Br}$, which is now equivalent to

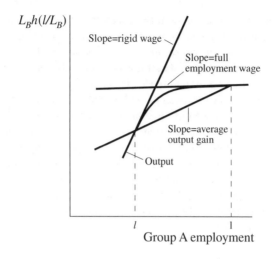

Figure 2.6. Feasibility of reform

$$L_B(h(1/L_B) - h(l/L_B)) > (1 - l)h'(l/L_B). \qquad (2.9)$$

This condition is similar to (2.8), with one key difference. The wage which is now imputed to the unemployed is no longer the *flexible* wage, but the *rigid* one. Not that job finders require that in order to accept the reform or to accept a job—simply, equal treatment implies that they get the same transfer as the insiders, so that the transfer scheme must yield an income of $h'(l/L_B)$ to each member of group A. Thus, more of the additional output must go to the unemployed, and this is enough to prevent (2.9) from ever being satisfied. This is again due to the concavity of h: its slope at l/L_B is now *greater* than its coefficient of variation between l/L_B and $1/L_B$. This concavity is illustrated in Figure 2.6.

This result is one of the important insights of our theory. Because transfers must be anonymous, it turns out to be impossible to put together a coalition of payers (group B) and incumbent employees that would agree to shift to the more efficient fiscal system. Those who bear the burden of redistribution in the rigid society—group B—actually support these institutions to the extent that the alternative would mean making a transfer to *more* people, and end up being poorer. This aspect is further developed in the next chapter where we deal with the 'cohesion effects' of relative income compression.

In order for the fiscal system to be adopted, it must be that group A has so much power that it can impose the fiscal system onto group B even though group B is then worse off; the considerations developed in the previous section then prevail. Or, if it was group B that had all the power, then it would remove any rigidity as it is better off, the larger the number of group A members who are employed. In that case, obviously, it would also not redistribute any money to other members of society. The point is that they favour rigidity to the extent that it is a substitute to taxation, but they naturally prefer to have none of it. Another possibility is to force the unemployed to somehow pay for their jobs, which allows again different transfers to be paid to the former insiders and the former jobless. In many cases the political viability of labour market reforms is achieved by designing some way of differentiating transfers; one illustration can be found in Chapter 8.

2.5.3 Employed vs. unemployed: back to external conflict

It follows from the preceding discussion that *both* the employed of group A and group B may prefer the rigid society to the flexible one, in spite of the fact that output is lower in the rigid society. How can this be?

So far we have mostly thought of rigidity as a tool to redistribute from group B to group A. This dimension cannot be forgotten, since group B will support rigidity only to the extent that the alternative is transferring more money to group A. However, it also seems that, relative to a package of flexibility and redistribution, rigidity is redistributing in favour of both group B and group A, and because of lower output such redistribution can only be at the expense of the rest of society—the unemployed.

That would not be surprising if we were in the fishing economy we discussed at the beginning of the chapter to introduce the notion of external conflict. Higher unemployment would then simply increase output per employed. However, here there are constant returns to scale: a proportional increase in L_A and L_B would increase output proportionately. Hence there would be no scope for external conflict *if* it were to lead to the same unemployment rate in the two groups.

But, precisely, we are considering institutions that create unemployment among the members of group A but not among the members of group B. There would be an element of external conflict if barring members of group A from employment increased output per employed (regardless of their group). Intuitively, that would be the case if these people's contribution to output were lower than average. This is indeed true, and is equivalent to group B having a greater marginal product than group A.

To see this, just compute the derivative of output per employed with respect to employment of group A:

$$\frac{\partial}{\partial L_A} \ln \frac{F(L_A, L_B)}{L_A + L_B} = \frac{F'_1}{F} - \frac{1}{L_A + L_B}. \tag{2.10}$$

This is negative if and only if A's marginal product is lower than average product:

$$F'_1 < \frac{F}{L_A + L_B}.$$

Because of constant returns to scale, we know that total output is equal to total factor cost:

$$\begin{aligned} F(L_A, L_B) &= F'_1 \cdot L_A + F'_2 \cdot L_B \\ &= w_A L_A + w_B L_B. \end{aligned} \tag{2.11}$$

Substituting (2.11) into (2.10) we find that output per capita falls with L_A if and only if

$$F'_1 < F'_2,$$

or

$$w_A < w_B.$$

It is because group B is more productive than group A, and consequently earns more, that reducing employment of type A people increases output per employed. This result tells us that when external conflict means excluding part of type A people from employment, there is a complementarity between internal and external conflict. This is because the income inequality between the two groups also gives us the gain, in per capita terms, to the two groups as a whole, from excluding some members of group A from employment. The greater the gap between group B's wage and group A's wage, the greater the incentive to redistribute from group B to group A, and the greater the incentive to exclude some members of group A from that redistributive game.

In the absence of internal conflict—if redistributing from group B to group A's employed people were impossible—group B would always want as many of group A's members as possible working, and group A's employed workers, as few of them as possible (except in the extreme case of a linear production function). Because of internal conflicts, the gains from maintaining some members of group A in unemployment are shared between the employed of the two groups, which may lead to members of group B actually supporting such exclusion.

Let us summarize this important result, which is further examined in the next chapter.

The existence of an institution that redistributes from group B to group A may create a consensus between the employed of both groups to exclude some of group A's members from employment.

In the absence of such an institution, such consensus would not exist, as group A's employed would be in favour of exclusion while group B's employed would be against it.

The gain from exclusion is increasing in the income differential between the employed of the two groups, i.e. in the degree of internal conflict.

We now proceed to analyse what happens when redistributive taxation may coexist with rigid labour market institutions.

3
Wage rigidity and social cohesion

3.1 Introduction

The preceding chapter has studied how labour market institutions can be used indirectly by insiders in order to improve their bargaining position in wage setting. We have showed that such institutions could be the outcome of redistributive conflict between these people and other groups, for example the most skilled workers. In studying why society might decide to redistribute that way rather than using fiscal transfers, we came across an important result: it is actually the group that is being taxed (in our case, the most skilled) that favours labour market rigidities over the fiscal option. That way, it is actually reducing the burden of redistribution because it is limiting the size of the recipient group.

Although the economy consisted of only two types of worker, labour market rigidity split it into three: group B, whose members were fully employed, the employed of group A, and the unemployed of group A. Implicitly, it creates a coalition of group B and the employed of group A that, by excluding the unemployed from redistribution, may increase the amount paid to each employed worker of group A while at the same time reducing the cost to workers of group B. In some sense, group B is bribing a fraction of group A (the employed) not to side with the others (the unemployed) to extract rents from group B. Under the fiscal system, i.e. when redistribution from group B to group A took place in the form of transfers, equal treatment was preventing that from occurring, but rationing in the labour market creates artificial differences in economic status among otherwise identical people.

Note that a benevolent central planner with distributive concerns would never elect to redistribute income in that fashion, as the creation of a class of unemployed people actually increases inequality. The benevolent central planner would surely prefer the fiscal option.

However, it is true that rigidity compresses the distribution of income *among* the employed. In Chapter 2, this was indirectly achieved by the fact that one was voting on an institution that increased the rent of group A employed workers but not of group B workers. In the real world, many institutions compress the distribution of wages, including not only the minimum wage but many collective bargaining agreements.[1] From the viewpoint of our altruistic social planner, all this is of no use as it leaves aside the poorest, who are unemployed. (Indeed if our social planner were altruistic in a Rawlsian way,[2] he or she would maximize the utility of those who are left aside and strongly object to rigidity.) But this compression of income within a large fraction of society may have effects that are likely to further enhance the political support for rigidity. It is these effects in which we are interested in this chapter.

Throughout the book we want to explain labour market institutions as the outcome of political choices by *selfish* agents, although our results are not incompatible with some degree of altruism. The question we want to answer is therefore the following: why do selfish agents care about the distribution of income, and why would they prefer to compress the distribution of wages rather than the distribution of welfare?

One answer is that an unequal distribution of income is associated with negative externalities exerted by the 'poor' on the rest of society. People do not only interact through the market (i.e. by selling to and buying from each other). They make collective decisions, share urban infrastructures, and cooperate at the workplace. An individual's welfare is affected by the characteristics of the people with whom he or she interacts in these spheres. Examples of negative externalities associated with an uneven distribution of income include political pressure in favour of populist government and high redistribution financed by distortionary taxes; increased crime and social unrest; and envy phenomena that may create tensions and low morale at the workplace.

It is then important to realize that these externalities are not determined by the same dimensions of the income distribution as, say, general measures of inequality such as the Gini coefficient. In other words, a society that wants to avoid or mitigate these negative effects will not make the same decisions as an altruistic social planner that

---

[1] One well known example is the now abandoned Italian *Scala Mobile,* which prevailed in the 1970's and was indexing wages on inflation by giving the same absolute pay rise to all workers.

[2] A Rawlsian social planner maximizes the welfare of the poorest agent in society. See Rawls (1971).

genuinely cares about the relative income of the poorest. Social conflict is reduced by making the economic characteristics of those who exert the externality more in line with the characteristics of those who suffer from the externality. A group may be eligible for the compassion of an altruistic social planner but the relevant question from the viewpoint of the bulk of society is: what are the externalities exerted by this group upon the rest of us?

While relative wage rigidity is an ill-designed tool for the altruistic social planner, it may be quite efficient if one wants to alleviate externalities. The altruistic social planner is genuinely averse to excluding somebody from work, while this may be fine to people who just want to avoid social conflict. Consider a hypothetical world where the unemployed would be deprived of their political rights and be locked in ghettoes where other people would never want to go. A benevolent social planner would certainly object to that. But the existence of unemployment would not increase social conflict (in our sense), as the unemployed would not interact at all with the rest of society.

Of especial relevance to the existence of institutions that compress the distribution of wages among the employed is the externality exerted by redistributive pressure. In this chapter, we show how the existence of redistributive taxation enhances the political support for labour market rigidity.

The exercise we perform here is different from what we did in Chapter 2. There, we studied what happened when people had the choice between two societies: an unregulated labour market along with a redistributive institution, or a regulated labour market without redistribution. Here, we analyse the choice between a regulated and an unregulated labour market when in both cases there exists such a redistributive institution, and when regulation affects the degree of redistribution.

3.2 Voting on redistributive taxation

In the previous chapter we discussed at length why group A and also group B might prefer rigidities to redistributive taxation; but the two options are not mutually exclusive. Once group A's insiders have determined their rent nothing prevents them from, on top of that, voting in favour of a transfer from the richest to the poorest. However, once we allow the two to co-exist, the point remains that rigidity and redistributive taxation are substitutes, at least for a wide range of the economy's underlying parameters, so that more rigidity implies less taxation. Here we study why and when.

Economic theory says that the level of redistributive taxation is determined by the median, or 'decisive' voter. His incentive to redistribute will depend on his income relative to the tax base, i.e. typically the average income. The poorer the median's income relative to the mean, the greater the equilibrium tax rate.

To illustrate that point, let us consider a simple model where people are indexed by $i \in [0, 1]$, and are distributed uniformly over that interval. Assume agent i has an income y_i so that average income is equal to $y = \int_0^1 y_i \, di$. Assume people vote on a redistributive scheme such that everybody gives up a fraction τ of his or her income in exchange for a flat transfer which is the same for everybody and equal to R. Finally, assume taxes are distortionary so that a fraction $b\tau$ of tax receipts are lost in the collection process (note that this fraction increases with the tax rate). The government's budget constraint implies that average tax receipts must be equal to the transfer, so that one has $R = \tau(1 - b\tau)y$. Consequently the income of agent i after taxes and transfers is equal to $w_i = y_i(1 - \tau) + R = y_i(1 - \tau) + \tau(1 - b\tau)y$. Agent i's preferred tax rate is the one that maximizes w_i, i.e.

$$\tau_i^* = \max((1 - y_i/y)/2b, 0).$$

According to this formula, agents poorer than average want a positive tax rate, while agents richer than average do not want any taxation. When people vote on the tax rate the majority winner is the tax rate preferred by the median voter, i.e. the median in the distribution of income.[3] In our case this is the agent with $i = 0.5$. More generally, political influence and participation may differ across income groups, so that the decisive voter would not be $i = 0.5$ but the median of a distribution weighted by some measure of political power.

Redistribution is clearly undesirable to those who pay more than they receive; moreover it has some efficiency loss. The key point to be noted is that to reduce redistributive pressure one must increase the income of the decisive voter relative to the mean, not the income of others. To the extent that the unemployed are at the bottom of the distribution of income the decisive voter is employed, not unemployed. For example, if the median agent characterized by $i = 0.5$ is decisive, and unemployment is

---

[3] Preferences are concave and therefore single-peaked.

10 per cent. the decisive voter is quite far away from the unemployed, who make up the bottom decile of the distribution of income.

Consider the previous chapter's example. Assume that group B is substantially smaller than group A, for example $L_A = 1$ and $L_B = 0.3$. As long as group B's workers are richer than those of group A, in equilibrium the poorest are the unemployed and the richest the members of group B, with the employed of group A between the two. As long as unemployment is not too large, the decisive voter is clearly an employed member of group A. For this not to be the case it would be necessary that either the unemployed or the members of group B represent more than half of the population. As long as group A's employed workers are decisive the equilibrium tax rate is the one that maximizes their welfare. Now, in the above setting people maximize their net income, and group A's welfare is different from their income because they have a positive probability s of losing their job. That is, their welfare V_e also reflects the income of the unemployed. Let us however assume $s = 0$, so that they will indeed set taxes so as to maximize their income (the role of exposure s is discussed further below). Then the equilibrium tax rate is

$$\tau^* = (1 - w_A/y)/2b, \tag{3.1}$$

where $y = Y/(L_A + L_B) = Y/(1 + 0.3)$ is income per capita. Clearly, an institution that increases the rent of group A's workers increases their wage while reducing income per capita. These two effects work in the direction of reducing the equilibrium level of redistributive taxation.

How does that affect the gains and losses from rigidity? To answer that question, let us parametrize our model. We assume a production function with constant elasticity of substitution so that, using the notation of the previous chapter, we have $Y = L_B h(l/L_B)$, with

$$h(x) = A(\alpha + (1 - \alpha)x^\sigma)^{1/\sigma},$$

where $x = l/L_B$. The elasticity of substitution between the two groups is given by

$$\eta = 1/(1 - \sigma).$$

We then compare a 'flexible society' where markets are free to operate with a 'rigid society' where wages of group A workers are set 10 per cent above market clearing level. In both societies people vote on redistributive taxation using the scheme described above. The parameter

A is normalized so as to yield a wage equal to 1 for group A workers under full employment. This implies that in the rigid world $w_A = 1.1$. As for α, which is nothing but the income share of skilled workers, we parametrize it so that the relative wage w_B/w_A is equal to some constant I at full employment. The greater is I, the greater the productivity (and therefore wage) differential between the two groups.

The model is solved as follows: first we can compute the value of employment of group A workers, l, which yields a wage 10 per cent above market clearing, i.e. equal to 1.1. This is simply done by inverting the relationship between w_A and x, which is given by

$$w_A = h'(x) = A(1 - \alpha)(\alpha x^{-\sigma} + (1 - \alpha))^{(1-\sigma)/\sigma}.$$

Then, knowing how many group A members are employed, one can straightforwardly compute y and τ^* (using (3.1) and the production function), as well as the wage of the fully employed group B given by

$$w_B = \alpha A(\alpha + (1 - \alpha)x^{\sigma})^{(1-\sigma)/\sigma}.$$

Finally, the net income of an employed worker is given by

$$\begin{aligned} z_i &= w_i(1 - \tau^*) + R \\ &= w_i(1 - \tau^*) + y\tau^*(1 - b\tau^*). \end{aligned}$$

3.3 The role of elasticity

Let us start by studying how the gains and losses from rigidity vary with the elasticity parameter η. Remember that the lower is η, the more the two groups cooperate in production, i.e. they are complements.

We compute numerically how elasticity affects the welfare of group A and group B employees, as well as the equilibrium tax rate and unemployment rate, for $b = 1$ and $I = 5$. Our results should be interpreted with some caution because we are making comparisons across economies with different production functions.

Figure 3.1 represents the evolution of the tax rate and the unemployment rate of group A workers in the rigid society. In the flexible society with the same parameter values, the equilibrium tax rate would be 0.24 (24 per cent).

Clearly, unemployment sharply rises with elasticity, as more people must be denied employment to sustain the same increase in wages. Since

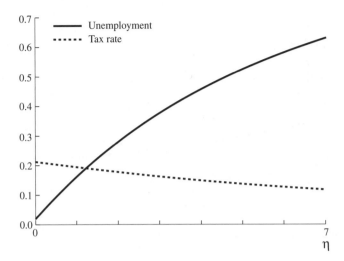

Figure 3.1. Impact of elasticity on taxes and unemployment

elasticity makes rigidity more costly in terms of jobs and therefore in terms of output per capita, the gains from redistributive taxation to group A employed members falls. There are two ways to interpret this: first, the tax base falls, making taxation more costly. Second, a larger share of tax receipts goes to the unemployed, making it less attractive to the employed decisive voter. Consequently, the tax rate falls when elasticity is larger.

Figure 3.2 represents the net welfare gain from rigidity (compared with flexibility) for both type A and type B employees, along with the tax rate, which we plot again for convenience.

In the simulation of Figure 3.2 an employed of type A is always better off in the rigid world than in the flexible one. This need not be the case. As elasticity increases to higher levels their gains eventually become negative. They get higher wages, but as output falls, so does the tax base for redistributive taxation. The latter effect becomes dominant for high elasticities. Furthermore, when we reintroduce exposure to unemployment ($s > 0$), group A insiders bear an extra loss due to the lower employment level. Here the loss from rigidity due to lower employment is irrelevant to the employed of group A because they are perfectly sheltered from unemployment.

One should also note that the gains to group A fall with elasticity, while the gains to group B rise with elasticity.

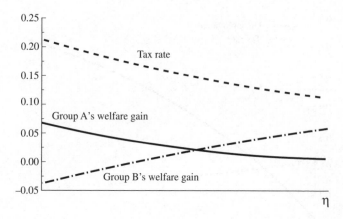

Figure 3.2. Employed's welfare gain from rigidity

That the gains to group A fall with elasticity has already been discussed in Chapter 2. However, here there is a subtlety. In Chapter 2 a higher elasticity reduced the gains because it reduced employment, and above all, the unemployed's job finding probability. As the employed of group A bore some unemployment risk they were less happy about rigidity when elasticity was larger. Here the linkage is totally different: group A dislikes unemployment not because it is exposed but because unemployment reduces the tax base and consequently the amount of transfers they get for a given tax rate.

What about group B? Rigidity affects their welfare in two ways. First, there are fewer people of type A to work with. This reduces their marginal product and consequently their wages. Second, there is less redistributive taxation. This makes them happier. Thus group B may either gain or lose from rigidity, depending on which effect is stronger. In Figure 3.2 we can see that group B loses from rigidity if elasticity is small but gains if elasticity is large.

It is true that a greater elasticity makes rigidity more costly in terms of jobs, and reduces the number of type A people cooperating in production with type B workers. But greater elasticity also means that there is less complementarity between the two types, so that the wage of type B is less responsive to the input of type A workers. At very low elasticities the two types are very complementary and the group B wage loss from even a small reduction in type A employment is very large. If elasticity was infinite, i.e. a linear production function with $\sigma = 1$, then group B's wage would be independent of rigidities.

On top of that, group B also benefits from the lower tax rate associated with greater elasticity. Given that they are net contributors to the transfer system, the fact that taxes are reduced is more relevant to them than the fact that the tax base is also reduced.

3.4 Rigidity as a source of cohesion

A crucial aspect of Figure 3.2 is that there exists a zone where *both* the employed of group A and those of group B prefer the rigid society over the flexible one. That would clearly never happen without redistributive taxation. In the previous chapter rigidity was always redistributing from group B to group A; group B was always worse off in the rigid society relative to a flexible society without transfers. Here, however, rigidity brings forward a reduction in the degree of conflict between the two groups, or, to put it another way, a reduction in the use of the alternative redistributive instrument.

How is it possible that both groups gain from rigidity? In principle, it could be that because of the lower burden of taxes, output per capita (net of tax distortions) is higher in the rigid world than in the flexible one. However, as Figure 3.3, which shows how net output varies with elasticity, makes clear, that gain can never be large enough to offset the loss that comes from the lower number of people employed. Therefore an increase in output per capita cannot be the reason why rigidity benefits both groups.

Remember that we are only talking about the *employed*. So it must be that they are made better off at the expense of the unemployed. The reason why both groups gain is that internal conflict generates external conflict, as was discussed at the end of the previous chapter; that is, if there is inequality within the employed, excluding the poorest from employment increases output per employed. Here the poorest employed are from group A, and the effect is stronger, the greater the productivity gap between the two groups. In the consensus zone the reduction in taxation automatically ensures that this greater output per employed is redistributed between the employed of the two groups in a way that makes both of them better off.

Note that the exercise we perform is not 'pure', in the sense that the unemployed are excluded from employment but not from the redistribu-

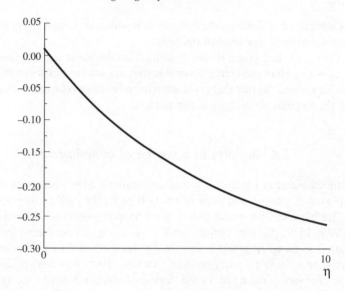

Figure 3.3. Net loss in output per capita in rigid society vs. flexible one

tive game. Part of the tax proceeds is paid to the unemployed. Consequently, the relevant average income which enters the determination of
the tax rate is not average income per employed, but per capita, which
is lower in the rigid society than in the flexible one (while income per
employed is higher). For that reason, group A's employed, who get lower
transfers in the rigid world, would not gain from rigidity if their pre-tax
wage did not rise. In other words, for high enough elasticities they end up
opposing the rigid society, since the loss from lower transfers eventually
outweighs the gains from higher wages, which tend to zero when the
two groups are more and more substitutes. If, instead, redistribution
only took place among the employed and no payment was made to the
unemployed, excluding some of group A's workers from employment
would increase the distributable income per recipient rather than reduce
it. Group A's employed would then support rigidity even if it did not
increase its *ex ante* wage—i.e. for an infinite elasticity.[4]

Consequently, institutions that redistribute among the employed are
more likely to generate a support for rigidity than institutions that redistribute among the whole population such as basic welfare assistance.

---

[4] But, in that case, group B would clearly oppose it.

3.5 Inequality

Let us now look at the impact of the inequality parameter, I.

In the previous section, the rigid society's wage was indexed on its market clearing level. This assumption was innocuous, because underlying inequality was held fixed. Now, however, we have to define more clearly what sort of institution the rigid society is representing.

We index the gap between the rigid wage and its market clearing level on the underlying level of inequality. If we were not doing so, the relative amount of wage compression achieved by the rigid society would fall when the level of inequality rises. That is, an institution that increases the lowest wage by 10 per cent compresses wages much more, relative to the free market outcome, when top wages are 20 per cent above bottom wages than when they are 1000 per cent above them. To avoid that, we assume that the rigid society achieves a degree of wage compression such that the inequality level in that society is

$$\frac{w_B}{w_A}\Big|_{\text{Rigid}} = I_{\text{Rigid}} = (I_{\text{Flexible}})^\gamma \, I_0^{1-\gamma},$$

where $\gamma \in [0, 1]$ is a parameter representing the degree of relative wage compression achieved, and I_0 the 'target' level of inequality. For $\gamma = 1$ the rigid society is in fact identical to the flexible one; as γ falls toward zero relative wages are more compressed; finally, for $\gamma = 0$ the rigid society achieves a target inequality level of I_0 regardless of the initial level of inequality. The smaller is γ, the lower the impact of underlying inequality on the relative wage structure achieved by that institution. Note that this structure implies that, unless $\gamma = 0$, if two societies have the same value of γ, and if one of them has a more unequal underlying distribution of productivity levels, it will also have a more unequal distribution of wages.

Figure 3.4 represents the impact of inequality on the equilibrium tax rate in both the rigid and the flexible societies, as well as the unemployment rate of the rigid world. We have chosen $\gamma = 0.9$, an elasticity of $\eta = 2$, and $b = 0.8$. These values allow us to have the greatest variety of regimes.

In both worlds, taxes are increasing with inequality, as the standard theory predicts. Unemployment is also increasing, although this feature should not be given too much weight given that α depends on I, so that we are not comparing unemployment under the same production functions.

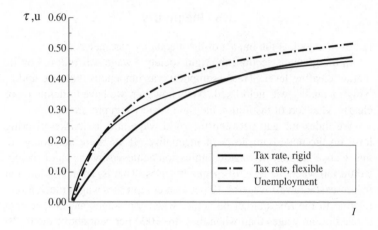

Figure 3.4. Impact of inequality on taxes and unemployment

At $I = 1$, the lowest value of inequality, the flexible and rigid societies are identical and there is no redistributive pressure so that taxes are zero.

Figure 3.5 represents the welfare gain from rigidity for both the employed of group A and group B.

As inequality increases, the gain to group A from rigidity increases and then falls. In Figure 3.5 it is always positive, but for other parameter values it may end up being negative for inequality large enough.

Under full equality rigidity cannot further compress the distribution of wages so it has no impact on type A's wages. If inequality is very small it only achieves a small degree of wage compression so the gain to group A is small. As inequality increases so does the wage increase achieved by rigidity for group A's employed members. Therefore their welfare increases. Their welfare eventually falls because as inequality increases the rigid society generates more unemployment. Recall that, despite their full job security, the employed are indirectly exposed to unemployment through the transfer system. Because of this effect the welfare of group A's employed ends up falling.

Let us now consider group B's welfare. Their gain is initially negative and falling with inequality, then increasing and then falling again. In Figure 3.5 it is first negative and then positive, but for other parameter values it may never become positive, or become positive and then negative again, as inequality increases.

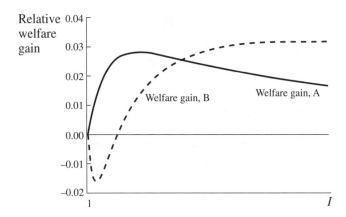

Figure 3.5. Impact of inequality on the employed's welfare gain from rigidity

What is the economic mechanism underlying this pattern? At low levels of inequality the effect that dominates is the reduction in group A's employment, which adversely affects group B's marginal product. Group B first starts losing, more so when inequality is greater. However beyond a certain level of inequality a second effect comes into play: namely that rigidity reduces redistributive conflict between the two groups. In that zone taxes are high and rigidity reduces them by an amount large enough to compensate group B for their fall in wages. Finally, when inequality becomes very large, the reduction in tax rates brought about by rigidity tends to be reduced, while group B also suffers from the fiscal costs of high unemployment. For these reasons their gain from rigidity ends up falling again.

This analysis suggests that the political support for rigidity will be larger for *intermediate* levels of inequality. At low levels of inequality there is not enough heterogeneity among the two groups for the gains (in terms of higher wages for group A and lower taxes for group B) to be large, while at large levels of inequalities the reduction in the degree of conflict is not large enough and the fiscal costs of unemployment are substantial.

3.6 Exposure

What happens, next, when we allow for some exposure of the employed to unemployment? An employed worker's welfare is no longer given by wages but by permanent income, which takes into account the expected time spent in future unemployment spells.

For type B workers nothing is changed as they are permanently employed. However, we now have to compute the steady state permanent income of type A workers. To do so, we can simply use the formulae derived in Chapter 1, under the assumption that there are no new entrants in the labour market:

$$rV_e = w + \dot{V}_e + s(V_u - V_e), \qquad (3.2)$$

$$rV_u = b + \dot{V}_u + a(V_u - V_e). \qquad (3.3)$$

Here w and b have to be interpreted as their net, post-tax income. So w has to be replaced by $w_A(1 - \tau) + R$ and b by R, where $R = \tau(1 - b\tau)y$. Finally, in steady state the job finding probability a is related to the unemployment rate via $u = s/(s + a)$.[5] Therefore,

$$a = \frac{sl}{1-l}.$$

Substituting this into (3.2) and (3.3) and making the appropriate substitutions we get that, in steady state,

$$rV_e = \frac{r(1-l) + sl}{r(1-l) + s} w_A(1 - \tau) + \tau(1 - b\tau)y. \qquad (3.4)$$

The left-hand side is the annuity value of the value of being employed, i.e. their permanent income. The right-hand side is the sum of the transfer R and of the post-tax wage $w_A(1 - \tau)$ multiplied by a factor representing the discounted fraction of time that this individual expects to be employed over his or her lifetime. This factor is given by

$$\psi = \frac{r(1-l) + sl}{r(1-l) + s}.$$

Clearly, we have $\psi \in [0, 1]$. It is larger, the larger the employment rate l, the smaller the exposure rate s, and the larger the interest rate r.

---

[5] a was equal to zero in the previous case where $s = 0$.

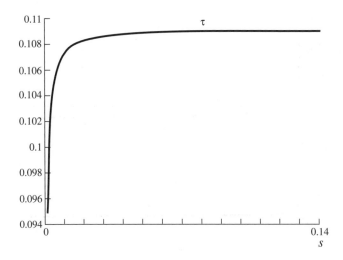

Figure 3.6. Impact of exposure on the rigid economy's tax rate

Also, it is more reactive to l, the larger the exposure rate s. At $s = 0$ it is equal to one and thus does not depend on l at all. At $s = \infty$ it is exactly equal to l. This would mean that people are constantly reshuffled at an infinite rate between employment and unemployment, so that it is as if the total amount of work were perfectly shared among the workforce.

Equation (3.4) tells us that a society with a higher exposure s will be more reluctant to vote for rigid institutions, as the associated rise in unemployment will have a greater adverse impact on the employment factor ψ. Furthermore, as s reduces ψ, the cost of taxes to an employed worker is lower relative to their benefit. A higher s should therefore increase the equilibrium tax rate. This is because the transfer system plays a role as unemployment insurance, and the employed are more in favour of it when more exposed to unemployment (this is further examined in Chapter 5, where we talk about unemployment benefits).

Our numerical analysis confirms this intuition. Figure 3.6 represents the evolution of the tax rate when s increases (we have chosen $I = 2$, $\gamma = 0.9$, $\eta = 0.4$).[6] The tax rate clearly increases with exposure. For some parameter values it may even end up higher than the flexible

---

[6] These values imply a tax rate equal to 0.12 in the flexible economy and an unemployment rate of 2.9 per cent in the rigid economy. This is illustrative and not meant to reproduce real-world features.

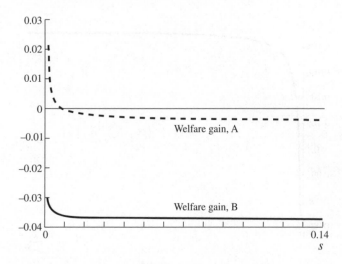

Figure 3.7. Impact of exposure on the welfare gain from rigidity

society tax rate. Figure 3.7 confirms that the gains from rigidity fall with exposure for both groups. Group A loses from higher unemployment risk and group B from higher taxes. Group A's gains become negative for a very small exposure level of 0.8 per cent, while the yearly job loss rate in the real world would be between 5 per cent and 20 per cent. This threshold level, however, obviously depends on the elasticity parameter, and can be higher for smaller elasticities. Also, we have assumed a uniform exposure level. If we take into account that exposure differs across workers, what is relevant is the exposure level of the *decisive* voter. It may be much lower than the economy's average, particularly if the bulk of labour turnover is concentrated on some categories of workers such as the young.

3.7   Lessons from a more general framework

In the above analysis we have assumed there were only two groups in society. But we can extend our approach by assuming that there is a large number of worker types, each with a different productivity level, who all cooperate in production. This extension is fully described in the appendix, but let us discuss the main results here. We assume that each worker's skill level is represented by an index $i \in [0, 1]$. Each skill has a productivity represented by a number a_i. The wage of a worker with type i, in a flexible, full-employment society, is proportional to his or her productivity a_i. Consequently, the ratio between the income of two workers of types i and j would be given by a_i/a_j. As above, there is a redistributive scheme among people. Everybody pays a flat tax rate τ on his or her income and receives a lump-sum transfer R. People vote on the tax rate, but prior to that they vote on a labour market institution represented by a parameter ρ, which is between 0 and 1. This institution compresses income among the employed, so that the ratio of wages between i and j is now $(a_i/a_j)^{\rho}$. ρ plays the same role as our γ. The smaller is ρ, the more 'rigid' the institution and the more it compresses wages. At $\rho = 0$ wages are fully equalized across skills, while $\rho = 1$ yields the free market outcome.

Wage compression is costly in terms of jobs because it increases the relative wages of the least skilled. The negative impact of rigidity on employment depends on the elasticity of labour demand. Our assumptions imply that

$$\frac{l_i}{l_j} = \left(\frac{\omega_i}{\omega_j}\right)^{-\sigma},$$

where σ is the elasticity of substitution between two labour types and ω_i is the ratio between the wage of type i and its productivity index, $\omega_i = w_i/a_i$.

3.7.1 Rank effects

One key insight that we get by extending the model is the existence of *rank effects*. In the above analysis we typically assumed that the decisive voter was always a member of group A. Therefore, the skill level of the decisive voter was the same in the rigid and in the flexible society.[7] When there is a large number of skill categories, the existence of unemployment will affect the skill level of the decisive voter. Suppose that people are uniformly distributed across skill levels as in Figure 3.8. Then, if everybody is fully employed, the median of the distribution of income is simply the middle of that interval. Suppose now that we force 10 per cent of the workforce into unemployment, that unemployment is distributed equally across skills, and that there are no unemployment

---

[7] This was true as long as the unemployed were not too numerous, otherwise the decisive voter would obviously be unemployed.

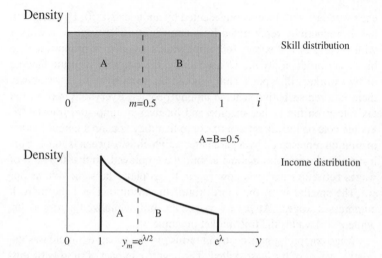

Figure 3.8. Median voter under full employment, uniform skill distribution

benefits. Then the distribution of income will be as illustrated in Figure 3.9. A mass of 10 per cent has been uniformly shifted from the positive income zone to a zero income level. The median is now the agent with rank $i = 0.44$.[8] The greater the unemployment, the smaller the rank of the median.

Thus, unemployment typically reduces the rank of the decisive voter in the distribution of skills, as it moves people from right to left in the preferences for redistribution.

This change in the identity of the decisive voter, who is now less skilled, has obvious consequences: the incentives to redistribute in the rigid society are increased by the rank effect, thus reducing or possibly overturning the cohesion effects of rigidity.

This rank effect is stronger, the larger the number of people who will lose their job as the result of wage compression. This depends on both inequality and elasticity. If the underlying distribution of skills is more unequal, rigid institutions will be more costly in terms of jobs. This further reduces the rank of the median. In addition, a given reduction in the decisive voter's skill levels will have a larger negative impact on his

[8] The median is such that 50 per cent of the people are richer than him or her. If m is the type of the median, there are $0.9 \times (1-m)$ people richer. Therefore $m = 1 - 0.5/0.9 = 0.44$.

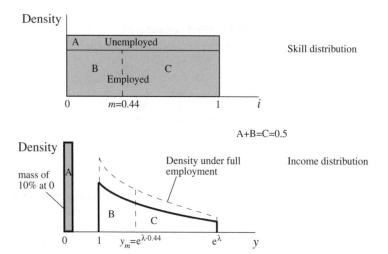

Figure 3.9. Median voter under a uniformly distributed unemployment rate of 10 per cent

income if productivity is more sensitive to skills—i.e. if a_i/a_j is greater for any given $i > j$. This sensitivity is also typically larger when there is more inequality. As for elasticity (σ), it works through the usual channel: a more elastic labour demand increases the unemployment created by rigidity, thus reducing the rank of the decisive voter.

The rank effect makes the rigid society more redistributive than otherwise, and therefore reduces its effects in terms of social cohesion. It may even be that the tax rate is higher in the rigid society than in the flexible one. It does not follow, however, that the poorest will support it, because transfers may still be lower because of the lower tax base.

Table 3.1 studies how the equilibrium tax rate depends on the degree of rigidity and on inequality. We have parametrized inequality by assuming that the productivity index a_i is an exponential function of the skill level i:

$$a_i = e^{\lambda i}.$$

Thus, if $i > j$, the income ratio between the two types for any given ρ is given by $e^{\lambda \rho (i-j)}$. The greater is λ, the wider the income gap between any two types. In Table 3.1, we can see that the tax-reducing effect of rigidity prevails only for not too large values of inequality. At $\lambda = 2$ a reduction in ρ (a more rigid society) always lowers the equilibrium tax

Table 3.1. Effect of λ and ρ on
the tax rate τ. $\eta = 0.2, b = 1$

λ ρ	2	3	5
0.6	0	0.35	1
0.7	0	0.28	0.97
0.8	0.05	0.27	0.77
0.9	0.1	0.28	0.65
1	0.15	0.3	0.59

rate. Because of the rank effect, however, this result is inverted at high levels of inequality: rigidity actually increases redistributive pressure. Finally, at intermediate levels of inequality, taxes are a U-shaped function of ρ. Rigidity reduces redistributive pressure up to some point, but increases it beyond that point.

Table 3.2 provides the same information, but for a lower level of the elasticity σ. A comparison with Table 3.1 tells us two things. First, given inequality, a greater elasticity makes it less likely that rigidity reduces redistributive pressure. For example, if we compare the second column across the two tables ($\lambda = 3$), we see that in the low elasticity case taxes are always lower in more rigid societies, while in the high elasticity case (Table 3.1) the pattern was U-shaped. This is because at high elasticities, rigidity creates more unemployment, thus having a stronger negative impact on the rank of the decisive voter. Second, given rigidity, an increase in inequality increases redistributive pressure less when elasticity is lower. This is again due to the rank effect: an increase in inequality increases unemployment more in the more elastic society, thus making the median voter poorer and more willing to redistribute. Without rigidity, however (if $\rho = 1$), an increase in inequality has, by construction, the same impact regardless of elasticity.

Finally, it is important to note that the rank effect is weaker, the more unemployment is concentrated at the bottom of the distribution of income. If it were fully concentrated (that is, if the 10 per cent unemployed were exactly the 10 per cent least skilled), then the rank effect would entirely disappear: unemployment would not change the decisive voter. So, an institution, like the minimum wage, that generates unemployment concentrated at the bottom of the distribution of income will have stronger cohesion effects, and will get greater support from the upper-middle class, than if its employment effects were more widely spread.

Table 3.2. Effect of λ and ρ on the tax rate τ. $\eta = -2$, $b = 1$

λ ρ	2	3	5	10
0.6	0	0.09	0.39	0.95
0.7	0.04	0.15	0.46	0.94
0.8	0.08	0.21	0.51	0.93
0.9	0.11	0.25	0.55	0.93
1	0.15	0.3	0.59	0.93

3.7.2 Extreme coalitions vs. the middle class: who votes for rigidity?

Once the tax outcome is computed as a function of labour market institutions, we can see what occurs when, in a first stage, people vote over ρ, the degree of rigidity. For simplicity we assume that people vote between two values, and that one of them is 1 (full flexibility). We also assume that people know for sure whether or not they will be employed.

The equilibrium is simply computed by calculating the net income of any worker under the two options, and assuming that this worker votes for the institution that yields the larger possible value. The outcome is then assumed to be the value of ρ with the largest number of votes.

Using numerical simulations one can uncover some interesting properties of the political support for rigidity. For a wide range of parameter values, the workers that will favour the rigid society over the flexible one are those who are employed whose skill level i belongs to an interval of *intermediate* values. That is, rigidity is opposed by the unemployed, the poorest, and the richest, while supported by a middle class of employed workers.

Another possibility, however, is that rigidity is supported by all employed workers whose skill level is below some threshold. But we find the 'middle class' case somewhat more instructive[9].

Table 3.3 illustrates these results by reporting, for the same parameter values as Table 3.2, the interval of skill levels whose employed workers favour rigidity over flexibility, along with the corresponding proportion of the population. It confirms that in many cases the 'middle class' sup-

---

[9] Our assumptions imply that the distribution of productivities is bounded away from zero. If there were people with arbitrarily small productivity, they would always oppose rigidity (just like the unemployed in our model). Therefore, the case where both ends of the distribution of income oppose rigidity is somewhat more generic.

Table 3.3. Intervals of values of i for which the employed prefer the rigid society, as a function of ρ and λ. Percentage of total population made up by these people

λ ρ	2	3	5	8
0.7	$0.00 - 0.69$	$0.00 - 0.79$	$0.26 - 0.92$	$0.58 - 0.90$
	60.6	66.1	54.8	26.8
0.8	$0.00 - 0.69$	$0.00 - 0.80$	$0.31 - 0.92$	$0.61 - 0.91$
	63.3	71.1	54.6	27.3
0.9	$0.00 - 0.70$	$0.04 - 0.81$	$0.35 - 0.94$	$0.63 - 0.91$
	67	73.6	56.6	27.2

ports rigidity, while the poorest and the richest oppose it. For example, with $\lambda = 5$ and $\rho = 0.9$ rigidity is supported by all employed agents with a skill level i between 0.35 and 0.94, who represent 56.6 per cent of the population. It is opposed by the unemployed, and employed agents with a skill level lower than 0.35 or greater than 0.94.

The explanation is as follows. The 'upper-middle class' benefits from the rigid institution because lower tax rates compensate them for the lower wages that they get. The richest, however, lose a lot from wage compression. Their productivity is very high and their wages can fall substantially if there is a reduction in the complementary input of less skilled people. The lower tax rate is insufficient to compensate these people for the sharp drop in their marginal productivity induced by the compression of wages.

The opposite occurs at the bottom of the distribution of income. The 'lower-middle class' gets lower transfers but rigidity increases their wages (as long as they remain employed); this extra wage is enough to compensate them for the lower transfers. The poorest, however, have a very low wage and the bulk of their income is due to transfers. They suffer a lot from the fall in transfers while their wage increase is not sufficient to compensate them.[10]

Other patterns emerge from Table 3.3. As inequality rises, the size of the support for rigidity goes up and then down. This confirms what

[10] This conclusion may be reinforced if the tax system is more complex so that the richest face a higher tax rate, which, being different from the one paid by the median voter, has no reason to fall when the median becomes richer relative to the mean. However, it is virtually impossible to tackle these aspects analytically because the median voter theorem typically only applies to one-dimensional collective decision problems.

we already saw in the two-group case, but this pattern now also reflects the influence of the rank effect. We also see that as inequality increases, the interval of workers who support rigidity shifts to the right, i.e. they have, on average, greater skills. This is because inequality increases the incentives to tax and therefore the value of the flexible world (where taxes and transfers are higher) to comparatively poor people, and its cost to comparatively rich people. The interval of support for rigidity consequently moves to the right.

3.8 Conclusion

The existence of a redistributive scheme considerably enhances the political support for labour market rigidities. Excluding part of the least productive workers from employment would always reduce the wages of the most skilled, because of the complementarities in production between these workers and the less skilled. Without a redistributive institution, this group of workers will therefore always oppose rigidity. When there exists a redistributive institution, these workers may be compensated by the lower transfers made by them to the rest of society. Excluding some of the poorest from employment increases the average output per employed worker, and therefore the income of each of them could increase if the income they generate was redistributed properly among them. Under certain conditions, the fiscal system automatically operates such redistribution, thus buying the support of a large fraction of the employed, including highly productive ones. This is because the pre-tax wage of the decisive voter, who remains employed and is less productive than the mean, increases relative to mean income, thus lowering incentives to tax. This is exactly what was necessary to support this coalition of skilled and unskilled workers.

While this discussion ignores the fact that part of the output is distributed to the unemployed because of the transfer system, it basically captures what is taking place in a society where the middle class supports labour rigidities. The higher welfare of this middle class is indirectly financed by the unemployed, and also typically by the two extremes of the distribution of income.

The mechanism studied in this chapter can be described in terms of the notions of internal and external conflict introduced in the previous chapter. Relative wage rigidity alleviates internal conflict, but makes external conflict more severe. However, those workers who are the source of internal conflict (type A workers) have greater political influence than those who generate external conflicts (the unemployed); consequently, a majority of the workforce may be willing to pay the cost of greater external conflict in order to alleviate internal conflict.

Appendix. The model with a continuum of agents

We now describe the model with a large number of worker types, which we used to get the simulations reported in Tables 3.1–3.3. There is a continuum of worker types, each indexed by its productivity a_i. Without loss of generality we assume that a_i is nondecreasing in i. These types cooperate in the aggregate production function, which is of the CES class:

$$Y = \left(\int_0^1 a_i l_i^\eta \, di \right)^{1/\eta}. \tag{A3.1}$$

The elasticity of substitution is $\sigma = 1/(1 - \eta)$. l_i is the employment density of workers of type i. We assume that the supply of workers of type i is normalized to 1: $\bar{l}_i = 1$. Firms are wage takers so that wages are equal to the marginal product of the corresponding type:

$$w_i = a_i \left(\int_0^1 a_i l_i^\eta di \right)^{1/\eta - 1} l_i^{\eta - 1}. \tag{A3.2}$$

This formula yields a relative labour demand curve:

$$\frac{l_i}{l_j} = \left(\frac{w_i}{w_j} \frac{a_j}{a_i} \right)^{-\sigma}.$$

Under full employment the relative wage of two types would therefore be equal to

$$w_i/w_j = a_i/a_j.$$

Changes in the underlying distribution of income are therefore captured by changes in the a_i. For example if $a_i = a(i)$, with $a(.)$ differentiable in i, and if average productivity is normalized to $\int_0^1 a_i \, di = 1$, the distribution of wages has a density equal to $1/(a'(a^{-1}(w)))$ at w.

Labour market institutions are captured by a parameter ρ which represents the degree of *relative* wage rigidity prevailing in that society. Institutions imply a compressed wage structure relative to the equilibrium one. More specifically we assume that it imposes a relative wage equal to

$$w_i/w_j = (a_i/a_j)^\rho .$$

Thus, the lower is ρ, the more compressed the distribution of wages. $\rho = 1$ corresponds to the full employment case, while $\rho = 0$ corresponds to an egalitarian society.

In order to sustain such a distribution, unemployment must exist in all groups except in the most skilled one. Using (A3.2) we see that the employment rate of group i must be such that

$$\left(\frac{a_i}{a_1}\right)^\rho = \frac{w_i}{w_1} = \left(\frac{a_i}{a_1}\right) l_i^{\eta-1}.$$

Hence

$$l_i = \left(\frac{a_i}{a_1}\right)^{\frac{1-\rho}{1-\eta}} . \tag{A3.3}$$

This allows us, next, to compute total output and absolute wages:

$$Y = \left[\int_0^1 a_i^{(1-\rho\eta)/(1-\eta)}\, di\right]^{1/\eta} a_1^{-(1-\rho)/(1-\eta)} \tag{A3.4}$$

$$w_i = a_i^\rho \left[\int_0^1 a_i^{(1-\rho\eta)/(1-\eta)}\, di\right]^{\frac{1-\eta}{\eta}} . \tag{A3.5}$$

Clearly, the ratio between an individual's wage in a 'rigid world' (with ρ small) and that same individual's wage in a flexible world (with ρ high) is decreasing in a_i, so that in the absence of redistributive schemes rigidity would be supported by a coalition of the poorest employed agents.

The redistributive system

As in the text, we assume that there exists a government which redistributes among agents by levying a flat tax rate on each individual's income and paying a lump-sum transfer to each individual. Consequently, tax receipts are given by

$$T = \tau(1 - b\tau)Y,$$

where $b\tau$ is the fraction of tax receipts lost due to distortions. An employed agent's post-tax income is therefore equal to

$$w_i(1 - \tau) + \tau(1 - b\tau)Y, \qquad (A3.6)$$

where w_i is determined by (A3.5), while for the unemployed it is given by T.

By concavity of preferences with respect to τ there exists a unique voting equilibrium determined by the median voter's preferences. This equilibrium tax rate is given by

$$\tau = \left(1 - \frac{w_m}{Y}\right)/2b,$$

where m is the type of the median voter, who will be employed as long as unemployment is less than 50 per cent, which we shall assume. The main difference with respect to the assumptions made in the text is that the median's type now varies smoothly with the model's parameters. Under full employment ($\rho = 1$), one would simply have $m = 0.5$. However, by creating unemployment, wage rigidity has a direct positive impact on the support for redistribution coming from the mass of unemployed workers. This mass shifts the type of the median voter so that he will be poorer than the median of the distribution of wages. This is what we call the *rank effect*. More specifically m is determined by

$$\int_m^1 l_i \, \mathrm{d}i = 1/2. \qquad (A3.7)$$

which, given that $l_i < 1$, implies $m < 0.5$.

Let us now sort out the effect of labour market institutions on the equilibrium tax rate. One can look at how the median/mean ratio varies with ρ. If it varies negatively then wage rigidity reduces redistributive pressure, since a higher ratio implies lower taxes. One can decompose this into two effects:

$$\frac{\mathrm{d}}{\mathrm{d}\rho} \ln \frac{w_m}{Y} = \left[\frac{\partial}{\partial\rho} \ln \frac{w_m}{Y}\right]_m + \frac{1}{w_m}\frac{\partial w_m}{\partial m}\frac{\partial m}{\partial\rho}.$$

The first term is the effect on the ratio between the median employed agent's income, and average income holding constant the identity of that agent (we call it the dispersion effect). We expect it to be negative, for two reasons. First, because this agent is likely to be poorer than the mean, which implies that a compression of the distribution of wages will make that agent richer. Second, because rigidity reduces average income since it reduces employment. The second term is the rank effect, which captures the fact that rigidity changes the type of the decisive agent, who is now poorer; it is always positive.

These contributions can be computed. From (A3.4) and (A3.5) we get that

$$\frac{w_m}{Y} = \frac{a_m^\rho a_1^{(1-\rho)/(1-\eta)}}{\left[\int_0^1 a_i^{(1-\rho\eta)/(1-\eta)} \, di\right]}.$$

This allows us to compute the dispersion effect:

$$\left[\frac{\partial}{\partial\rho} \ln \frac{w_m}{Y}\right]_m = \left(\ln a_m - \int_0^1 \ln a_i \cdot \theta_i \, di\right) - \int_0^1 \frac{1}{1-\eta} (\ln a_1 - \ln a_i) \theta_i \, di,$$

(A3.8)

where the θ_i's are weights given by

$$\theta_i = \frac{a_i^{(1-\rho\eta)/(1-\eta)}}{\int_0^1 a_j^{(1-\rho\eta)/(1-\eta)} \, dj}.$$

The first term $\left(\ln a_m - \int_0^1 \ln a_i \cdot \theta_i \, di\right)$ is an index of the decisive voter's productivity relative to the mean. It says that the decisive voter is more likely to be made richer by an increase in rigidity (a fall in ρ) when its productivity is smaller relative to the average (as defined by $\int_0^1 \ln a_i \cdot \theta_i \, di$). It is typically negative if the median is poorer than the 'mean' (computed using the θ_i's as weights), and the gap between the two is likely to increase with inequality. The second term is an index of inequality: it is a weighted sum of the log productivity gap between each agent and the most productive one. It says that a fall in ρ has a larger negative impact on Y when there is more inequality in the sense that people are on average more remote from the top agent. This is because a fall in ρ then destroys more jobs.

As for the rank effect, we can compute it by substituting (A3.3) into (A3.7), yielding

$$\int_m^1 \left(\frac{a_i}{a_1}\right)^{\frac{1-\rho}{1-\eta}} \, di = 1/2.$$

Differentiating, we get

$$\frac{\partial m}{\partial \rho} = \int_m^1 \frac{1}{1-\eta}(\ln a_1 - \ln a_i)\left(\frac{a_i}{a_m}\right)^{\frac{1-\rho}{1-\eta}} \, \mathrm{d}i > 0.$$

We see that the right-hand-side is a measure of inequality of the same sort as the last term in (A3.8). This formula tells us that when inequality is higher, rigidity destroys more jobs, which further reduces the rank of the decisive voter among the employed.

Next, noting that

$$\frac{1}{w_m} \frac{\partial w_m}{\partial m} = \frac{\rho}{a_m} \frac{\mathrm{d}a_m}{\mathrm{d}m}$$

we get

$$\frac{1}{w_m} \frac{\partial w_m}{\partial m} \frac{\partial m}{\partial \rho} = \frac{\rho}{a_m} \frac{\mathrm{d}a_m}{\mathrm{d}m} \cdot \int_m^1 \frac{1}{1-\eta}(\ln a_1 - \ln a_i)\left(\frac{a_i}{a_m}\right)^{\frac{1-\rho}{1-\eta}} \, \mathrm{d}i > 0. \tag{A3.9}$$

This formula tells us two things. In addition to its effect on the rank of the decisive voter m, inequality also affects the income of the decisive voter. The factor $\frac{1}{a_m}\frac{\mathrm{d}a_m}{\mathrm{d}m}$ is a *local* inequality measure around the median voter, which is just the elasticity of income with respect to the worker's rank type. The larger this number, the more income is sensitive to worker type in this zone, and the greater the reduction in the median voter's income due to the rank effect.

Consequently, through the rank effect inequality tends to mitigate or offset the tax-reducing impact of rigidity. However, the net impact of inequality on $\frac{\mathrm{d}}{\mathrm{d}\rho}\ln\frac{w_m}{Y}$ is ambiguous since inequality also magnifies the dispersion effect, which goes in the other direction.

In the exponential case where $a_i = \mathrm{e}^{\lambda i}$ one can explicitly compute the type of the decisive voter. Making the appropriate substitutions into (A3.7) we get that

$$\frac{1-\eta}{\lambda(1-\rho)}\left[1 - \mathrm{e}^{\lambda(m-1)(1-\rho)/(1-\eta)}\right] = 1/2,$$

or, equivalently,

$$m = 1 + \frac{1-\eta}{\lambda(1-\rho)}\log\left(1 - \frac{1}{2}\frac{\lambda(1-\rho)}{1-\eta}\right). \tag{A3.10}$$

We can clearly see that $\frac{\partial m}{\partial \rho}$ is positive and that its magnitude is proportional to λ, our measure of inequality. As for the other factor

$$\frac{\rho}{a_m} \frac{da_i}{di} \Big|_{i=m},$$

it is simply equal to $\rho\lambda$, and also contributes to increasing the size of the rank effect when inequality is higher.

One can in the same way compute the dispersion effect. Substituting the values of a_i into (A3.8) and integrating we get

$$\left[\frac{\partial}{\partial \rho} \ln \frac{w_m}{Y} \right]_m = \lambda \left(m - \frac{e^{\lambda k}}{e^{\lambda k} - 1} + \frac{1}{\lambda k} \right) - \frac{\lambda}{1 - \eta} \left(-\frac{1}{e^{\lambda k} - 1} + \frac{1}{\lambda k} \right),$$

where $k = (1 - \rho\eta)/(1 - \eta)$. One can show that the first term is always negative because

$$m < 1/2 < \frac{e^{\lambda k}}{e^{\lambda k} - 1} - \frac{1}{\lambda k}.$$

Taking the derivative and using that inequality one can see that it is always falling with λ. The second term is always negative because $\frac{1}{e^{\lambda k}-1} > \lambda k$. Its derivative with respect to λ can be shown to be negative too. This confirms that the dispersion effect is magnified by an increase in inequality.

(A3.5) and (A3.4) can also be used to explicitly compute the median's wage and output as a function of m as well as pre-tax output per capita:

$$w_m = e^{\lambda \rho m} \left[\frac{e^{\lambda k} - 1}{\lambda k} \right]^{\frac{1-\eta}{\eta}}.$$

As for output we get

$$Y = \left(\frac{e^{\lambda k} - 1}{\lambda k} \right)^{1/\eta} e^{-\lambda(1-\rho)/(1-\eta)}.$$

Labour market institutions

The model is then closed by computing the welfare of each type of worker under the flexible and rigid systems, using (A3.6), and computing the total mass of workers who are better off in the rigid society. Rigidity is then the political equilibrium if that number is greater than 0.5.

4
Employment protection

The preceding chapters have helped us to understand how employee rents arise. We have seen that they may come from microeconomic imperfections such as the ones we discussed in Chapter 1. We have also seen that they may be affected by the political process; in some circumstances, there is scope for distributive conflict to be mediated by labour market rigidities that increase the rents of some categories of workers at the expense of the wages of others. We have also established how the existence of a fiscal system of redistribution may increase the political support for rent-generating rigidities.

In this chapter we make a further step in our understanding of how various rigidities fit together. We take as given the existence of rents and we discuss how the existence of employee rents leads to political support in favour of employment protection. By employment protection we refer to all institutions that make it more costly for firms to dismiss their workers. Such institutions are prevalent in many countries, most notably in Europe.

In the preceding chapters, by manipulating the rents, incumbent employees were exploiting a trade-off between job finding and wages. They could choose either high wages and a low job finding rate, or the converse. The trade-off involved when voting over employment protection is somehow a dual one. Incumbent employees are now able to trade a lower job loss rate against lower wages. We first postulate the existence of such a trade-off by introducing it into the framework discussed in Chapter 1, assuming a fixed total rent. We show that the support for employment protection increases with the rent, but that both the employed and the unemployed would vote for the same level of job protection, and that this level would be the one unilaterally adopted by firms if they could commit on their dismissal policy. We then consider what happens if the total rent is an increasing function of expected job tenure, and show that the employed will want more employment protection than the unemployed, who are happy to leave that decision to firms. Finally, we explicitly analyse the process by which firms become obsolete, which allows us to derive the wage/job loss trade-off rather than postulate it. This allows us to compare the politically determined level of employment protection with the socially efficient one, and to show, in particular, that the employed's preferred level is strictly greater than the socially efficient one, which is above the market-provided one if there is no other instrument available to the policymaker. It also gives us some further results, in particular that more 'mobile' societies are likely to pick up a lower level of employment protection.

4.1 The wage–exposure trade-off

When dealing with the economic effects of employment protection, two important things have to be kept in mind.

First, employment protection reduces the incentives to hire, as do most constraints imposed on firms. Since the set of actions available to the employer is reduced, the expected profits made out of any newly employed workers necessarily fall, and so do the incentives to hire. Hence labour market tightness—the exit rate from unemployment—falls. Unemployment duration increases. At the same time, however, fewer dismissals will take place since these are made more costly. Therefore, employment protection also reduces the inflow into unemployment. It follows that the net effect of employment protection on employment is ambiguous, even though its effect on hiring and unemployment duration is unambiguous.

Second, employment protection artificially maintains people in activities that would not take place otherwise. Such activities are unproductive relative to some alternative value of human time, which reflects higher productivity elsewhere in the economy. Therefore, employment protection typically reduces average productivity. This has to be reflected in living standards and wages. More employment protection therefore reduces wages.

Consequently, in deciding their most preferred level of employment protection, people trade lower living standards against lower exposure to unemployment. This trade-off is represented in Figure 4.1. We assume that it is given by a function $w(s)$, which represents which wage w is achievable as a function of the job loss rate s. We assume it is concave for

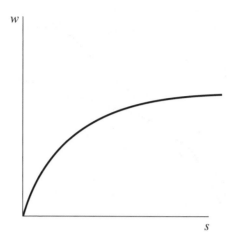

Figure 4.1. The wage–exposure trade-off

expositional convenience: it rules out technical problems when dealing with optima.

In the preceding chapters the job loss rate s was treated as exogenous. Now it is endogenous and depends on the degree of job protection. By picking up the degree of job protection, workers thus indirectly choose their exposure to unemployment s. $w(s)$ is an increasing function of s, although it may eventually be decreasing for high values of s, reflecting the adverse impact of too high turnover on productivity due to incentives and other considerations such as on-the-job training.

What is a worker's most preferred point on this curve? To know that, we need to know how their welfare is affected by exposure and wages. Let us use the small model developed in Chapter 1. In this chapter we assume there are no new entrants ($p = 0$), therefore using (1.18) we have

$$V_e = \frac{w - sQ}{r}. \tag{4.1}$$

This simple formula implies that the marginal rate of substitution between wages and unemployment exposure is equal to Q, the intertemporal rent. That is, to maintain V_e constant to compensate the worker for an increase in the job loss rate by ds, we must increase the wage by $dw = Q\, ds$. Every time the worker loses his job, he loses that rent. How much is he willing to give away in wages to lose his job less often, say

Employment protection

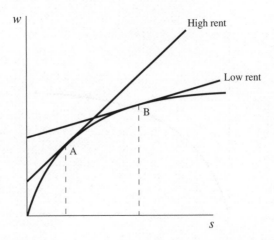

Figure 4.2. Indifference curves and preferred employment protection level

1 per cent of the time less often? The answer is 1 per cent times the rent Q.

In Figure 4.2 we have drawn the indifference curves for workers in two economies: a high rent one (A) and a low rent one (B). The indifference curve is steeper in the economy with high rents—these people gain more from a given reduction in exposure, and are willing to accept a greater reduction in wages for that. Consequently, the degree of job protection most preferred by the high rent economy is larger than in the low rent one; point A has lower exposure and lower wages than point B. The first-order condition for maximizing (4.1) with respect to s is

$$w'(s) = Q. \tag{4.2}$$

This simple result implies that the existence of rents is a crucial determinant of the support for employment protection. Without the rent s would not appear in (4.1). Job loss is not associated with any cost in the no-rent society because people are indifferent between being employed and unemployed—as we have seen, job seekers find work instantaneously. An increase in the rent means that the labour market is less competitive; outsiders are less able to underbid insiders, who are able to increase the gap between their wages and their alternative value of time. This gap is what they lose if they end up unemployed; so their support for employment protection increases with the rent.

This important result tells us that *employment protection will arise in societies with less competitive labour markets.*

Our discussion conveys the flavour of a conflict of interest between insiders and outsiders about the degree of employment protection. This idea is very natural, since the former, not the latter, enjoy the rent. However, it should be qualified. What are the unemployed's workers preferences for employment protection? From Chapter 1 we get the welfare of an unemployed person

$$V_u = \frac{w - (r + s)Q}{r}.$$ (4.3)

We can see from that formula that the marginal rate of substitution between w and s—the slope of the indifference curve—is exactly equal to Q, just as for the employed. Thus, as long as Q is fixed, the unemployed's preferred level of employment protection is exactly the same as the employed's!

The difference between the employed's and the unemployed's welfare is always pinned down by the exogenous rent Q. A change in any other parameter therefore affects the welfare of both the employed and the unemployed by the same amount: there cannot be any conflict of interest between the employed and the unemployed unless the policy change affects the total rent Q.

If wages were *fixed*, an increase in employment protection would benefit the employed much more than the unemployed. The unemployed put greater weight on the reduced job finding probability than the employed, since they are more directly affected by that event. The employed only care about lower job finding to the extent that they have a positive probability of becoming unemployed in the future. Conversely, the employed more directly benefit from longer job tenure than the unemployed. Therefore if wages were fixed there would be a sharp conflict of interest between the employed and the unemployed over the degree of job protection. However, in equilibrium, wages adjust so as to bring the welfare of both groups in line with each other. When employment protection increases, at the initial level of wages the employed's welfare is too far above their alternative option so that employers are able to impose reduced wages on them; this at the same time increases both recruitment incentives and the exit rate from unemployment, until the point where the equality $V_e = V_u + Q$ is restored.

This level of employment protection that is preferred by both the employed and the unemployed, is also the one that would be adopted by a social planner wishing to maximize the total welfare of the employed and of the unemployed. As discussed in Chapter 1, this is the appropriate welfare criterion if all existing firms have a value of zero. However, the essence of employment protection is that it maintains the life of a number of jobs whose net value is negative. This result can therefore not be applied here, and in order to make a proper welfare analysis one has to explicitly formalize the layoff decision, as we will do further below.

What we can prove, for now, is that the employed's and unemployed's level of job protection will automatically be provided by the *market, if* firms can actually elect the value of s when entering the market and make a credible commitment over it. That is, firms entirely internalize the workers' gains and losses from reducing unemployment exposure. As for the losses, this is obvious: these losses are due to lower productivity that directly reduces profits. But the gains are also internalized, because commitment to longer tenure allows firms to pay lower wages.

Assume that productivity is an increasing function of s, $m(s)$. In equilibrium of course one must have $w(s) = m(s)$: free entry of firms must drive profits to zero, and therefore wages are equal to productivity.[1] Firms would like to provide the level of employment protection which maximizes their value, given labour market conditions. This value is given by (1.22), which can be rewritten as

$$J = \frac{m(s) - w}{r + s}. \tag{4.4}$$

Now, w is not taken by firms as exogenous. Firms know that they must set wages so as to match the wage formation equation (1.15), which is now equivalent to

$$w = rV_u + (r + s)Q. \tag{4.5}$$

In (4.5) V_u is taken as given but s is a variable to be chosen by the firm. Smaller exposure to unemployment reduces wages, because the payment of the total rent Q can be spread over a longer period (in the next section, where the total rent depends on s, this effect will not be present). Workers ask for less if they have more job security. Hence

---

[1] This identity is due to our assumption, made for convenience, that m is constant throughout the life of the firm, so that the trade-off between s and m arises *exante*, at the time the firm enters the market. Further below we introduce productivity shocks, getting different results.

it is in the interest of firms to reduce s. It is through this effect that they internalize the gains from employment protection.[2] Which value of s will they set? They will maximize their present discounted value J. Substituting (4.5) into (4.4) we can see that

$$J = \frac{m(s) - rV_u}{r + s} - Q. \tag{4.6}$$

The first-order condition is

$$m'(s) = \frac{m(s) - rV_u}{r + s}. \tag{4.7}$$

At face value this looks very different from (4.2). In fact it gives the same value for s. Recall that under free entry profits are equal to zero. Labour market tightness adjusts so as to yield $m(s) = w = rV_u + (r + s)Q$. Therefore the numerator of (4.7) is just $(r + s)Q$. Hence in equilibrium (4.7) is just equivalent to (4.2). So, not only do all workers vote for the socially optimal degree of job protection, but private firms deliver it as well in the absence of regulation! A unit reduction in s reduces productivity by $m'(s)$, and reduces the wage that workers ask by Q. These are the two effects that were present when we looked at the effect of s on V_e, and they are entirely internalized in firms' profits. Finally, a reduction in s also reduces the rate at which profits are discounted (the denominator of (4.4)). However, since profits are zero in equilibrium, this effect is zero. Consequently, firms would spontaneously elect the value of s that maximizes V_e.

This result is a special case of the one we established at the end of Chapter 1, where we saw that the unemployed wanted to leave the determination of job characteristics to the market, while the employed agreed if the rent was zero or fixed. However, there is a subtlety here. This result hinges crucially on one implicit assumption we have made: namely, that firms can make a *commitment* over the rate of job destruction s.[3]

---

[2] If the wage level w were fixed, say because productivity is fixed, a reduction in s would increase firms' incentives to hire and therefore equilibrium labour market tightness. Recall that from Chapter 1 we have

$$a = w/Q - (r + s).$$

If wages were constant, a unit fall in unemployment exposure would increase the equilibrium job finding rate by a unit. This is why both the employed and the unemployed benefit from it to the same extent.

[3] This effect is discussed at length in Saint-Paul (1996c, Ch. 3).

Workers ask for lower wages *now* because they *anticipate* a lower value of s to prevail *in the future*. Such commitment will naturally hold if firms elect between various production opportunities, each characterized by a pair $(m(s), s)$ when entering the market. But if job destruction is a response to adverse productivity shocks, and if the decision to destroy a job is made at the time of that shock, it will be typically inefficient, for reasons that we further explain below.

On the other hand, a planner, or politician, who cares about employment rather than output will always pick up a degree of employment protection greater than optimal. To show this we use equation (1.17), which determines unemployment in steady state, where for simplicity we have assumed $b = p = 0$. We have

$$u = \frac{sQ}{w - rQ}. \tag{4.8}$$

Taking the derivative and equating it to zero yields the first-order condition for the degree of job protection that minimizes unemployment:[4]

$$w'(s) = \frac{w - rQ}{s}. \tag{4.9}$$

As one must have $u < 1$ in any reasonable equilibrium, (4.8) implies that one must have $w - rQ > sQ$. Substituting that into (4.9) we see that it implies $w'(s) > Q$. At the employment-maximizing point, an increase in turnover would increase wages by more than the rent. This means that the employment maximizer is willing to pay more for employment protection than private agents. Figure 4.3 illustrates that as $w(s)$ is concave it will choose a point with a lower value of s than private agents.

This is not surprising. For private agents, the reduction in productivity due to increased employment protection is costly both because income is lower and because there is less hiring. The employment maximizer only takes into account the latter effect, ignoring the adverse impact of job protection on productivity. As we see below, however, this result is likely to be overturned when we relax the assumption of a fixed total rent.

---

[4] Strictly speaking, this is an approximation. When one chooses a value of s the long-run corresponding level of unemployment is generally different from the initial one. Hence unemployment has transitional dynamics that we neglect since we minimize its steady-state level.

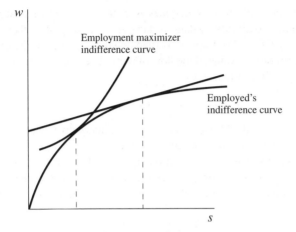

Figure 4.3. The employment maximizing level vs. the employed's preferred level

4.2 Beyond unanimity: impact of tenure on the total rent

The above discussion captures the basic motivation for employment protection. However, in this simplified world, employment protection is
not associated with any sort of conflict since both the employed and the
unemployed would vote for the socially efficient level of s. And, under
commitment, private firms would provide that level in equilibrium even
in the absence of any regulation.

However, we have made important simplifications. So far, the
total rent Q has been treated as exogenous, as well as the exposure–
productivity trade-off $w(s)$ (or equivalently $m(s)$).

That Q is fixed is just one possibility, and not the most plausible, as
discussed in the appendix to Chapter 1. In particular, the assumption of
a fixed Q is especially problematic here. As (4.5) makes clear, it has
the implication that as tenure goes to zero (s goes to infinity) the wage
that must be paid by the firm to the worker becomes infinite, which is
not very realistic. This is because, regardless of the expected duration
of a job, workers must earn a fixed total rent in intertemporal, or present
discounted, terms.

It is more reasonable to assume that the total discounted rent that the worker is able to earn declines with the job's expected duration.[5] One simple possibility is that workers are able to grab a fixed rent q *per unit of time.* Total rent Q is then equal to $q/(r + s)$, the expected present discounted value of the flow of rents. The equation giving wages, equation (4.5), is replaced by

$$w = rV_u + q. \tag{4.10}$$

Wages are a fixed additive markup over the alternative wage rV_u. They are insensitive to unemployment exposure s.[6]

We will use the wage formation equation (4.10) in the next section, but for now let us be more general and simply assume that the total rent Q is a decreasing function of s, $Q(s)$. The employed's welfare is then given by

$$V_e = \frac{w(s) - sQ(s)}{r}.$$

The first-order condition for maximization with respect to s is

$$w'(s) = Q(s) + sQ'(s). \tag{4.11}$$

As $Q'(s) < 0$, this yields a value of s which is actually higher than if Q did not depend on s. While each individual worker likes to have a rent, they recognize that in general equilibrium higher rents for everybody are enforced through lower job finding probability. Thus, the recognition that a reduction of s further increases Q *reduces* the employed's net gain from employment protection.

What about the unemployed? Their welfare is now given by

$$V_u = \frac{w(s) - (r + s)Q(s)}{r}.$$

Their first-order condition is

$$w'(s) = Q(s) + (r + s)Q'(s). \tag{4.12}$$

---

[5] This is implied not only by the 'trying-to-steal model' described at the end of the appendix to Chapter 1, and that we use here, but also, more indirectly, by matching models. In such models the total rent is a fraction of the hiring cost, which rises with labour market tightness. An increase in s reduces the duration of a job and therefore the present discounted profit of the firm, through the denominator of an equation such as (4.4). In equilibrium, to compensate, firms must spend less on hiring, which reduces the total rent. As s goes to infinity the firm's value goes to zero, so do hiring costs, and the total rent goes to zero.

[6] Such a formulation is implied by the 'trying-to-steal' version of the efficiency wage model—see the appendix to Chapter 1.

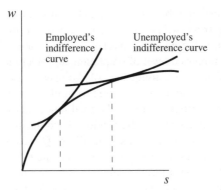

Figure 4.4. Employed's vs. unemployed's preferences for employment protection

The unemployed would choose a higher value of s than the employed. This is illustrated in Figure 4.4: the indifference curves of the unemployed are flatter than those of the employed; they are willing to accept a lower reduction in wages in exchange for a given increase in job protection. One way to view this is that a reduction in s increases the rent Q, i.e. the welfare difference between the employed and the unemployed, so that the latter gain necessarily less from it than the former. Another way to interpret it is by saying that the cost of reduced job finding weighs more in the unemployed's welfare than in the employed's welfare. The reason is that the unemployed have already lost their jobs and will be affected by the event of job finding before the event of job loss, while the converse holds for the employed. Unless the full credibility effects of the previous section hold, we therefore expect the employed to benefit from employment protection more than the unemployed.

What about firms? What level of protection would they offer to workers? They now have to take into account that the rent paid to workers increases with employment protection. The first-order condition from maximizing (4.6) is now

$$m'(s) = \frac{m(s) - rV_u}{r + s} + (r + s)Q'(s).$$

Substituting the free entry condition $m(s) = w = rV_u + (r+s)Q(s)$ we get

$$m'(s) = Q(s) + (r + s)Q'(s),$$

which, given the equilibrium identity between wages and productivity, is no different from (4.12). Therefore, provided firms, as above, can commit on the value of s, the market will spontaneously provide the *unemployed's* preferred level of employment protection, rather than the employed's. This is a consequence of the result proved at the end of Chapter 1, that the unemployed are in favour of letting the market determine job characteristics. Here, as the total rent is not fixed, there is no unanimity about that between the employed and the unemployed.

Hence, whenever the total discounted rent Q falls with s, there will be a conflict of interest between the employed and the unemployed. The latter will opt for a lower level of employment protection than the former, indeed they will be partisan to not regulating it and leaving it to the market.

We do not yet address social welfare, for the reasons already explained above. However, we can again look at the degree of employment protection that maximizes employment. One now has to take into account that Q depends on s in (4.8). The first-order condition becomes

$$\frac{\mathrm{d}\ln u}{\mathrm{d}s} = \frac{1}{s} + \frac{Q'(s)}{Q(s)} - \frac{w'(s) - rQ'(s)}{w(s) - rQ(s)}$$
$$= 0.$$

This is equivalent to

$$w'(s) = \frac{w(s)}{s}(1 - \eta) - \frac{rQ}{s}(1 + \eta),$$

where $\eta = -sQ'(s)/Q(s) > 0$ is the absolute value of the elasticity of the rent with respect to s. The greater is η, the lower the right-hand side, and the lower the employment gain from increasing employment protection. This is because the greater η, the more likely it is that the wage moderation effects of employment protection that were present in the previous section are absent or reversed. Hence, the position of the employment-maximizing level of s relative to the market- and politically-determined levels crucially depends on the value of η.

In the case where the employed are able to collect a fixed rent per unit of time, i.e. when wage formation is given by (4.10), the right-hand side of (4.12) is given by

$$Q(s) + (r + s)Q'(s) = \frac{q}{r + s} - (r + s)\frac{q}{(r + s)^2}$$
$$= 0.$$

This means that the marginal benefit to the unemployed of reducing unemployment exposure is equal to zero; they are not willing to have any degree of employment protection and will vote for the highest possible value of s. By the same token, firms will not provide any employment protection in equilibrium, because according to (4.10) a reduction in s has no moderating impact on wages. By contrast, the employed's marginal gain is given by

$$Q(s) + sQ'(s) = \frac{q}{r+s} - s\frac{q}{(r+s)^2} \qquad (4.13)$$
$$= \frac{rq}{(r+s)^2}.$$

It is increasing with the rent q.[7] As we have already seen, the greater the rent, the greater the employed's political support for employment protection. It is also increasing in r for low values of r, but eventually falls with r. A higher value of r makes the employed more myopic and less willing to consider the costs of employment protection in terms of reduced job destruction, since they will only be affected by these costs in the future, in the event that they lose their job. This effect dominates at low values of r. There is, however, another effect, which is that as the future is more heavily discounted the total intertemporal rent Q falls. Greater myopia also means that people care less about the duration of their current job. This effect ends up dominating for large values of r. One can check that the right-hand side of (4.13) is increasing in r for $r < s$ and decreasing for $r > s$.[8] As the first inequality is more plausible, the likely prediction is that higher discounting increases the support for employment protection.[9]

4.3 Deriving the wage–exposure schedule: introducing productivity shocks

So far, we have considered this society to have selected a point on the trade-off between unemployment exposure and wages, and we have con-

---

[7] It is also decreasing with s, implying that (4.11) is valid only if $w(.)$ is concave enough. Otherwise, the second-order condition for maximization would not be satisfied.

[8] The logarithmic derivative is $1/r - 2/(r+s)$, which is positive if and only if $1/r > 2/(r+s)$, or equivalently $r < s$.

[9] While the order of magnitude for real interest rates is 0–5 per cent , job destruction is about 8–12 per cent on an annual basis in most OECD countries. See Davis *et al.* (1996).

sidered this trade-off as exogenous, ignoring that it results from unproductive jobs being forced to remain in existence. We now explicitly take into account that phenomenon.

To do so, we extend our model as follows. Firms may be in one of two states, high (H) or low (L). When they enter the market, their productivity is m_H. Furthermore, there is free entry at that productivity level. With probability γ per unit of time, they fall into the low state. Their productivity then becomes $m_L < m_H$. Furthermore, firms in either state disappear (go bankrupt) with probability σ per unit of time. This event cannot be affected by labour market institutions. By contrast, employment protection may force firms to continue operating even though they have fallen to the low state. This will reduce expected profits, which will eventually affect the incentives for job creation and thus wages.

We assume wages are determined by (4.10), the specification with a fixed rent per unit of time. This has the convenient properties that wages are the same in all firms.

Contrary to the preceding section, the degree of employment protection is no longer a continuous variable. Instead, we assume that society must choose between a *flexible* system where firms can freely get rid of their workers and a *rigid* one where firms cannot dismiss their employees when falling into the low productivity state. However, in the appendix, we consider an extension of the model where productivity in the low state can take a large number of values and where different degrees of employment protection may be imposed.

To compute the effect of employment protection on wages, we compute the value of a firm and use the free entry condition.

One can readily apply (4.4) to firms in the low state, getting

$$J_L = \frac{m_L - w}{r + \sigma}, \tag{4.14}$$

where J_L is the expected present discounted profits of a firm in the low state. This formula is valid for any firm which is continuing to operate in the low state, either because it is profitable to do so or because regulation prevents the firm from closing.

In the flexible world, firms will continue operating in the low state if and only if this yields a positive net value, i.e. $J_L \geq 0$. Otherwise, firms instantaneously close the day they fall into the low state. Therefore, in the flexible system, the value of a firm which has just fallen into the low state is given by $\hat{J}_L = \max(J_L, 0)$. In the rigid world, firms are forced to continue in the low productivity state. Therefore, we then have $\hat{J}_L = J_L$.

As for firms in the high state, their present discounted value reflects the fact that they may fall into the low productivity state, in which case they make a capital loss equal to $J_H - \hat{J}_L$, where J_H is the firm's value in the high state. Consequently J_H is determined by

$$r J_H = m_H - w - \sigma J_H + \gamma(\hat{J}_L - J_H). \tag{4.15}$$

The term in $m_H - w$ is the flow of profits, the term in σJ_H is the capital loss made when the job is destroyed, and the last term is the (negative) capital gain when falling into the low state.

The free entry condition implies $J_H = 0$. Substituting this into (4.15) allows to compute the equilibrium wage as

$$w = m_H + \gamma \hat{J}_L. \tag{4.16}$$

4.3.1 The flexible economy

In the flexible economy, one necessarily has $\hat{J}_L \geq 0$. Firms cannot do worse than closing, which yields a zero value. (4.16) then implies that $w = m_H + \gamma \max[J_L, 0] \geq m_H > m_L$. Wages are above productivity in the low state. Hence, firms that continue in the bad state always have a negative value. Firms will therefore always fire when falling into the bad state, and we have $\hat{J}_L = 0$, implying

$$w = m_H = w_f,$$

where subscript f refers to the flexible economy. Competition from entrants in the high productivity state drives up wages to m_H, which makes it impossible for firms in the low state to survive. In the flexible economy all employed workers are allocated to the most productive sites, although there is a mass of involuntarily unemployed workers because the rent q prevents wages from adjusting to restore full employment.

Consequently, the separation rate in the flexible economy is the sum of the exogenous job destruction rate and the transition rate to the low state:

$$s = \sigma + \gamma = s_f.$$

Before proceeding, one may ask, as we did before, whether firms would like to provide some employment protection, despite the absence of a regulation forcing them to do so. The answer is no, for two reasons. First, firms decide on dismissals *at the time of the shock*. That is, they do not make any commitment over their future separation policy. Second, even if they could commit, they would not provide any employment protection, because, as we have argued in the preceding section, equation (4.10) is such that employment protection does not moderate wages.

One can also compute the job finding probability a and the unemployment rate u. To do this just apply (1.16) with $p = b = 0$, $Q = q/(r+s)$, $w = m_H$ and $s = s_f$, yielding

$$a = \left(\frac{m_H}{q} - 1\right)(r + \sigma + \gamma) = a_f. \qquad (4.16a)$$

In steady state the unemployment rate u is $s/(s+a)$, hence

$$u = \frac{q(\sigma + \gamma)}{m_H(r + \sigma + \gamma) - rq} = u_f. \qquad (4.17)$$

This concludes the characterization of the equilibrium steady state in the flexible economy. Finally, we need to compute the employed's and unemployed's utility. We can simply apply (4.1) and (4.3) to get

$$V_u = \frac{m_H - q}{r} = V_{uf} \qquad (4.18)$$

$$V_e = \frac{m_H}{r} - q\frac{\sigma + \gamma}{r(r + \sigma + \gamma)} = V_{ef}. \qquad (4.18b)$$

4.3.2 The rigid economy

In the rigid economy, firing is prevented when firms fall into the 'low' state, and $\hat{J}_L = J_L$. Substituting this and (4.14) into (4.15) allows us to compute the equilibrium value of the wage:

$$w = \frac{(r + \sigma)m_H + \gamma m_L}{r + \sigma + \gamma} = w_r = \bar{m}. \qquad (4.19)$$

That is, the wage is equal to the properly weighted average $\bar{m}$ of the firm's productivity over its lifetime. The weights reflect the expected fraction of time spent in each state as well as discounting. In both the flexible and the rigid economies, free entry ensures that wages and living standards reflect the economy's average productivity. In the rigid system, contrary to the flexible one, a fraction of employment is allocated to low-productivity firms. Consequently, average productivity and wages are lower :

$$w_r < w_f.$$

The greater is γ, the more frequently firms fall into the low state, and the greater the weight given to low productivity in wages.

Note that $m_L < \bar{m} < m_H$. Firms make profits in the high state and losses in the low state. In expected present discounted terms, the two cancel each other. When γ increases, firms expect to spend a lower fraction of their lifetime in the high state. To compensate for that, profits must rise in the high state and/or losses must fall in the low state. Hence wages must fall.

The separation rate is now simply equal to σ, the exogenous rate of job destruction:

$$s = \sigma = s_r < s_f.$$

Job loss is clearly less likely in the rigid world.

Finally, (4.1), (4.3), and (1.16) allow us to compute the job finding probability and the employed's and unemployed's utility, by applying these formulas with $w = \bar{m}, s = \sigma$ and $Q = q/(r + \sigma)$. We get

$$V_u = \frac{\bar{m} - q}{r} = V_{ur} \qquad (4.20a)$$

$$V_e = \frac{\bar{m}}{r} - q\frac{\sigma}{r(r + \sigma)} = V_{er} \qquad (4.20b)$$

$$a = \left(\frac{\bar{m}}{q} - 1\right)(r + \sigma) = a_r. \qquad (4.20c)$$

As we have already seen, $a_r < a_f$. Employment protection reduces the outflow from unemployment—increases unemployment duration. Maintaining jobs that yield negative profits reduces the incentives to hire *ex-ante*.

We can also compute unemployment, and decompose employment into employment in high-state firms l_H and in low-state firms l_L. The outflow from employment in low-state firms is determined by exogenous job destruction, and given by σl_L. The inflow comes from high-state firms, and is equal to γ, the transition probability, times l_H, high-state employment. In steady state, the inflow and the outflow are equal. Therefore

$$\sigma l_L = \gamma l_H. \qquad (4.21)$$

The inflow into high-state firms comes from the pool of unemployed workers who find jobs. It is equal to a, the job finding probability per unit of time, times the number of unemployed workers $u = 1 - l_H - l_L$. The outflow from high-state firms comes from workers who lose their jobs due to exogenous job destruction, and from workers who end up in low-state firms. Therefore the outflow rate from high-state employment is given by $(\sigma + \gamma)l_H$. Consequently in steady state we must have

$$(\sigma + \gamma)l_H = a(1 - l_H - l_L). \tag{4.22}$$

(4.21) and (4.22) allow us to compute employment in both states in steady state; using the above expression for a_r we finally get:

$$l_{Hr} = \frac{r + \sigma}{\sigma + \gamma} \frac{(\bar{m} - q)\sigma}{\bar{m}(r + \sigma) - rq}$$

$$l_{Lr} = \frac{r + \sigma}{\sigma + \gamma} \frac{(\bar{m} - q)\gamma}{\bar{m}(r + \sigma) - rq}.$$

This allows us to compute total unemployment:

$$\begin{aligned} u &= 1 - l_H - l_L \\ &= \frac{q\sigma}{\bar{m}(r + \sigma) - rq} \\ &= u_r. \end{aligned} \tag{4.23}$$

4.3.3 The support for rigidity

We now analyse the political support for the rigid society. For this we need to compute how each arrangement affects the utility of the employed and the unemployed. We will then assume that the employed are decisive so that the political process will deliver their preferred outcome.

Starting with the unemployed, comparing (4.20) and (4.18) shows what we expected, namely that they always prefer the flexible society over the rigid one. Both wages and the job finding rate are larger in the former than in the latter, and the higher job loss rate weighs less, as we have seen, in their utility function. Turning now to the employed, we see that they will prefer rigidity if and only if[10]

$$V_{er} = \frac{\bar{m}}{r} - \frac{q\sigma}{r(r + \sigma)} > V_{ef} = \frac{m_H}{r} - \frac{q(\sigma + \gamma)}{r(r + \sigma + \gamma)}, \tag{4.24}$$

---

[10] This discussion ignores that the status quo may sometimes matter, something we analyse in Chapter 6.

which may be rewritten as

$$m_H - m_L < rq/(r + \sigma).$$ (4.25)

This condition tells us a number of interesting things. First, it is more likely to be satisfied, the greater is q. The employed's support for employment protection arises when rents are large. This confirms the results of the previous sections, which have already established a tight link between insider rents and their gains from employment protection. They will support the rigid society provided $q > q^e$, where $q^e = (r + \sigma)(m_H - m_L)/r$.

Second, the support for the rigid society falls when there is more turnover. Here, turnover has two components. One source of turnover, captured by σ, is exogenous and thus unaffected by employment protection. When it is larger, (4.25) is less likely to hold. The reason is that exogenous turnover increases the employed's exposure to unemployment, thus increasing the negative impact of reduced job creation in the rigid world on their welfare. The second component is γ, the rate of transition toward the low productivity state. γ has two effects on the gains from rigidity. First, the greater is γ, the greater employment protection increases expected tenure. If γ were equal to zero employment protection would have no effect and the rigid and flexible systems would yield identical outcomes. This effect is captured by the last term in the right-hand side of (4.24), which tells us that the expected loss from dismissal is increasing with γ. On the other hand, a larger γ increases the expected length of time spent by firms in the low productivity state, thus lowering the wage $\bar{m}$. This is captured in the first term of the left-hand side of (4.24), since $\bar{m}$ is a decreasing function of γ. These two effects cancel out, so that γ has disappeared from (4.25). It has no impact on the threshold beyond which the employed vote for rigidity. Overall, this suggests that more 'mobile' societies, or societies where the employed are more exposed to unemployment, are less likely to support employment protection. Note that we could not answer this question within the framework of the preceding sections, since there was no exogenous variable representing labour turnover.

Third, a higher discount rate r increases the employed's support for rigidity, since they put less weight on the reduction in their future job finding rates when unemployed. This confirms our previous analysis.

Fourth, the support for rigidity is greater when $m_H - m_L$, the size of the productivity loss experienced by firms when they fall into the low state, is smaller. This is because when this gap is smaller, rigidity exerts less downward pressure on wages. When the less productive firms are only marginally less efficient than the most productive ones, maintaining the former in operation only entails small costs in terms of living standards. Therefore, the rigid society is more likely to arise.

This last result tells us in some sense that there is a link between the support for rigidity and how severe the process of obsolescence is. The lower the productivity of old firms relative to new firms, the lower the value of maintaining these old firms. The analysis can be extended to encompass the idea that such obsolescence is the by-product of growth (see Saint-Paul 1999a, b). In economies with a faster rate of renovation or technological progress, the employed will be less in favour of employment protection.

4.3.4 Employment

The preceding analysis tells us when the employed will favour employment protection but does not give us any benchmark against which to gauge that result. That insiders hold political power may not be problematic, after all, if they end up supporting the 'right' decision. The most appropriate alternative criterion is clearly aggregate welfare. It is also of interest, however, to look at how employment protection affects employment. Above we saw an example where a policymaker who cares about employment would actually provide more employment protection than the employed would choose for themselves. This result was, however, in great part due to the wage-moderating effects of employment protection, and therefore severely qualified when the assumption of a fixed intertemporal rent Q was relaxed.

What do we get here? Comparing (4.23) and (4.17) we can see that employment is higher in the rigid society if and only if

$$\frac{\sigma}{\bar{m}(r+\sigma) - rq} < \frac{\sigma + \gamma}{m_H(r+\sigma+\gamma) - rq},$$

or equivalently:

$$q < \frac{r^2 - \sigma^2 - \sigma\gamma}{(r+\sigma+\gamma)r}m_H + \frac{(\sigma+\gamma)(r+\sigma)}{r(r+\sigma+\gamma)}m_L = \tilde{q}.$$

Recall that employment may a priori be larger or smaller in the rigid society compared with the flexible one: the rigid society creates fewer jobs, but it also destroys fewer jobs. So in steady state it may well be that employment is higher in the rigid society. The above formula tells us that the rigid society has a higher employment level than the flexible one if the rent q is smaller than $\tilde{q}$, and lower employment if the rent is large enough. This is because a given increase in the rent has a more damaging impact in the rigid society than in the flexible one because productivity is on average lower in the former. Or, to put it another way, a given fall in productivity, as the one implied by rigidity, reduces employment creation more when the rent is high.

The important point is that the effect of the rent on employment in the flexible society relative to the rigid society is the opposite of its effect on the employed's welfare. Typically, as we saw, there will be support for rigidity when the rent is high, which is precisely when rigidity reduces employment. The converse holds when the rent is low, but note that the smaller the rent, the closer both economies are to full employment, and the lower the associated employment differential.

One can also see that $\partial \tilde{q} / \partial \gamma < 0$ and $\partial \tilde{q} / \partial \sigma < 0$. Exposure therefore has the same effect on the employment differential between the two societies as on the employed's welfare differential: low exposure increases both the support for rigidity and employment in the rigid relative to the flexible society. The lower is σ, the longer the time firms spend in the low productivity state, and the greater the employment-augmenting effect of maintaining firms in that state.

4.3.5 Welfare

We now turn to the question of whether employment protection may be desirable from the viewpoint of aggregate welfare. The answer is that *some* degree of employment protection (beyond that generated by the market) is always desirable, but that this level is always lower than the one the employed vote for.

Here we establish these results while using our simple model. But in the appendix we show how it can be extended to allow people to choose between different degrees of flexibility.

Let us assume that at date $t = 0$ the economy is flexible and in steady state and that a central planner decides on whether or not it should become rigid. In the initial situation there are no rigid firms and all existing firms have a zero value. If the economy becomes rigid then the degree of labour market tightness a falls instantaneously to its new level a_R. Therefore, the outflow from unemployment falls. The value of existing firms, that are in the high productivity state, remains equal to zero. The wage instantaneously adjusts downwards to reflect the lower expected productivity. As time passes some firms fall into the low state, where their present discounted value is negative. Employment in the low productivity firms gradually rises to its new steady state level l_{Lr}.

In Chapter 1 we discussed various ways of computing aggregate welfare. The simplest, here, is to add the welfare of all agents in the economy at date $t = 0$, *including* firms. Originally all firms are in the high state—since the economy is initially flexible—so that their value is equal to zero, both prior to and after the policy change. Consequently, welfare is simply given by

$$\Omega = uV_u + (1 - u)V_e,$$

where u is the initial unemployment level. Using the above formulae for V_e and V_u we can compute aggregate welfare if the economy decides to become rigid:

$$\Omega_r^f = u_f V_{ur} + (1 - u_f)V_{er}$$
$$= \frac{\bar{m} - q}{r} + (1 - u_f)\frac{q}{r + \sigma}, \qquad (4.26)$$

where superscript f refers to the fact that the economy is originally flexible. If the economy remains flexible welfare is given by

$$\Omega_f^f = u_f V_{uf} + (1 - u_f)V_{ef} \qquad (4.27)$$
$$= \frac{m_H - q}{r} + (1 - u_f)\frac{q}{r + \sigma + \gamma}.$$

The rigid society will be preferred by the social planner if and only if $\Omega_f^f \leq \Omega_r^f$. Using (4.19) along with (4.26) and (4.27) we see that this is equivalent to

$$m_H - m_L \leq \frac{rq}{r + \sigma}(1 - u_f). \qquad (4.28)$$

This equation should be compared with (4.25), which gave us the condition for the employed to support rigidity. Equation (4.28) is always less likely to hold than (4.25). If rigidity increases aggregate welfare, then the employed must support it. This is not surprising, since the unemployed lose from it. On the other hand, the employed may support it even though it reduces aggregate welfare. In that sense, the employed always want more employment protection than the social planner. However, there is a zone in which employment protection is welfare improving. Furthermore, (4.28) apparently obeys the same logic as (4.25): high rents, high discount factors, low productivity gaps, and low turnover all increase the social value of rigidity, just like they increase their value to the employed.

Here employment protection is an all-or-nothing decision. So there is a zone where it is socially optimal, and a zone where it is not. But if the degree of employment protection can vary, we can show (this is done in the appendix) that for any parameter values the social planner will always elect a degree of employment protection strictly above the market one.

An important aspect of (4.28) is that the *initial* value of employment, $1 - u_f$, enters. So far, we have not expressed it as a function of parameters because the formula is valid not only if the economy is originally in steady state, but also for any initial level of employment— that is, u_f in (4.28) can be interpreted not only as the steady state level of unemployment, but as any initial level. Note that this inequality is more likely to hold, the smaller is u_f. Equation (4.28) therefore implies that the social value of employment protection is greater, the greater the initial employment level. Before we discuss why, let us stress that this has important implications: it tells us that it is precisely in situations of high unemployment that labour market flexibility is most desirable.

It may be surprising that some degree of employment protection is welfare improving. The key reason is that the separation decisions made by firms are socially inefficient. Separation is too high because firms perceive a cost of labour which is greater than its true social cost. The true social cost of labour (in an equilibrium which in itself is inefficient) is the value of being unemployed. An unemployed would be just indifferent between earning a wage $r V_u$ for ever or remaining unemployed. Thus, the social cost of labour is $r V_u$, which is also the employed's alternative option. But, because the employed are able to earn rents, wages are above the social cost of labour , by an amount precisely equal to the rent q. When firms consider whether closing or not once they are in the low state they compare their productivity m_L to their wage w. Thus, they would like to close if $m_L < w$, whereas the social planner would like them to close if $m_L < r V_u$. So, if $r V_u < m_L < w$, the social planner would like to prevent them from closing. One can indeed check that if (4.28) holds, the flexible economy is such that $r V_{uf} < m_L$.

This inefficiently high level of separation explains the social benefits of employment protection. If one could prevent firms in the low state from closing while not affecting the incentives for firms in the high state to enter the market, one would indeed implement employment protection as long as $r V_{uf} < m_L$. However, this is impossible; the government cannot commit to a policy that prevents existing firms in the low state from getting rid of their workers and at the same time promise new entrants that they will freely be able to do so. That is, employment protection also entails social costs, since it reduces the number of jobs created.[11] For this reason, if the degree of employment protection can vary, as in the appendix, the social planner will opt for a level of employment protection such that the level of separation is still 'too high'; that is, even the worst jobs being destroyed have a productivity greater than the social cost of labour $r V_u$. Even the employed's preferred level of job protection has that property, for reasons that are explained in the appendix.

While the above argument seems to validate the view that employment protection may be good, this conclusion strongly depends on the fact that we have ruled out alternative instruments for the social planner. Here we have a market imperfection; wages are above the social cost of labour. This imperfection is not intrinsically associated with the decision to destroy jobs, but more generally to any decision regarding the *quantity* of labour being employed. It simply implies that employment is too low. It makes both hirings too low and separations too high at the same time. Employment protection is only an imperfect instrument in order to solve that market failure; while it moves the economy in the right direction for separations, it moves it in the wrong one for hiring. The best instrument is, quite simply, an employment subsidy such that the government pays an amount q to employers for each person employed. If such a subsidy can be used then the economy can reach full employment in high-state firms and no employment protection is necessary. That instrument, however, is more costly in financial terms than employment protection; so the case for employment protection as a welfare instrument is not totally dead.

We now understand why the initial employment level affects the optimal degree of employment protection. If employment is high many people already have jobs and the social planner does not care so much about lowering job creation; at the same time the total number of people whose separation rate will be reduced is higher, so the gains are higher. Employment protection is an imperfect instrument to increase employment by reducing separations. That instrument is more efficient, the greater the initial employment level. High employment initially gives

---

[11] This reduction in job creation is stronger, the lower m_L is relative to m_H: hence the role of $m_H - m_L$ in the left-hand side of (4.28).

the central planner an opportunity to get high employment in the future by simply preventing firms from dismissing people.

However, there is again a commitment problem associated with that strategy. Once a reform is implemented employment will change so that the economy may end up in a situation where the social planner would again want to revert to the initial situation. For example, we have just argued that rigidity is more desirable, the greater the initial employment level. So, if employment is greater in the flexible society than in the rigid one, it may well be that the social planner wants to shift to rigidity if institutions are initially flexible and vice versa.

This dependence of the desired institution on initial conditions is an important feature, which we shall discuss in Chapters 6 and 7. For the time being, this observation leads us to look for situations where the decision made by the social planner is self-sustaining; that is, we need to know under what conditions he will want to remain in the flexible society if this is the initial state of the economy, and under what conditions he will want to remain in the rigid one.

4.3.6 Self-sustaining social optima

The flexible society will be self-sustaining if (4.28) is violated when the economy is initially in the flexible steady state. Substituting (4.17) we get the following condition:

$$m_H - m_L \geq \frac{rq}{r+\sigma} \frac{(m_H - q)(r + \sigma + \gamma)}{m_H(r + \sigma + \gamma) - rq}. \tag{4.29}$$

This condition now reflects the fact that the initial unemployment rate depends on all the parameters. In particular, the condition no longer implies that rigidity is more likely to be socially preferable when the rent is larger. This is true when *controlling* for the initial unemployment rate, but the rent actually increases initial unemployment, thus increasing the weight of job creation in the social planner's objective. As (4.29) makes clear, flexibility prevails for q low enough but also when q becomes large. The right-hand side of (4.29) is first increasing and then decreasing in q. Rigidity will be preferred over flexibility by the social planner for intermediate values of the rent q.

Similarly, we now need to determine when a social planner will wish to maintain a society in the rigid regime. The social planner now has to take into account that there exists a mass of people working in low productivity firms. The contribution of these people to aggregate welfare is lower than their own welfare, because the firms that employ them are making losses. That is, if society continues to be rigid, aggregate welfare is given by

$$\Omega_r^r = (l_{Lr} + l_{Hr})V_{er} + u_r V_{ur} + l_{Lr} J_L.$$

The last term represents the present discounted value of the profits of those firms in the low state, which is negative. Remember that $J_L = (m_L - w)/(r + \sigma) = (m_L - \bar{m})/(r + \sigma)$. Using that and the preceding calculations we can compute Ω_r^r as

$$\Omega_r^r = \frac{\bar{m} - q}{r} + (l_{Hr} + l_{Lr})\frac{q}{r + \sigma} - l_{Lr}\frac{\bar{m} - m_L}{r + \sigma}. \tag{4.30}$$

If the social planner now decides to shift to flexibility, the hiring rate a will instantaneously jump to its new value, and so will wages. Firms in the low state will fire all their workers: unemployment will jump to a higher value, equal to $1 - l_{Hr}$. As time passes, unemployment gradually falls to the new steady state level u_f. So, an interesting aspect of that reform is that even if it may increase employment in the long run, in the short run massive layoffs take place and unemployment sharply rises. [12]

From now we can proceed and compute aggregate welfare in the event that the economy decides to shift from rigidity to flexibility. If the economy shifts to flexibility, right after the reform the unemployment rate is $1 - l_{Hr}$, so that we can compute aggregate welfare in that case by replacing u_f by $1 - l_{Hr}$ in (4.27). We get

$$\Omega_f^r = (1 - l_{Hr})V_{uf} + l_{Hr}V_{ef} \tag{4.31}$$
$$= \frac{m_H - q}{r} + l_{Hr}\frac{q}{r + \sigma + \gamma}.$$

[12] These layoffs, as such, may or may not be socially efficient, depending on whether the right-hand side of (4.30) is increasing or decreasing with l_{Lr}. If it is decreasing, then social welfare in the rigid society would actually be greater if those who work in low productivity firms were unemployed instead. The condition for these layoffs to be efficient is $q \leq \bar{m} - m_L$. This is a condition for society to gain from suppressing low productivity firms even though the remaining ones will remain rigid. It is sufficient, but not necessary, for flexibility to be preferred to rigidity. It is actually identical to the rule a discretionary social planner would follow, as discussed at the end of the chapter.

The left-hand side is the rent, while the right-hand side is the difference between the wage and the output of those workers, i.e. the unit loss made by those firms. This condition means that if firms in the bad state lose more than the worker's rent, then the net social value of these jobs is negative; one could not cover the losses of these firms even by paying their workers a wage that would make them no better off than the unemployed. The converse occurs if losses are lower than the rent.

One could then derive a condition for the social planner to want to remain in the rigid world if the economy is originally in that situation. Such a condition will be like (4.29), with a reversal of the sign of the inequality.

An interesting question, anticipating Chapters 6 and 7, is whether the social planner would have a bias in favour of the status quo; that is, whether rigidity is more likely to be preferred if society is initially rigid. This can be formally stated as

$$\Omega_r^f \geq \Omega_f^f \Rightarrow \Omega_r^r \geq \Omega_f^r,$$

meaning that if the central planner wishes to change a flexible society into a rigid one, then *a fortiori* he would like to preserve the rigid society. The answer to that question is as follows (see the appendix for more detailed computations). If rigidity is not too costly in terms of jobs, then there is status quo bias. However, if rigidity costs many jobs, the converse holds. In that case there exists a zone of parameter values where the central planner would like to establish employment protection if society is originally in a steady state where it does not exist, but to scrap it if one is in the rigid steady state. For example, in the extreme case where $\bar{m} = q$, there is no employment in the rigid steady state. So, starting from that steady state the social planner always prefers to have flexibility in order to create jobs. But once these jobs exist, there may be an incentive to put employment protection back into place, as the zero-employment steady state will only be reached in the long run.

However, this possibility of cycles crucially hinges on the assumption that the choice between rigidity and flexibility is a zero/one one. If one allows the degree of rigidity to be optimally chosen, as in the model analysed in the appendix, then one can show that the degree of rigidity chosen by the central planner will always be greater, the greater the *initial* level of rigidity. The explanation for this stems from the above-mentioned fact that the social planner will always want to pick a degree of rigidity such that job destruction is inefficiently high: those jobs just at the margin of being destroyed have a surplus greater than the opportunity cost of labour . The greater the initial degree of rigidity, the greater the number of such jobs that would be destroyed if society were to shift to a given, more flexible, arrangement, and the greater the associated welfare loss.

The above discussion suggests that in a world with imperfect labour markets, 'sclerosis' is not necessarily a disease but may actually be chosen by a benevolent central planner—*provided there is not a more adequate instrument to foster employment*. As we expect the employed to decide on employment protection, it is likely that there will be too much of it relative to the social optimum. However, one may be tempted to look at a formula like (4.28) and claim that if unemployment is of the order of 10 per cent, the social planner's rule is not that different from the political outcome given by (4.25). After all, this is not that surprising: if the employed are 90 per cent of the population, maximizing aggregate welfare is not very different from maximizing the utility of the employed. Of course, that conclusion would be totally reversed if the central planner was Rawlsian, in which case he would maximize the utility of the unemployed. But even in our utilitarian case, this claim is likely to be erroneous. The reason is that while we have assumed for simplicity that all employed workers earn the same rent q, in practice q is likely to differ across workers. Some workers work in sectors with high rents, others in sectors with low rents. The latter's preferences will be much more like those of the unemployed. So, if the decisive voter has a high rent, but if there are enough workers in low-rent sectors, the politically determined level of employment protection will be substantially higher than the socially desirable one.

4.3.7 Discretionary employment protection

In the above discussion, we have assumed that either the employed or the social planner chose an employment protection legislation once and for all, and that such legislation applied in all cases. In practice there is a considerable degree of discretion in the way the law is applied, with many issues decided on a case-by-case basis. Here we argue that such discretion is likely to lead to an even higher degree of employment protection. This is because every time it is decided to prevent a given job from being destroyed, the adverse consequences of that practice on the rest of the economy, i.e. lower wages and lower job finding rates, are now ignored; it is not this particular decision which can change firms' expectations as to whether they will be prevented to close when hit by a bad shock.

Assume that the economy is flexible. Consider a single firm falling into the low state. What if a social planner could step in and save that particular job, preventing the firm from closing? The social planner will do so provided the productivity of that job, m_L, is strictly greater than the social opportunity cost of labour, $r V_u$. Thus the firm will be prevented from closing if and only if $m_L > rV_u$. Substituting (4.18) we see that this is equivalent to

$$m_H - m_L < q. \qquad (4.32)$$

This is more likely to be satisfied than (4.28), which gives the social planner's choice if employment protection is determined by law rather than discretionary intervention.[13] So, there will be more employment protection under discretion. Indeed, (4.32) is more likely to be satisfied than (4.25), meaning that the discretionary, benevolent social planner will impose more rigidity than the employed will vote for! The reason is that even the employed, when they vote on employment protection legislation, internalize its adverse effects. In the model of the appendix, we can show a similar result: the discretionary social planner will maintain all jobs whose productivity is greater than rV_u, picking up a degree of job protection such that the productivity of the worst jobs is exactly equal to rV_u. Thus job destruction is efficient, but at the cost of a too low level of job creation, and welfare could be increased by raising both.

---

[13] If society is initially rigid, we get

$$m_H - m_L < q\frac{r + \sigma + \gamma}{r + \sigma},$$

which is even more likely than (4.32). The reason is that the social value of saving a given job is higher, the lower V_u, i.e. the lower job creation. Therefore, this is more likely to occur if the economy is rigid, since job creation is lower in the rigid economy.

This means that over the zone where that equation is satisfied but (4.32) is not, there are two equilibria. In one equilibrium (the rigid one) job creation is low because firms expect the social planner to prevent them from laying off, and it is indeed optimal for the social planner to do so, given the level of job creation. In the other equilibrium, job creation is high because firms expect the social planner to allow them to lay off, and because job creation is high the social planner will indeed be willing to allow layoffs.

This mechanism is reminiscent of one studied in Saint-Paul (1995), where it is the worker's decision to quit, rather than the policymaker's choice, which leads to multiple equilibria. We will return to this phenomenon in Chapter 9, where we deal with policy complementarities.

This multiplicity is different from the status quo bias phenomenon discussed here and in Chapters 6 and 7. Here the status quo is irrelevant to the policymaker's choice. What is relevant is V_u, the present discounted value of being unemployed, which reflects the *future* job finding rates and the productivity of future jobs. Hence, rigidity is self-sustaining not because an initially rigid economy is associated with an initial distribution of employment such that it is optimal to continue being rigid, but because private agents' expectations over the future course of policy being rigid leads the policy maker to actually prevent jobs from being destroyed, thus validating these expectations. As in the vast literature on monetary policy (see Cukierman (1995) for a survey), multiplicity is a consequence of the policymaker's inability to commit over its future decisions—when policy is not discretionary but follows pre-established rules as in the rest of the chapter, multiplicity does not arise.

What if, now, it is the employed who discretionarily decide whether jobs should be protected or not? That is, at the time of a bad shock hitting a firm, its employees can force it to continue. In that case, rigidity will *always* prevail, since the employed will compare V_e, their value of continuing, with V_u, the value of being unemployed, and V_e is always greater than V_u.

4.4 Conclusion

In this chapter, we have examined some extensions of the model outlined in Chapter 1, which allowed us to discuss the determination of employment protection. Our results inevitably depend on the assumptions being made, and we have considered different assumptions regarding the wage formation process and the nature of the wage–exposure trade-off.

The most fundamental results, however, do not depend on these assumptions. We always get that the employed will be more likely to support employment protection, the greater the rent, so that we expect such regulation to arise in labour markets that are already uncompetitive. Furthermore, while some degree of employment protection may be optimal, the employed will always choose a more stringent regulation than the social planner.

Appendix

In this appendix, we first formally analyse the possibility of status quo bias when employment protection is decided by a benevolent social planner. We then describe an extension of the model which allows the degree of employment protection to vary continuously rather than being elected between two variables.

Status quo bias

We already know that the flexible society will remain, from the social planner's view point, if and only if

$$m_H - m_L \geq \frac{rq}{r + \sigma}(1 - u_f). \tag{A4.1}$$

The rigid society is stable if and only if $\Omega^r_r > \Omega^r_f$, or equivalently, using our formulas,

$$\frac{\bar{m} - q}{r} + (l_{Hr} + l_{Lr})\frac{q}{r + \sigma} - l_{Lr}\frac{\bar{m} - m_L}{r + \sigma} \geq \frac{m_H - q}{r} + l_{Hr}\frac{q}{r + \sigma + \gamma},$$

which can be rewritten as

$$m_H - m_L < \frac{rq}{r + \sigma}\left[\frac{\gamma l_{Hr} + (r + \sigma + \gamma)l_{Lr}}{\gamma + r l_{Lr}}\right]. \tag{A4.2}$$

There will be status quo bias if and only if (A4.1) and (A4.2) can hold simultaneously, that is if

$$\left[\frac{\gamma l_{Hr} + (r + \sigma + \gamma)l_{Lr}}{\gamma + r l_{Lr}}\right] > 1 - u_f.$$

Clearly, for that to hold l_{Hr} and l_{Lr} must be large enough. So if rigidity is not too costly in terms of jobs there is status quo bias, while in the converse case policy cycles may arise.

Status quo bias should not be mixed with multiple equilibria, which means that given the initial conditions, there are several equilibrium paths for the economy. Here, given initial conditions, there is a unique outcome. But it is dependent on initial conditions in such a way that it reinforces them, leading to multiple steady states, which is different from multiple equilibria.

A more general model

Here we describe a simple extension of our model where the degree of employment protection can be chosen among a continuum of values. As in the text, firms enter the market at the highest possible productivity level m_H; they stay at that level until they fall into a low productivity state, which occurs with probability γ per unit of time. At the time they fall into that state, their productivity becomes m, which is drawn from the interval $[\underline{m}, m_H]$ with a density $f(m)$. They remain in that state until they disappear, which occurs with probability σ per unit of time. Note that the productivity loss at the time of the shock can be arbitrarily small, since the upper bound of the interval of new values of m is m_H.[14] As in the text, wages are set according to (4.10). There exists a cutoff level

---

[14] This structure is somewhat similar to the one used in Mortensen and Pissarides (1994).

of productivity in the low state, m^*, such that firms close if they have a level of $m < m^*$. We will represent employment protection by assuming that society directly imposes the level of m^* (without such a regulation one can check that the market would deliver $m^* = m_H$). Thus, voting on employment protection amounts to voting on m^*. The lower is m^*, the greater the level of employment protection. The present discounted value of a firm in a low state with productivity m is $(m - w)/(r + \sigma)$. Consequently the value of a firm in the high state obeys the following equation:

$$r J_H = m_H - w + \gamma F(m^*)(-J_H) + \int_{m^*}^{m_H} \gamma (\frac{m - w}{r + \sigma} - J_H) f(m) \, dm.$$
(A4.3)

This equation has the standard asset value interpretation. The term $\gamma F(m^*) (-J_H)$ is the expected capital loss made when the productivity shock is below m^*, in which case the firm closes. The last term is the contribution of the expected capital losses for all the productivity shocks above m^*, when the firm continues to operate. It is equal to the flow probability of having a shock γ times the integral over all the values of m greater than m^* of the difference between the new value of the firm $\frac{m-w}{r+\sigma}$ and the old one J_H.

The free entry condition implies $J_H = 0$. Substituting that into (A4.3) allows us to compute the equilibrium wage

$$w = \frac{(r + \sigma)m_H + \gamma(1 - F(m^*))E(m \mid m \geq m^*)}{r + \sigma + \gamma(1 - F(m^*))}.$$
(A4.4)

As in the text, wages are equal to an appropriately discounted weighted average of the various productivity levels that a firm may experience during its lifetime. One can readily see that $w > m^*$ unless $m^* = m_H$. Since in the free market case all continuing firms must make nonnegative profits, one must have $w \leq m^*$ which implies $m^* = m_H$. This proves that without regulations only firms in the highest productivity level would exist.

What if firms could commit on the value of m^*? They would set it so as to maximize J_H. Using (A4.3) we see that

$$\frac{\partial J_H}{\partial m^*} = (w - m^*)\frac{\gamma}{r + \sigma} f(m^*).$$

This is strictly positive since $w > m^*$, unless $m^* = m_H$. So if employment protection was left to the market, in equilibrium there would be none of it.

The above equation allows us to compute V_u as a function of m^*, since $V_u = (w - q)/r$. The value of being unemployed is maximized at the highest possible wage, which is at $m_H = m^*$. Thus the unemployed support the market outcome, which is zero employment protection.

What about workers in low-productivity firms? Their utility is[15]

$$V_e(L) = \frac{w + \sigma V_u}{r + \sigma} = V_u + \frac{q}{r + \sigma}. \tag{A4.5}$$

This formula suggests that the level of employment protection that maximizes w and V_u would also maximize the welfare of workers in low productivity firms. However, this would only be true if they kept their jobs, which is not the case under zero employment protection. Consequently, a worker in a low productivity firm m will vote for the lowest possible level of employment protection conditional on him keeping his job, that is for $m^* = m$.

As for workers in high productivity firms, their utility is given by [16]

$$V_e(H) = \frac{w + \gamma(1 - F(m^*))V_e(L) + \gamma F(m^*)V_u}{r + \gamma} \tag{A4.6}$$

$$= V_u + \frac{q}{r + \gamma}\left(1 + \frac{\gamma}{r + \sigma}(1 - F(m^*))\right).$$

The last term is the rent q times the expected discounted time over which it is reaped. In order to compute their most preferred level of employment protection we need to compute the derivative of $V_e(H)$ with respect to m^*. We get

$$\frac{\partial}{\partial m^*}V_e(H) = \frac{\partial V_u}{\partial m^*} - \frac{q\gamma}{(r + \gamma)(r + \sigma)}f(m^*).$$

Their marginal gain from increasing m^* is clearly lower than from the unemployed, since a higher m^* reduces the duration of employee rent. To compute $\frac{\partial V_u}{\partial m^*}$, one can simply use (A4.4), getting

$$\frac{\partial V_u}{\partial m^*} = \frac{1}{r}\frac{\partial w}{\partial m^*} \tag{A4.7}$$

[15] The evolution equation for $V_e(L)$ is

$$rV_e(L) = w + \sigma(V_u - V_e(L)) + \dot{V}_e(L),$$

from which we derive (A4.5) in steady state.

[16] As for (A4.5), this is obtained from the evolution equation for $V_e(H)$, used in steady state.

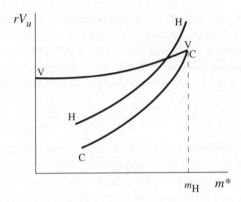

Figure 4.5. Market and employment determined levels of employment protection

$$= \frac{\gamma f(m^*)(w - m^*)}{r(r + \sigma + \gamma(1 - F(m^*)))}.$$

At the preferred level of employment protection for workers in high state firms, we must have $\frac{\partial}{\partial m^*} V_e(H) = 0$. Substituting (A4.7) and using (4.10) we see that this is equivalent to

$$m^* = rV_u + \frac{\gamma q}{(r + \gamma)(r + \sigma)}(\sigma + rF(m^*)). \qquad (A4.8)$$

Assume that these agents are politically decisive. Then the politico-economic equilibrium is as represented in Figure 4.5, in the (m^*, rV_u) plane. The flat VV curve represents how m^* affects labour's alternative value rV_u, via its effect on the wage (equation (A4.4)) (alternatively, the y axis may be thought of as representing wages, which only differ from rV_u by an additive constant). The greater is m^*, the greater the wage, and the greater the value of being unemployed. The economy must lie on VV regardless of how m^* is chosen. The steep curve HH represents equation (A4.8), which determines the preferred level of employment protection for workers in high productivity firms. Because the second term in (A4.8) is always lower than q, HH is above VV at $m^* = m_H$. Consequently it intersects VV at some $m^* < m_H$. This proves that the employed in high state firms will always vote for a strictly positive level of employment protection.

The CC curve represents the first-order condition for the market provided level of employment protection. It is determined by $m^* = w =$

$rV_u + q$, since firms are willing to continue operating if and only if productivity is above wages. CC is below HH, and intersects VV at the no employment protection level $m^* = m_H$.

We now consider how a social planner would determine employment protection. Let us assume that the economy is originally in a steady state with an initial value of m^* equal to m_0. We have to consider two cases.

Case 1: $m^* < m_0$.

Let us first consider what happens if the social planner chooses a value of m^* lower than m_0, that is if employment protection is increased. Then all workers in unproductive firms keep their jobs. Total social welfare is the sum of the utilities of all workers, plus the (negative) value of unproductive firms

$$\Omega(m_0, m^*) = l_H V_e(H) + l_L V_e(L) + u V_u$$
$$+ \int_{m_0}^{m_H} \left(\frac{m - rV_u - q}{r + \sigma} \right) g(m) \, dm,$$

where $g(.)$ refers to the initial distribution of *employment* across unproductive firms, with $l_L = \int_{m_0}^{m_H} g(m) \, dm$. Using (A4.5) and (A4.6) this can be rewritten as

$$\Omega(m_0, m^*) = V_u + l_H \frac{q}{r + \gamma} \left(1 + \frac{\gamma}{r + \sigma} (1 - F(m^*)) \right) - \frac{rV_u}{r + \sigma} l_L$$
$$+ \int_{m_0}^{m_H} \frac{m}{r + \sigma} g(m) \, dm.$$

This allows us to compute the first-order condition for maximization of Ω with respect to m^*. We get

$$\frac{dV_u}{dm^*} \left(1 - \frac{rl_L}{r + \sigma} \right) - l_H \frac{q\gamma}{(r + \gamma)(r + \sigma)} f(m^*) = 0. \qquad (A4.9)$$

The second term, $-\frac{rl_L}{r + \sigma} \frac{dV_u}{dm^*}$, represents the fact that a higher V_u reduces the social value of existing unproductive jobs, as this higher V_u represents the better job prospects elsewhere in the economy—this signal is actually transmitted to those firms via greater wages and heavier losses, but does not lead them to close as long as $m^* < m_0$. The third term represents the losses of lower job protection to workers employed in high productivity firms. Substituting (A4.7) into (A4.9) we now get

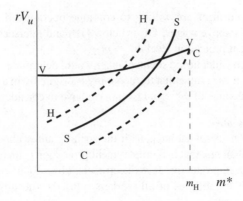

Figure 4.6. The socially optimal level of employment protection

the first-order condition for the social planner's preferred level of employment protection

$$m^* = rV_u + q \left[\frac{1 - \frac{r}{r+\sigma}l_L - \frac{r}{r+\gamma}(1 + \frac{\gamma}{r+\sigma}(1 - F(m^*)))l_H}{1 - \frac{r}{r+\sigma}l_L} \right].$$

(A4.10)

This formula defines a relationship SS between m^* and rV_u which is depicted on Figure 4.6. This relationship lies between HH and CC, meaning that the social planner will always elect a strictly positive value of employment protection, contrary to the market, but that this level is always lower than the one the employed in high productivity firms would choose.[17]

Why is optimal employment protection always positive? This arises from the fact that low productivity firms can be arbitrarily close to the high productivity level m_H. If the economy were at full flexibility the losses from increasing employment protection marginally would only be of second order, because the unproductive firms that would remain in operation as a result of that policy measure would only be marginally

[17] To prove this, we need to prove that $\left[1 - \frac{r}{r+\gamma} \left(1 + \frac{\gamma}{r+\sigma}(1 - F(m^*))\right) \frac{l_H}{1-rl_L/(r+\sigma)}\right]$
$> \frac{\gamma q}{(r+\gamma)(r+\sigma)}(\sigma + rF(m^*))$. Multiplying both sides by $(r+\sigma)(r+\gamma)$ and rearranging we see that this is equivalent to $(r + \sigma + \gamma)(1 - \frac{l_H(r+\sigma)}{r+\sigma-rl_R}) + \frac{\gamma l_H(r+\sigma)F(m^*)}{r+\sigma-rl_R} > \gamma F(m^*)$. This is equivalent to $(r + \sigma + \gamma) > \gamma F(m^*)$, which is always true.

less productive than the best ones. This can be checked by noting that the right-hand side of (A4.7), which gives us the effect of an increment in employment protection on wages and/or the value of being unemployed, is equal to zero at $m^* = m_H = w$. By contrast, the gains from employment protection remain of first-order magnitude as long as $q > 0$ and $f(m_H) > 0$. As in the text, it is because firms perceive the wrong price of labour and have too high incentives to close that some degree of protection is optimal.

Case 2: $m^* > m_0$.
All this reasoning is clearly only valid if the intersection between SS and VV yields a value of m^* which is indeed below m_0. If this is not the case we cannot be in that regime. In that case we have to look at what happens when $m^* > m_0$. In that case, the day of the reform a mass of jobs are destroyed. These firms no longer make losses and their workers end up being unemployed. Consequently, aggregate welfare is now given by

$$\Omega(m_0, m^*) = l_H V_e(H) + \left[\left(\int_{m_0}^{m^*} g(m) \, dm \right) + u \right] V_u$$
$$+ \int_{m^*}^{m_H} \left(\frac{m - rV_u - q}{r + \sigma} + V_e(L) \right) g(m) \, dm.$$

The first term is the welfare of the workers employed in high state firms, the second term the welfare of the unemployed, who include the originally unemployed and those who lose their jobs as the result of reform, and the last term is the sum of the welfare of workers who remain in low productivity firms and the negative profits of their employers. Using (A4.5) and (A4.6) we can re-express that as

$$\Omega(m_0, m^*) = V_u + l_H \frac{q}{r + \gamma} (1 + \frac{\gamma}{r + \sigma} (1 - F(m^*)))$$
$$+ \int_{m^*}^{m_H} \frac{m - rV_u}{r + \sigma} g(m) \, dm.$$

The first-order condition for maximization with respect to m^* is

$$\frac{dV_u}{dm^*} \left(1 - \frac{r}{r + \sigma} (l_L - G(m^*)) \right) - l_H \frac{q\gamma}{(r + \gamma)(r + \sigma)} f(m^*)$$
$$- \frac{m^* - rV_u}{r + \sigma} g(m^*) = 0. \quad \text{(A4.11)}$$

Substituting (A4.7) we can write it in a form analogous to (A4.8) and (A4.10):

$$m^* = rV_u + q \left[\frac{1 - \frac{r}{r+\sigma}(l_L - G(m^*)) - \frac{r}{r+\gamma}(1 + \frac{\gamma}{r+\sigma}(1 - F(m^*)))l_H}{1 - \frac{r}{r+\sigma}(l_L - G(m^*)) + \frac{r}{r+\sigma} \frac{r+\sigma+\gamma(1-F(m^*))}{\gamma} \frac{g(m^*)}{f(m^*)}} \right].$$

$$(A4.12)$$

This defines a relationship SS' between m^* and rV_u. The key point is that at $m^* = m_0$ that relationship is always above SS.[18] Consequently it is smaller, meaning that SS' is above SS at $m^* = m_0$. What does that mean? It means that there is a discontinuity in the social marginal gain from employment protection at the status quo level. This discontinuity comes from the fact that if employment protection is reduced marginally, there is a mass of job destruction from existing unproductive firms, while these firms would survive if employment protection is increased marginally. This discontinuity induces status quo bias in the social welfare function by generating a corridor of inaction. This is illustrated in Figure 4.7. The relevant decision rule for the social planner is given by the SS–SS' schedule, which matches SS in the $m^* < m_0$ zone and SS' in the $m^* > m_0$ zone. If it crosses VV along its vertical portion, this means that the status quo is optimal. The social gain from increasing employment protection is strictly negative, but so is the social gain from reducing it. If the status quo was more rigid than m_1, the intersection point of SS' and VV, the social planner would reduce employment protection, increasing m^* from m_0 to m_1. If the status quo was more flexible than m_2, the intersection point of SS and VV, the social planner would increase rigidity, reducing m^* from m_0 to m_2. For any value of m_0 between m_1 and m_2 it is optimal to remain at the status quo. Thus, the outcome is always more rigid, the more rigid the initial conditions.

An important aspect of this analysis is that, whether chosen by the employed, the unemployed, the market, or a central planner, m^* is always greater than rV_u in equilibrium. This is implied by (A4.10), (A4.12), and (A4.8). This implies that the productivity of even the least productive job is always greater than the social opportunity cost of labour in equilibrium. It is this feature that explains why there

---

[18] To see this, just note that at $m^* = m_0$ we have $G(m^*) = 0$, so that the term in brackets in (A4.12) has the same numerator as the term in brackets in (A4.10), with a greater denominator.

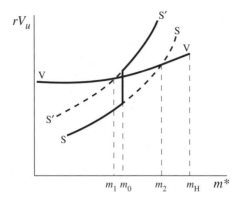

Figure 4.7. The social planner's status quo bias

is status quo bias. It is costly for society to destroy existing jobs in low productivity firms because in equilibrium each of these jobs has a positive net social value.

Why is that so? For the social planner, this is not surprising: it is trading off the value of maintaining unproductive plants against the cost of employment protection in terms of lower job creation. As that cost is positive, the optimum must be such that the marginal social value of maintaining an unproductive plant is strictly positive. The employed, however, do not care about the social value of jobs in declining industries, yet they also elect a degree of employment protection moderate enough to maintain it above zero.

The intuition is as follows. Expected future losses are passed to workers in the form of lower wages. That is, (A4.4) can be rewritten as

$$w = m_H - \frac{\gamma}{r + \sigma} \int_{m^*}^{m_H} LOSS \cdot f(m) \cdot \mathrm{d}m,$$

where $LOSS = m - w$ is the loss per unit of time. The welfare of an employed worker can be decomposed into three terms: current wages, expected welfare if the firm falls into the low state, and expected rents lost if fired when the firm falls into the low state. That is, the numerator of (A4.6) can be rewritten as

$$(r + \gamma)V_e = w - \gamma F(m^*)\frac{RENT}{r + \sigma} + \gamma V_e(L),$$

where $RENT = q$ is the rent.

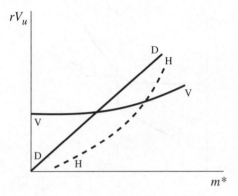

Figure 4.8. The discretionary social planner's choice

An increase in m^* increases wages by an amount exactly equal to the expected discounted loss made by the marginal firms that are forced to close. It increases rents lost by an amount equal to the expected discounted rent generated by these firms. If workers were ignoring the general equilibrium effects of employment protection they would just consider these two effects. As long as $LOSS < RENT$, they would have an incentive to increase employment protection because their gain from the rents that are saved outweighs the reduction in wages due to the transmission of losses to workers. Therefore, they would increase employment protection up to the point where $LOSS = RENT$, which is precisely equivalent to $w = rV_u + q = m^* + q$. That is, $rV_u = m^*$. So the employed would elect precisely the point where the net social value of a marginal job is exactly equal to zero (as we have seen, this point is *not* the social planner's preferred point since one has also to consider the negative impact of employment protection on job creation). However, workers also take into account the general equilibrium effects of employment protection and recognize that it reduces job prospects and therefore the term $V_e(L)$. Because of that general equilibrium effect they actually want a level of job protection which is below the one that satisfies $LOSS = RENT$. Therefore they pick up a point where the net social value of the lowest productivity job is strictly positive.

A discretionary social planner, however, will always maintain jobs whose productivity m is greater than the social opportunity cost of labour. Therefore, his preferred level of employment protection is determined by

$$m^* = rV_u.$$

This defines an upward sloping locus DD, which, as represented in Figure 4.8, is strictly above HH. The discretionary social planner will elect a stronger level of employment protection than the employed would vote for.

5
Unemployment benefits and other measures for the unemployed

So far in this book we have adopted the view that labour market institutions are set by incumbent employees in order to fit their own interests, at the expense of other groups of employees, the unemployed, or both. We saw that while microeconomic frictions could generate employee rents, incumbent employees could support institutions that increased such rents, whenever there is scope for redistribution between various groups of workers. We then showed that the existence of such rents led to the rise of employment protection.

Yet if the world works in this way, why do we observe public unemployment insurance? It is a transfer to the unemployed financed by a tax on the employed. If the employed are so powerful, why do they engage in such a scheme? Indeed, this paradox seems to be reinforced by the observation that unemployment benefits are most generous in countries where unions are most powerful and rigidities are most prominent. How can a society choose institutions that reduce the unemployed's job prospects and at the same time tax the employed to pay the unemployed? It is this puzzle that we tackle here.

5.1 Insurance effects

The most straightforward answer to this question is that unemployment benefits provide insurance to the employed against the event of job loss. Therefore, they are set in the interests of the employed, just like other institutions, but play a different role. They do not mediate any sort of redistributive conflict but are society's best response to the risk generated by the misfunctioning of the labour market. One may ask why, rather than unemployment insurance being a public good, one would not have people directly buying insurance on the market. It is not difficult to come up with an answer to that question. The market for privately provided unemployment insurance is likely to collapse because only the most exposed workers will want to buy it—a standard adverse selection argument.[1]

Once a unitary system of unemployment insurance exists, it is not without conflicts. More exposed workers want a higher degree of insurance than less exposed ones. The unemployed will want more insurance than the employed.

Let us illustrate this point in a world where people move between employment and unemployment, and where there are new entrants. Assume, as we have so far, that the job loss rate is s and the job finding rate is a. Assume the employed earn a wage w, out of which they pay a tax τ to finance unemployment benefits b.

Furthermore, contrary to what has been assumed so far, we assume that workers are risk averse. That is, if y is their income they derive a utility $u(y)$ which is concave in y. This assumption implies that they prefer a certain income to a variable one that has the same average value. We must make it in order to get an insurance motive for unemployment benefits.[2]

Then the evolution equations for the value of being employed and unemployed, respectively, are given by, in steady state

$$rV_e = u(w(1 - \tau)) + s\,[V_u - V_e] - pV_e$$

$$rV_u = u(b) + a[V_e - V_u] - pV_u.$$

This is just (1.9) and (1.10), but written in steady state, with wages and benefits being replaced by the utility flows $u(w(1 - \tau))$ and $u(b)$.

Solving for these two equations we get

$$(r + p)V_e = \frac{(r + p + a)u(w(1 - \tau)) + su(b)}{(r + p + s + a)} \tag{5.1}$$

---

[1] Following Akerlof (1970), there is a vast literature studying how a market can collapse because of adverse selection, insurance markets being a prominent example. See Kreps (1990) for an introduction.

[2] Furthermore, we are also assuming that borrowing and lending is impossible, thus equating consumption to income in each period. Relaxing that assumption has important consequences, discussed in Hassler and Rodriguez (1996). See also Hassler *et al.* (1999) on the political determination of employment benefits.

$$(r+p)V_u = \frac{au(w(1-\tau)) + (s+r+p)u(b)}{(r+p+s+a)}. \qquad (5.2)$$

The value of being employed (in annuity terms) is a weighted average of the utility of post-tax wages and the utility of unemployment benefits. The weight on unemployment benefits is proportional to s, the degree of exposure to unemployment. The weight on employment income is proportional to $r+p+a$, the sum of the job finding rate, the exit rate from the workforce, and the interest rate. The dependence on the interest rate reflects the fact that being employed now, the employed put a greater weight on employment income relative to unemployment benefits. The exit rate p plays a similar role: the future is more heavily discounted when p is larger because the individual is less likely to be around at any given future date. The dependence on the job finding rate a reflects the fact that when jobs are found more often people expect to spend a greater fraction of their lifetime in employment, so that the weight of employment income in their welfare is greater.

A similar formula holds for the welfare of the unemployed. The discount rate, however, now appears in the weight of unemployment benefits, which is therefore larger for the unemployed than for the employed. Note that if $r=p=0$ the welfare of both types of workers is the same; people give the same weight to future events as to current ones. Both the employed and the unemployed then maximize utility weighted by the average time spent in each state.

The unemployment rate, in steady state, is given by (1.11), rewritten for convenience as

$$u = \frac{s+p}{s+p+a}. \qquad (1.11)$$

We assume that the budget of the unemployment benefit system must be balanced. We also assume that new entrants are paid unemployment benefits. This is not meant to be realistic, but will allow us to analyse the impact of an increase in unemployment exposure s holding its direct impact on the financial burden of unemployment benefits constant. This implies that receipts $\tau w(1-u)$ must be equal to expenditures bu or, equivalently, using (1.11):

$$\tau = \frac{b(s+p)}{wa}. \qquad (5.3)$$

The tax rate is the product of two terms. b/w is the replacement ratio, i.e. the fraction of wages that is replaced by unemployment benefits.

$(s + p)/a$ is the entry/exit ratio: i.e. the ratio of the entry rate into unemployment over the exit rate from unemployment to employment.[3]

The tax rate must be greater, the greater the benefit level b, the smaller the wage w, the greater the inflow into unemployment, and the smaller the outflow from unemployment.

What is the level of unemployment benefits preferred by the employed and the unemployed? To answer that question, it is convenient to start with the assumption of an exogenous value of a. Substituting (5.3) into (5.1) and (5.2), then differentiating with respect to b, we get the first-order condition for the employed's and unemployed's preferred value of b.

The employed's first-order condition is

$$\frac{u'(w(1-\tau))}{u'(b)} = \frac{a}{r+p+a}\frac{s}{s+p} < 1. \tag{5.4}$$

The left-hand side is the ratio of the marginal utility of consumption between the employed and the unemployed. That is, the numerator is the disutility cost, in the employment state, of increasing unemployment benefit contributions by one unit, while the denominator is the utility gain, in the unemployment state, of increasing unemployment benefits by one unit.

The right-hand side is the terms of trade between consumption in the unemployment state and consumption in the employment state, seen from the point of view of the employed. It is equal to the product of two terms. $a/(s + p)$ is the ratio between the employed and the unemployed: it is the marginal rate of transformation of income between the two states implied by the budget constraint (5.3). $s/(r + p + a)$ is the ratio between the expected time an employed expects to spend in unemployment over the expected time spent in employment, adjusted for time preference.

The product of these two ratios is lower than one, implying $c_e = w(1 - \tau) > c_u = b$. The employed want less than full insurance, more so, the greater the discount rate r and the retirement rate p. This reflects the fact that they are employed right now and will only be unemployed in the future.

For the unemployed, the first-order condition is

$$\frac{u'(w(1-\tau))}{u'(b)} = \frac{r+p+s}{s+p} > 1. \tag{5.5}$$

---

[3] One can check that if new entrants are not eligible for benefits then the tax rate is $\tau = sb/(a + p)w$.

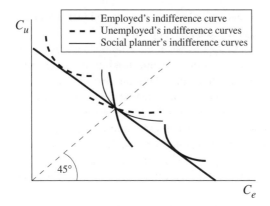

Figure 5.1. Preferences for unemployment benefits

The unemployed would actually prefer overinsurance, i.e. a net income larger for the unemployed than for the employed.

As r and p fall, both the employed's and the unemployed's preferred insurance level converge toward the full insurance one, in which consumption is the same for the employed and the unemployed.

What would be a central planner's preferred insurance level? He would simply maximize $(1 - u)V_e + uV_u$, which is proportional to $au(w(1 - \tau)) + (s + p)u(b)$. The corresponding first-order condition is $u'(b) = u'(w(1 - \tau))$. So, not surprisingly, the central planner would elect for full insurance—as he is maximizing the weighted average of two utility levels, and utility is concave, he wants to redistribute income in such a way that these two levels are equal.

The solution is illustrated in Figure 5.1. The downward sloping straight line represents the terms of trade between the consumption (or income) of the employed and the consumption of the unemployed, i.e. society's budget constraint. Its slope is $-(s + p)/a$, the ratio between unemployment and employment. This slope tells us how much money must be taken out of the pocket of an employed to increase an unemployed's income by one unit. Along the 45° line a central planner, at the margin, values the employed's and the unemployed's income equally. Consequently, along the 45° line the slope of the social indifference curve is equal to the slope of the budget line; so the social planner will pick up a point where consumption of the employed equals consumption of the unemployed. The employed value the former more than the latter, so they have a steeper indifference curve and pick up a suboptimal level of b. The unemployed do the opposite.

Finally, what happens when the employed's exposure to unemployment s increases? To do so while holding employment constant, we assume that p, the entry rate, falls one for one with s, so that $s + p$ remains constant. One can then see that the right-hand side of (5.4) must increase, meaning that the employed are willing to trade more dollars in the employment state to get an extra unit of income when unemployed; being more exposed to unemployment, they value unemployment benefits more, and their preferred level of insurance increases. By contrast, the unemployed's preferred level does not, as the right-hand side of (5.5) is constant.

The model can also be extended to pick up differences in unemployment exposure among the employed. This is done by replacing s by an individual-specific s_i in (5.1) and (5.2), while interpreting s as the *average* job loss rate in (5.3). The first-order conditions then become

$$\frac{u'(w(1 - \tau))}{u'(b)} = \frac{a}{r + p + a} \frac{s_i}{s + p},$$

for the employed and

$$\frac{u'(w(1 - \tau))}{u'(b)} = \frac{r + p + s_i}{s + p},$$

for the unemployed.

The preferred level of insurance is now higher for individuals with a greater degree of exposure relative to the average.[4] A highly exposed employed might want more than full insurance, a lowly exposed unemployed may want less than full insurance. The one-size-fits-all unemployment benefit system automatically redistributes income from the less exposed to the more exposed.

5.2 Employment effects

As we saw in Chapter 1, unemployment benefits increase workers' outside option and reduce job creation. The unemployed are more vulnerable to reduced job creation than the employed. That effect may potentially lead them to like unemployment benefits less than the employed. Who benefits most from that institution is then no longer clear.

---

[4] This is the central insight of Wright's (1986) seminal paper.

To better see how our results are qualified when people recognize the adverse effect of unemployment benefits on job creation, let us assume that in equilibrium there is a negative relationship between the job finding rate a and the unemployment benefit level b. That is, $a = a(b)$, $a' < 0$. Taking that into account in the maximization of (5.1) and (5.2), and denoting by

$$\eta = -\frac{b}{a(b)}a'(b)$$

the elasticity, in absolute value, of a with respect to b, we find that the first order conditions become:

$$\frac{u'(w(1 - \tau))\,[1 + \eta]}{u'(b) - \eta\frac{a}{b}[u_e - u_u]/(r + p + s + a)} = \frac{a}{r + p + a}\frac{s}{p + s} < 1 \quad (5.6)$$

for the employed, and

$$\frac{u'(w(1 - \tau))\,[1 + \eta]}{u'(b) - \eta\frac{a}{b}[u_e - u_u]/(r + p + s + a)} = \frac{r + p + s}{s + p} > 1 \quad (5.7)$$

for the unemployed.

If we compare these formulas with (5.4), (5.5), we see (looking at numerators) that when unemployment benefits increase, the marginal disutility to the employed must be incremented by a factor $1 + \eta$. This represents the increase in the tax cost of unemployment benefits brought about by the associated rise in unemployment. Looking now at denominators, we see that the utility gain to the unemployed must be reduced by a quantity $\frac{da}{db}[u_e - u_u]/(r + p + s + a)$, which represents the average annualized loss to the unemployed of the reduction in the job finding rate, in utility terms.

Therefore, these formulae tell us that when unemployment benefits have an adverse impact on job creation, people take that into account, which reduces the support for unemployment insurance.

Does that change our predictions very much? It is still true that the unemployed want more insurance than the employed. If (5.6) is satisfied then (5.7) cannot hold because its left-hand side is lower than its right-hand side, meaning that the unemployed would like to increase unemployment benefits.

To the extent that unemployment benefits have a direct negative impact on the employed's consumption flow, they must be compensated for that. Otherwise they will not support any unemployment benefits. That compensation must come in the form of greater utility when they become

unemployed. At the employed's preferred level of benefits, the direct
cost in terms of lower consumption of an extra unit of unemployment
benefits is exactly equal, at the margin, to the indirect benefit when unemployed. But this *must* imply that the marginal gain to the unemployed
is strictly positive, i.e. that they would like to increase the degree of
benefits. Formally, we have

$$V_e = \frac{u(w(1-\tau)) + sV_u}{r+s+p}, \tag{5.8}$$

implying that at the employed's preferred point, which satisfies
$\mathrm{d}V_e/\mathrm{d}b = 0$, we have

$$\frac{\mathrm{d}}{\mathrm{d}b} u(w(1-\tau)) = -s\frac{\mathrm{d}}{\mathrm{d}b}V_u, \tag{5.9}$$

implying $\frac{\mathrm{d}}{\mathrm{d}b}V_u > 0$ if b reduces $w(1-\tau)$.

What about the impact of unemployment exposure on unemployment
benefits? When s increases while p falls to maintain $s + p$ constant, the
right-hand side of (5.6) increases, implying that the marginal utility of
consumption when employed increases. So it is still true that greater
exposure increases the employed's desired benefit level—this, despite
the fact that greater exposure makes them more vulnerable to unemployment, and therefore care more about the reduction in the job finding
probability. Again, insurance considerations dominate at the margin
because the employed always elect a value of b which yields a positive
marginal effect of b on V_u. So, when unemployment is given a heavier
weight in the employed's utility, as is the case when exposure increases,
the employed's desired value of b necessarily increases.

Our provisional conclusion is therefore that if we allow benefits to
reduce a, that effect will lower the employed's desired benefit level, but
will not change the qualitative determinants of unemployment benefits.

Furthermore, (5.6) and (5.7) tell us that an important determinant of
unemployment benefits is the elasticity η of the job finding rate with
respect to the benefit level b. This elasticity is associated with the distortionary cost of unemployment benefits. The higher η, the greater that
cost, and the lower the employed's and unemployed's preferred benefit
level. It is also true, not surprisingly, that a social planner would also
elect for a lower value of b, the larger η.

η is intimately related to the degree of 'wage rigidity', that is, the
elasticity of wage setting with respect to labour market tightness. If

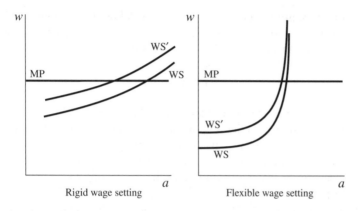

Figure 5.2. Employment effects of an increase in unemployment benefits

wage formation is very flexible, a slight deterioration of employment prospects will trigger a lot of wage moderation. In that case, an increase in unemployment benefits will only have a low impact on a, the job finding probability.

The underlying logic is illustrated in Figure 5.2, which is similar to Figure 1.1. The wage formation schedule WS shows how wage setting depends on labour market tightness a. The horizontal schedule MP is the marginal product schedule, which under constant returns to scale is horizontal. An increase in unemployment benefits shifts WS vertically. The more flexible is wage formation, the more vertical the wage setting schedule WS, and the lower the fall in a in response to an increase in b.

5.2.1 The fixed total rent case

By maintaining a relationship between the value of being employed and the value of being unemployed, the wage formation mechanism limits the scope for insurance. The rise in the unemployed's welfare brought about by an increase in unemployment benefits may be partially offset by the fall in the job finding rate triggered by the employed's increased ability to get higher wages.

If the wage formation process is such that the total rent is fixed, as in Chapter 1, people will not want any unemployment benefit, because the market mechanism for wage formation will defeat any attempt to insure all workers against unemployment.

Let us return to our wage formation model used in Chapter 1. We assumed that wages were set at the point where the employed's welfare exceeded the unemployed's by a fixed amount:

$$V_e = V_u + Q. \tag{1.14}$$

In that world, the utility loss made when losing one's job cannot be different from Q. What would happen if society increased the level of unemployment benefit? Incumbent employees would try to bid up wages, which, so far, we have ruled out because of constant returns to scale. So to maintain equilibrium the job finding rate a must fall to the point where, despite their higher income, the unemployed's job prospects have deteriorated so much that they are still worse off than the employed by an amount Q. It is not difficult to realize that in such a world, provided that voters understand this economic mechanism, there will be no social demand for unemployment insurance—we proved this in Chapter 1, in the absence of risk aversion, and it is still true if people are risk averse.[5] Both the employed and the unemployed then oppose any level of benefits. Any attempt to narrow the gap between the two is defeated by the market mechanism, so there is no insurance effect, only the adverse effect on job creation remains.

This example illustrates that the negative impact of benefits on job creation may reduce the value of unemployment benefits to such a point that everybody opposes them. Equation (1.14) implies that if people take into account the general equilibrium effects of policy, there cannot be any conflict of interests between the employed and the unemployed over a measure that leaves Q unaffected; so any policy that leaves Q unaffected and does not increase the overall welfare of the employed and the unemployed will be rejected by both groups. This is the case of an increase in b, which reduces the size of the cake to be shared between the employed and the unemployed, so that the welfare of both types of worker cannot increase at the same time.

---

[5] Using (5.1), (5.2), and (1.14) we can simply compute a:

$$a = \frac{u(w(1-\tau)) - u(b)}{Q} - (r + p + s).$$

This implies $da/db = -u'(b)/Q - su'(w(1-\tau))/aQ$, and one can then check that the denominator of (5.6) and (5.7) is always negative, meaning that the marginal utility to the unemployed of an increase in benefits, corrected for its effect on job finding, is actually negative.

5.3 Wage effects: reintroducing distributive conflict

Unemployment benefits become more like other 'rigidities' once we allow for equilibrium wages to vary. Let us again assume that because of the existence of another factor (group B), wages may actually increase in equilibrium if employment of group A is reduced. Then an increase in b also increases the pre-tax wage w. How will that affect the employed's preferred level of benefits if they take that into account? Let us assume $w = w(b)$, $w' > 0$. Then, differentiating (5.1) and (5.2) we get the following first-order conditions:

$$\frac{u'(w(1-\tau))\left[1 + \eta - \frac{a}{s+p}\frac{\mathrm{d}w}{\mathrm{d}b}\right]}{u'(b) + \frac{\mathrm{d}a}{\mathrm{d}b}[u_e - u_u]/(r+s+p+a)} = \frac{a}{r+p+a}\frac{s}{s+p} < 1 \tag{5.10}$$

for the employed and

$$\frac{u'(w(1-\tau))\left[1 + \eta - \frac{a}{s+p}\frac{\mathrm{d}w}{\mathrm{d}b}\right]}{u'(b) + \frac{\mathrm{d}a}{\mathrm{d}b}[u_e - u_u]/(r+s+p+a)} = \frac{r+p+s}{s+p} > 1 \tag{5.11}$$

for the unemployed. There is now an extra corrective term in the marginal disutility of increasing unemployment benefits. This corrective term,

$$-\frac{a}{s+p}u'(w(1-\tau))\frac{\mathrm{d}w}{\mathrm{d}b},$$

represents the extra wage gains, to the employed, of increasing unemployment benefits. It is negative, meaning that unemployment benefits are higher when wage effects are taken into account.

In terms of the logic of Figure 5.2, the MP schedule is now downward sloping. As illustrated in Figure 5.3, the gains from increasing b in terms of wages are greater, and the losses in terms of employability smaller, the steeper the MP schedule, i.e. the more inelastic labour demand is.

An important aspect of (5.10) is that it may be matched under two configurations. If the denominator and numerator are both positive, we are in a configuration where unemployment benefits, at the margin, redistribute from the employed to the unemployed. In that case, their determinants are motivated by an insurance logic. It is still true, for example, that an increase in unemployment exposure—an increase in s holding $s + p$ constant—will increase the employed's optimal benefit level.

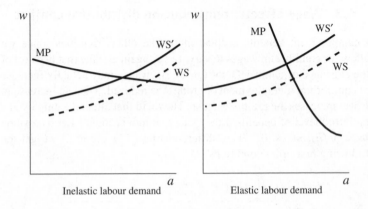

Figure 5.3. Wage effects of an increase in unemployment benefits

But, given that both the numerator and the denominator now have negative corrective terms, it may be that (5.10) is satisfied with a negative numerator and denominator. This means that, at the margin, unemployment benefits will actually redistribute from the unemployed to the employed. The losses to the unemployed in terms of reduced job finding are then greater than their gains in terms of increased current income, while the gains to the employed in terms of increased wages are greater than the costs in terms of higher taxes and lower job finding rates. If this regime prevails, the logic is then inverted. Insurance effects are dwarfed by wage effects.

For example, (5.9) is now equivalent to

$$\frac{as}{s+p}\frac{\mathrm{d}V_u}{\mathrm{d}b} = u'(w(1-\tau))\left[1+\eta-\frac{a}{s+p}\frac{\mathrm{d}w}{\mathrm{d}b}\right].$$

The right-hand side is simply the numerator of (5.10). So, in the regime where it is negative, the employed will always pick up a point such that $\mathrm{d}V_u/\mathrm{d}b < 0$: at the margin, they actually like unemployment benefits more than the unemployed themselves.

Also, an increase in exposure now may well reduce the employed's preferred benefit level: they now give more weight to the unemployment state, where the marginal benefit of unemployment insurance is negative;

accordingly they want to reduce benefits.[6]

This 'inverted' regime is more likely to prevail, the greater $\mathrm{d}\dot{w}/\mathrm{d}b$, that is, the greater the scope for increasing wages via unemployment benefits. Here again we see the important role of the elasticity of labour demand. The smaller that elasticity, the greater $\mathrm{d}w/\mathrm{d}b$, and the more strongly are benefits affected by wage-setting considerations.

At that stage, the reader may be tempted to believe that these arguments are a bit far-fetched, since they seem to imply that unemployment benefits actually harm the unemployed. Remember, however, that what matters is what is taking place *at the margin*. The first units of unemployment benefits achieve a large insurance function. And large reductions in benefits would clearly harm the unemployed more than the employed. But wage effects lead the employed to choose a benefit level beyond the one preferred by the unemployed.

5.3.1 The fixed total rent case

To illustrate the importance of wage effects, we go back to the case where the total rent Q is fixed. We know that the denominator of the left-hand side of (5.10) is then always equal to zero. But we may now be in the knife-edge case where there is an interior solution for b, because (5.10) is matched with a numerator also equal to zero. That is, the left-hand side is indeterminate, so that equality is satisfied in a general sense. In that case, wage effects are strong enough to prompt the employed and the unemployed to agree on a strictly positive benefit level even though it has no general equilibrium insurance effects. The first-order condition now collapses to

$$\frac{\mathrm{d}w}{\mathrm{d}b} = (1 + \eta)\frac{s + p}{a}.$$

Unemployment benefits will be set at the level that maximizes the

---

[6] Differentiating (5.9) with respect to s we get

$$0 = \frac{\partial^2 u(w(1-\tau))}{\partial b \partial s} + \frac{\partial^2 u(w(1-\tau))}{\partial b^2}\frac{\mathrm{d}b}{\mathrm{d}s} + \frac{\mathrm{d}V_u}{\mathrm{d}b} + s\frac{\partial^2 V_u}{\partial b \partial s} + s\frac{\partial^2 V_u}{\partial b^2}\frac{\mathrm{d}b}{\mathrm{d}s}.$$

Therefore,

$$\frac{\mathrm{d}b}{\mathrm{d}s} = \frac{\frac{\mathrm{d}V_u}{\mathrm{d}b} + s\frac{\partial^2 V_u}{\partial b \partial s} + \frac{\partial^2 u(w(1-\tau))}{\partial b \partial s}}{-\left(\frac{\partial^2 u(w(1-\tau))}{\partial b^2} + s\frac{\partial^2 V_u}{\partial b^2}\right)}.$$

The second-order condition for maximization of (5.8) implies that the denominator is positive. In the numerator, we have $\mathrm{d}V_u/\mathrm{d}b < 0$. If the other terms are negative or not too positive, then $\mathrm{d}b/\mathrm{d}s < 0$.

post-tax wage $w(1 - \tau)$. Here they play the same role as the rent-enhancing institutions analysed in Chapter 2, of redistributing from group B to group A by reducing the supply of group A's workers. The big difference, here, is that because unemployment benefits work their way through the outside option rather than the rent, the unemployed of group A totally agree with the employed over their optimal level.

If the whole of group A behaved as a monopoly union,[7] and if the elasticity of demand were low enough, it would set wages at a level above full employment and redistribute from its employed to its unemployed members in such a way that they would all be perfectly insured and get an income greater than their full employment wage.

This is not exactly what is taking place here as full insurance is not achievable because of the rent Q. However, the logic is somewhat similar; an increase in unemployment benefits allows group A as a whole to increase the surplus it is extracting from group B, while the wage formation mechanism ensures that any increase in group A's overall welfare is equally shared between its employed and unemployed members, despite the fact that the latter remain worse off than the former.

5.3.2 A graphical illustration of the two regimes

The two regimes are illustrated in Figures 5.4 and 5.5. The backward bending curve BB represents the trade-off between the employed's utility flow $u(w(1 - \tau))$ and the utility of the unemployed V_u. The arrows represent the direction of motion of the economy along this trade-off as unemployment benefits increase. The indifference curves, labelled $I(s)$, are those of the employed, as defined by (5.8). Their slope is equal to $-s$. In the standard regime where insurance effects dominate, the employed's income falls while V_u rises, up to point A where the unemployed's maximum utility is reached. The employed will always elect a point E left of that point, and an increase in their exposure from s to s' shifts E to E′, where benefits are higher than at B but still lower than at A.

When wage formation effects dominate, the direction of motion of the economy along BB is inverted (Figure 5.5). At low benefits level an increase in b increases both the employed's net wage and the unemployed's utility. One eventually reaches point A where further increases

---

[7] See the appendix of Chapter 1 for a brief discussion of union-based models of wage setting.

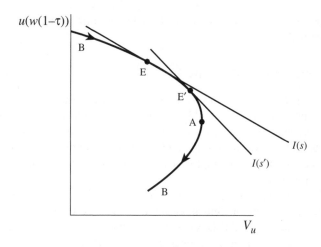

Figure 5.4. The normal (insurance) regime: impact of an increase in exposure

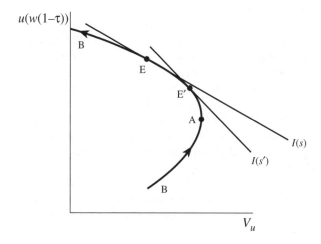

Figure 5.5. The inverted (wage) regime

in b harm the unemployed, because of the reduced job finding prospects. The employed's preferred level, given by E, is now at a higher benefit level than the one preferred by the unemployed. Just as before, an increase in s moves that point closer to A, but that now means a reduction in benefits.

5.3.3 Alternative instruments

The above discussion seems to settle the apparent paradox discussed at the beginning of this chapter. That is, we have established that if unemployment benefits have strong enough positive effects on wages, then at the margin they will benefit the employed and harm the unemployed— the politically powerful employed will set them too high relative to the social optimum.

Now, the paradox is not completely settled, because we have assumed that the only instrument available to insiders was unemployment benefits. But, we established in Chapter 2 that if the employed had the choice of manipulating wages using a policy instrument that affects their rent, they would do so rather than use an instrument, such as unemployment benefits, that affects their outside option in wage setting. If such an alternative instrument is available, unemployment benefit will then only obey insurance considerations.

That is, there are now two degrees of freedom. The alternative instrument is used to achieve the best possible trade-off between employment and wages, while unemployment benefits are simultaneously used to achieve the most desirable degree of insurance. The intuition is very simple. Suppose the trade-off between wages and labour market tightness, i.e. the marginal product schedule, is unaffected by the other instrument. Then that instrument can be used to adjust the position of the wage formation schedule to best exploit that trade-off. Therefore, at the optimum, any slight deviations from that point along the labour demand schedule generates only second-order losses. When considering the marginal gains and losses from unemployment benefits, the employed can therefore ignore the gains and losses associated with the effect of b on w and a. Consequently, the only effects they will take into account are insurance effects.

More formally, assume that we have $w = w(b, c)$, and $a = a(b, c)$, where c denotes the alternative instrument. We assume $\partial a/\partial c < 0$ and $\partial w/\partial c > 0$, meaning that a greater value of c increases wages at the expense of job creation. The marginal product of labour depends on employment: $w = h'(l)$, with $h'' < 0$. Employment is given by $l = l(a) = a/(s + p + a)$. Therefore if the two instruments b and c change neither the production function nor $s + p$, both will move the economy along the same trade-off between wages and tightness, given by $w(a) = h'(a/(s + p + a))$. Therefore the $w(.,.)$ and $a(.,.)$ functions must satisfy

$$\frac{\partial w/\partial b}{\partial a/\partial b} = \frac{\partial w/\partial c}{\partial a/\partial c} = w'(a).$$

The employed simultaneously decide on a and c in order to maximize (5.1). The optimality condition with respect to b is still given by (5.10). The optimality condition with respect to c is

$$-s\frac{\partial a}{\partial c}\frac{u(w(1 - \tau)) - u(b)}{r + p + s + a}$$
$$= u'(w(1 - \tau))(r + p + a)\left[\frac{\partial w}{\partial c} + \frac{b(s + p)}{a^2}\frac{\partial a}{\partial c}\right].$$

Substituting that into (5.10) we get

$$\frac{u'(w(1 - \tau))}{u'(b)} = \frac{a}{r + p + a}\frac{s}{s + p},$$

which is exactly (5.4). All arbitrages between a and w are entirely exploited by using the instrument c. At the margin only insurance considerations remain when setting unemployment benefits.

Does that bring us back to our previous arguments? Not at all. Take, for example, the previous result that under sole insurance considerations, the employed want less insurance than the unemployed. It no longer necessarily holds. While insurance considerations end up being the only effects taken into account by the employed at the margin, this is due to the fact that wage and employment effects only have a second-order impact on their utility, because the other instrument c is determined optimally. But, it is optimal from the viewpoint of the employed, not of the unemployed. The employment and wage effects therefore have a first-order impact on the unemployed's welfare, and if the employment effects are strong enough, they may still prefer a benefit level lower than the employed. That is, (5.4) holds but (5.5) does not. The unemployed's preferred insurance level is still determined by (5.11), which does not necessarily yield a greater value of benefits than (5.4).

More generally, the unemployed's preferred pair of institutions (b, c) will be different from that of the employed, and it may well be that they would prefer a value of c such that the associated value of b will be lower than the one elected by the employed. Similarly, an increase in exposure s will increase the employed's demand for insurance given the other institution c, but they also will want to alter the level of c, so that the net effect on benefits b is unclear.

5.4 Active labour market policies: a case of conflicts between the short-term and the long-term unemployed[8]

The above discussion suggests that the logic of political insider models may apply to the determination of unemployment benefits, and that these effects may dominate if the elasticity of demand for the group we are considering is small enough.

Another example of how policies toward the unemployed may be determined by political insider effects is the case of active labour market policies. A common argument in favour of these policies is that the long-term unemployed have a low probability of finding a job. These policies are efficient at reducing unemployment if they bring them back into the workforce, thus exerting pressure for wage moderation, and increasing the incentives for job creation. But how is the *employed's* welfare affected by such policies? If the wage moderation that they bring implies wages that are actually lower in equilibrium, they might well object to it. If that effect is small, however, they may support it for two reasons. First, they may end up in long-term unemployment themselves, and second, the tax burden of unemployment benefits may be reduced.

Here we have a case of disagreement among the unemployed. The short-term unemployed are solidaristic with the employed, as their welfare defines the latter's outside option in wage formation. Roughly speaking, both suffer from the increased competition of the long-term unemployed. The long-term unemployed always would like more active labour market policies than the short-term unemployed.

It is possible to slightly modify our framework developed in Chapter 1 in order to introduce a distinction between the short-term and the long-term unemployed and to analyse the political support for active labour market policies. Insiders are now able to manipulate labour market programmes that directly affect search intensity.

We introduce 'long-term' unemployment as follows. Instead of assuming that people retire from the workforce with probability p, we assume that they fall into a state called 'long-term' unemployment, which is similar to short-term unemployment but characterized by a lower probability of finding a job. The only modification with respect to equations (1.9) and (1.10) is that now long-term unemployment is

---

[8] This section is based on Saint-Paul (1998b), to which we refer the reader for further details.

associated with a value V_l, whereas the value of retirement was assumed to be zero. Thus we now have

$$r V_e = w(1 - \tau) + \dot{V}_e + s(V_u - V_e) - p(V_e - V_l) \qquad (5.12)$$

$$r V_u = b + \dot{V}_u + a(V_u - V_e) - p(V_u - V_l), \qquad (5.13)$$

where V_u is now defined as the welfare of the short-term unemployed. Note that we assume that both the employed and the short-term unemployed may fall into 'long-term' unemployment, and this with the same probability. This somewhat simplifies the analysis, relative to the case where people would move first from employment to short-term unemployment, then from short-term to long-term unemployment.[9] Note also that we no longer discuss insurance effects, so that we go back to the assumption of a utility flow which is linear in income.

We still assume a wage formation mechanism with a fixed intertemporal rent, as given by (1.14). The important point is that the employed's outside option is now defined by the value of being short-term unemployed, capturing the hypothesis that the long-term unemployed exert little pressure on wages, contrary to the short-term unemployed. A fall in V_u will directly reduce the outside option of employed workers in wage formation, which is not the case when V_l goes down. The long-term unemployed's welfare does not affect the wage formation relationship.

Taking differences between (5.12) and (5.13) and using (1.14) we again get (1.16):

$$a = \frac{w(1 - \tau) - b}{Q} - (r + s + p). \qquad (1.16)$$

We assume that the long-term unemployed find a job with a lower probability than the short-term unemployed; their welfare therefore evolves according to

$$r V_l = b + \dot{V}_e + \varphi a(V_e - V_l).$$

The parameter φ is exogenous and lower than one; it tells us that the long-term unemployed's probability of finding a job is only a fraction

---

[9] In terms of plausibility, the relative merits of the two approaches are debatable. On the one hand, it is reasonable that it is precisely the fact of having stayed long in unemployment which discourages workers and reduces their job prospects. On the other hand, our assumptions capture the view that the long-term unemployed are people who have lower job prospects from the beginning, and end up endogenously having longer spells. For example, the shock p may be interpreted as a fall in the demand for one of the individual's skills, due to some demand shift or technical progress.

φ of the short-term unemployed's probability of finding a job. Thus if $\varphi = 0.5$; and if 50 per cent of the short-term unemployed find a job per month, only 25 per cent of the long-term unemployed will find a job in any given month. When the labour market becomes less tight, a falls, and the job finding probability of both the short-term and the long-term unemployed fall, while the ratio between the two is maintained constant.

We can compute the steady state level of short-term and long-term unemployment by equating inflows and outflows. Let u_s and u_l be the short-term and long-term unemployment rates, respectively. The inflow into short-term unemployment is equal to $sl = s(1 - u_s - u_l)$, while the outflow is $(p + a)u_s$. Consequently

$$u_s = \frac{s(1 - u_l)}{s + p + a}.$$

The inflow into long-term unemployment is $p(1 - u_l)$, while the outflow is $\varphi a u_l$. Therefore

$$u_l = \frac{p}{p + \varphi a}.$$

Given a, a higher value of φ means fewer long-term unemployed, which implies more short-term unemployed. This is only possible if employment l rises. Therefore, total employment l is an increasing function of a and φ.

If we assume a decreasing relationship between wages and employment, equilibrium is again represented as in Figure 5.3, with a downward sloping labour demand schedule, and an upward sloping wage formation schedule.

How can we use this framework to think about active labour market policy? One simple way is to assume that by engaging in such programmes, society is increasing the long-term unemployed's search intensity φ. This captures at least the motivation of a variety of programmes that prevail in the real world, although we also observe the use of relief jobs, which are considered to have little impact on the search intensity of the long-term unemployed.

The effect of an increase in φ is depicted in Figure 5.6. In this figure we have represented three relationships: the link between wages and employment as implied by the production function, the wage formation schedule which relates wages to labour market tightness, and the steady state relationship between employment and labour market

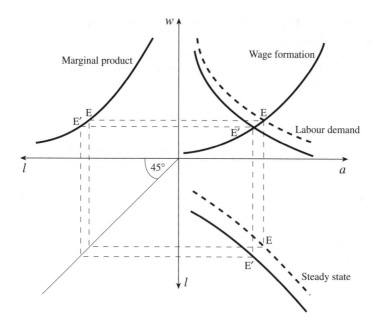

Figure 5.6. Impact of active labour market policy on tightness, employment, and wages

tightness, which is given by

$$l = 1 - u_s - u_l$$
$$= \frac{\varphi a(p + a)}{(p + \varphi a)(s + p + a)}.$$

Using the 45° line in the lower left quadrant we can substitute that relationship into the marginal product schedule to get a relationship between wages and labour market tightness representing labour demand. Equilibrium is then determined by the crossing of that schedule and the wage-setting schedule.

An increase in φ means that there is more employment for any value of a, implying a lower marginal product. While the true marginal product schedule is unaffected, the 'labour demand' schedule shifts downwards in the (a, w) plane. This does not mean that employment falls (it rises), but that the same employment level can be reached with a lower labour market tightness, as the long-term unemployed are now more active in seeking jobs. To absorb this increase in job seekers, wages and labour market tightness must fall.

Under what circumstances will incumbent employees support such an increase in φ, despite falling wages? Using the above formulae we can compute their welfare; we get

$$rV_e = w(1 - \tau) - (s + p)Q - \frac{paQ(1 - \varphi)}{r + p + \varphi a}.$$

The first term is the wage; the second term represents the rents lost when falling into unemployment; the third term represents the loss from having a lower probability of finding a job if falling into long-term unemployment. This last term increases with exposure to long-term unemployment p—if p is small one is unlikely to fall into long-term unemployment, with labour market tightness a—if a is very small it does not make a big difference to be short-term rather than long-term unemployed, and with the rent Q—if the rent is very low it does not make a big difference to be employed instead of unemployed. Finally, it is lower, the lower the relative search intensity of the long-term unemployed φ.

It is through this last term that the employed may gain from active labour market policy. Again, their support for such policies depends on their likelihood of falling into long-term unemployment p, and on the wage elasticity of labour demand. The smaller is p, the lower the political support for active labour market policy. The lower the elasticity, the more wages must fall to absorb the increase in employment brought by active labour market policies. Finally, the larger the unemployment benefit level b, the more taxes fall in response to an increase in φ, and the more likely it is that the employed will support active labour market policies.

This brings us to an interesting aspect of unemployment benefits; while in themselves they tend to increase unemployment, by generating a negative effect of high unemployment on the employed's income they create some 'solidarity' between the two. The tax burden of financing unemployment compensation creates additional incentives for the employed to fight unemployment, in a way similar to a higher exposure to unemployment.

We conclude from this discussion that political opposition to active labour market policies is likely to arise in situations of low elasticity and low exposure to unemployment, while a generous benefit system increases the support to such policies.

5.5 Conclusion

If the scope for increasing wages is limited, unemployment benefits will chiefly play the role of providing the employed with insurance against job loss, and we expect benefits to be too low relative to the social planner's optimum. If wage effects are strong, unemployment benefits are much more like other institutions that allow wages to be bid up. The employed will set them too high relative to the social optimum, and they will be greater, the smaller the elasticity of labour demand and the smaller the employed's exposure to unemployment. Interestingly, this conclusion may still hold if one allows an alternative institution to be used in order to target the employed's most desired wage level. Finally, the same sort of considerations apply to the determination of active labour market policies targeted at the long-term unemployed, in which case the short-term unemployed are likely to have the same interests as the employed, since both may suffer from the competition of the long-term unemployed.

Part II

The political economy of labour market reform

6
The constituency effect

This chapter and the remaining ones are devoted to the analysis of labour market reform. By reform we mean a change in any of the institutional parameters of the economy, and we will mostly focus on reforms aimed at making the market more 'flexible', i.e. such that the job finding rate a is higher after the reform than before. This includes any institutional change that reduces employee rents, reduction in employment protection, and reductions in the generosity of unemployment benefits.

The key questions we are interested in are: how should reform be designed to be politically viable, and what is the economic environment most favourable to reform? These questions are driven by the observation that measures like the ones just referred to often face strong political opposition. Therefore, the issue arises of how to implement them so as to overcome such opposition.

6.1 Reform: a conceptual problem

At the outset one should recognize that formulating the problem in this way is in contradiction with the political economy approach that has prevailed in this book so far. If policy is undertaken by a government which is elected by a majority of voters, and represents that majority, then that government will want to make a reform if, and only if, it is politically viable in the sense of being accepted by that majority. If a reform is unpopular, then why should that government ever consider it in the first place? For that to be the case, there must be some discrepancy between the preferences of that government and those of its constituency; but then, why is it that people have not elected, instead, *another* government, less inclined to the reforms they dislike?

The other side of this difficulty is that even if the government wants a reform which is unpopular, and if by some mechanism it manages to implement it, why should the resulting situation be stable? In principle, voters might want to go back to the old days.

Thus it is only meaningful to consider reforms that lead to a stable outcome, that is, a *political equilibrium* that will not be overturned by the next election (or more generally, the next decision process).

If, given the underlying parameters that characterize the behaviour of the economy, there is a unique political equilibrium, then the economy can only end up at that equilibrium. There is scope for reform only if the economy is not initially at that equilibrium, and in that case reform will indeed take place; there is no need to worry about its political viability—it is simply the process by which equilibrium is reached.

Hence, the question of reform is interesting only if the initial situation is *also* a political equilibrium. That is, we understand reform as the attempt to move from one self-sustaining situation to another equally self-sustaining one. This, still, does not solve the paradox of why policymakers want to do that rather than remain in the initial equilibrium, but at least it poses the problem of reform in a fruitful way.

In the first place one must understand why there can be several stable political outcomes: i.e. situations where policy A is preferred to policy B if policy A is already in place, and the converse occurs if it is policy B which is already in place. For such a configuration to arise, there must exist mechanisms that lead to *status quo bias*. It is these mechanisms that we study in this chapter and the next one.

The key message of this chapter is that labour market imperfections are a powerful source of status quo bias, not only against labour market reform, but against policy changes in general.

6.2 Rents and the constituency effect

By *constituency effect* we refer to the fact that institutions create their own political support, by maintaining a fraction of the population in jobs that would not exist without those institutions. This is a mass of people who are likely to oppose reform because of two interacting factors.

First, institutions and policy alter the allocation of human resources across different activities. Any change in policy must be associated with some reallocation of labour from some activities to other activities. Such reallocation implies that some people will lose their jobs.

Second, in an imperfectly competitive labour market where there are employee rents, losing one's job means losing that rent. Consequently, workers who expect to lose their job because of the reform are more likely to oppose it than those who don't. This mass of people forms a constituency in favour of the status quo. They are likely to be more opposed to the reform, the greater the rent, i.e. the more imperfect the labour market.

Clearly, both ingredients are necessary in order to have a constituency effect. Without the reallocative effects of reform, none of the employed would feel that their job is threatened. Without the rent, job losers would not be worse off than those who remain employed.

Many institutions create rents directly for some groups of people, because their nature is to redistribute in favour of these groups—think about agricultural subsidies, for example. In such cases it is obvious that the beneficiaries will support the institution. Here, however, we have a more subtle mechanism. The institution does not in itself create rents in favour of some groups; it does so only indirectly, both because it maintains people in activities that they would not do otherwise, and because the labour market is imperfect, so that those who change activity are made worse off.

The constituency effect is not enough to generate a status quo bias. It will do so, however, under some plausible circumstances, i.e. when employment adjusts slowly because job creation is sluggish, or when the employed are more powerful politically than the unemployed.

To illustrate the arithmetic of the constituency effect, let us consider the following, fairly general, example. Assume a vote between two alternatives, one which we call 'rigid' (R) and the other 'flexible' (F), although at this point such terminology is only a matter of labelling. The allocation of people across employment in the two sectors and unemployment is summarized in Table 6.1. We assume that there are more people working in sector B in the flexible society than in the rigid one: $l_B^f > l_B^r$, while the converse is true for sector A.

As we have assumed already at various points throughout the book, in both worlds wage formation is such that the employed earn a rent Q over the value of being unemployed (equation (1.14)). This rent is assumed to be the same in the flexible and the rigid worlds. Therefore, for analytical convenience, we rule out any effect of the reform on the rent Q. People are heterogeneous: they differ according to some characteristic i. There is a different micro labour market for each characteristic i. Within each market the value of being unemployed in equilibrium may

Table 6.1. Allocation of labour in the 'rigid' and 'flexible' economies

	Rigid	Flexible
Employed in A	l_A^r	l_A^f
Employed in B	l_B^r	l_B^f
Unemployed	$u^r = 1 - l_A^r - l_B^r$	$u^f = 1 - l_B^f - l_A^f$

differ; but the rent is assumed to be the same across these markets, an assumption we again make for the sake of simplicity. Therefore

$$V_e(i, \alpha) = V_u(i, \alpha) + Q,$$

where i is the type of the individual and $\alpha = r, f$ refers to the type of society one is considering, rigid or flexible.

In what follows we shall consider a rigid economy that votes over becoming flexible. In order to assess the extent of status quo bias we will compare the political support for flexibility with what it would be if the economy were initially flexible.

We shall assume that any individual knows for sure what will happen to him or her after the reform. Thus, workers in any sector will be split into three groups: those who know for sure that they will keep their job, those who know they will be moved to the other sector, and those who know for sure that they will become unemployed. Similarly, the unemployed may be split between those who know that they will remain unemployed, and those who know that they will find a job because of the reform. Introducing uncertainty about one's fate after reform has important consequences, which we analyse in the next chapter.

6.2.1 The case of instantaneous job creation

The existence of a status quo bias depends on the way labour reallocation takes place following the reform. In order to make clear that the constituency effect does not necessarily generate a status quo bias, we first assume that all employment levels jump instantaneously to their new steady state level. That is, if the economy decides to shift from rigidity to flexibility, a mass of $l_A^r - l_A^f$ workers employed in sector A lose their job instantaneously, while there is a mass of $l_B^f - l_B^r$ jobs created in sector B.

This is not a very realistic description of the labour market, but is helpful to illustrate under what conditions status quo bias arises.

If an individual of type i keeps the same labour market status when the economy moves from rigidity to flexibility, then his gain is

$$V_e(i, f) - V_e(i, r) = V_u(i, f) - V_u(i, r) = G(i).$$

If, on the other hand, he is employed and loses his job, then his net gain from the reform is

$$V_u(i, f) - V_e(i, r) = G(i) - Q.$$

Finally, if an unemployed worker finds a job because of the reform, his net gain is

$$V_e(i, f) - V_u(i, r) = G(i) + Q.$$

To complete the description of labour reallocation following reform, it is necessary to make assumptions about what fraction of the newly created jobs go to the unemployed and what fraction is obtained by workers from sector A who lost their jobs. To simplify matters, we rule out direct job-to-job mobility, so that all the workers of sector A who lose their jobs become unemployed, while all the jobs created in sector B go to the unemployed.[1]

We assume that the distribution of people types is the same across employment statuses. That is, there is the same proportion of people of any type i among the unemployed, among workers in sector A, and among workers in sector B. Within each of these groups the proportion of people whose gain from reform is lower than G is given by the same cumulative density $H(G)$; the local density is $h(G) = H'(G)$.

Workers who keep their jobs or remain unemployed at the time of reform have a gain equal to $G(i)$. They will support the reform provided $G(i) > 0$. The total number of workers who keep their jobs is $l_A^f + l_B^r$, while the number of unemployed workers who do not find a job in sector

---

[1] Clearly, this is feasible only if $l_B^f - l_B^r < u^r$. More generally, we can denote by ϕ_{jk} the mass of workers being shifted from status j to status k at the time of reform, where j and k can take the labels A, B, and u, representing employment in sector A, employment in sector B, and unemployment, respectively. Thus at the time of reform there are ϕ_{AB} people who move from sector A to sector B, and ϕ_{uB} people who move from unemployment to sector B. If we assume that nobody loses their job in sectors where employment jumps upwards, and that there are no hirings in sectors where employment falls, then we have $\phi_{uA} = \phi_{BA} = 0$ and $\phi_{uB} + \phi_{AB} = l_B^f - l_B^r$, while $\phi_{AB} + \phi_{Au} = l_A^r - l_A^f$.

B is $u^r - (l_B^f - l_B^r)$.[2] Adding these two quantities, and recall that $l_A^r + l_B^r + u^r = l_A^f + l_B^f + u^f = 1$, we see that the total number of workers whose labour status is not affected by reform is

$$1 - (l_A^r - l_A^f) - (l_B^f - l_B^r),$$

that is, the total labour force minus the gross flow of job destruction and job creation brought about by the reform.

Among those there are $(1 - (l_A^r - l_A^f) - (l_B^f - l_B^r))(1 - H(0))$ workers who support the reform. Similarly, there are $l_A^r - l_A^f$ workers of sector A who lose their jobs. They support the reform provided that $G(i) > Q$. Among those there are $(l_A^r - l_A^f)(1 - H(Q))$ workers who support the reform. Finally, there are $l_B^f - l_B^r$ unemployed workers who find a job in sector B. They support the reform provided that $G(i) > -Q$. Thus among these we have $(l_B^f - l_B^r)(1 - H(-Q))$ workers who support the reform.

Adding up all supporters, and rearranging, we see that reform will pass majority voting if and only if

$$H(0) + (H(Q) - H(0))\left(l_A^r - l_A^f\right) - (H(0) - H(-Q))\left(l_B^f - l_B^r\right) < \tfrac{1}{2}. \tag{6.1}$$

The left-hand side of (6.1) is the total number of workers who oppose the reform, which has to be lower than $\tfrac{1}{2}$. The first term, $H(0)$, is the total number of opponents if the rent was zero or, more generally, if reform was not associated with any redistribution of rents among labour market participants. The second, positive term, is the increment in opponents to the reform due to job losers in sector A, while the third, negative term, represents the reduction in opponents due to the unemployed who find jobs.[3]

Equation (6.1) tells us whether the shift from rigidity to flexibility is politically viable or not. In order to assess whether there is a bias in favour of the status quo, we need to compare it with what the support

[2] In the more general case outlined in the previous footnote, these numbers are $l_A^f + l_B^r + \phi_{AB}$ and $u^r - \phi_{uB}$, respectively. The support for reform from workers whose status is unaffected is $(l_A^f + l_B^r + \phi_{AB} + u^r - \phi_{uB})(1 - H(0))$. Similarly, there are $\phi_{Au}(1 - H(Q))$ job losers from sector A who support the reform, and $\phi_{uB}(1 - H(-Q))$ job finders from the pool of unemployed who support it.

[3] The equivalent formula in the more general case described in the preceding footnotes is $(l_A^f + l_B^r + \phi_{AB} + u^r - \phi_{uB})(1 - H(0)) + \phi_{Au}(1 - H(Q)) + \phi_{uB}(1 - H(-Q)) > \tfrac{1}{2}$.

for flexibility would be if the society was originally flexible. For this we can repeat the same computations as above, but in the case of a shift from flexibility to rigidity instead of the converse. If we do that, then the condition for flexibility to be viable is exactly the same as above. Therefore, the political support for flexibility does not depend on whether society is originally rigid or flexible.[4]

Therefore, the existence of a constituency of job losers against a reform is not enough, in itself, to generate a status quo bias. The number of unemployed people made happier by a shift from f to r because they find jobs is exactly the same as the number of employed workers made worse off by a shift from r to f because they lose jobs. The former create a constituency in favour of rigidity in the flexible society that is exactly as large as the constituency in favour of the status quo in the rigid society made by the latter. Consequently, there is no status quo bias.

6.2.2 The case of sluggish job creation

The instantaneous job creation described above is certainly not the most realistic description of how the labour market operates. It is plausible to assume that job destruction may be massive, because the cost of a dismissal, even if it is high, does not increase with the size of the layoff. Thus if a firm finds it profitable to get rid of some workers it will typically reduce employment by a large fraction—say 20 per cent. On the other hand, the job creation process is much more sluggish as new workers have to be located, screened, and trained, so that it is much more difficult

---

[4] Given the symmetry of the problem, in order to obtain the number of opponents to a shift from flexibility to rigidity, we simply have to make the following steps in the left-hand side of (6.1). First, replace labels f with r and A with B. Second, given that the gain from 'reform' for individual i is now $-G(i)$ instead of $G(i)$, the number of people whose gain exceeds x is now $H(-x)$ instead of $1 - H(x)$. So we have to replace $H(x)$ with $1 - H(-x)$.

If we do that, we get that the total number of opponents to a shift from f to r is

$$1 - H(0) + (-H(-Q) + H(0))\left(l_B^f - l_B^r\right) - (-H(0) + H(Q))(l_A^r - l_A^f).$$

For flexibility to have a majority of supporters, this quantity must be greater than $\frac{1}{2}$, which is strictly equivalent to (6.1).

It is easy to check that the same result holds in the more general case where job-to-job mobility is allowed, provided the reallocation flows induced by an institutional change are symmetrical; that is, provided the flow from sector A to unemployment at the time of a shift from rigidity to flexibility is exactly equal to the flow from unemployment to sector A in the reverse case, and so on. That is, as long as the amount of churning generated by a change does not depend on the direction of a change, there is no status quo bias.

for employment to jump upwards than downwards. Thus we shall now analyse what happens when sectors may destroy jobs instantaneously but job creation only takes place gradually. Hence if the economy shifts from rigidity to flexibility, the impact effect on employment is a mass $l_A^r - l_A^f$ of layoffs in sector A, so that unemployment jumps to $u^r + l_A^r - l_A^f$. Then only gradually are jobs created in sector B, so that employment in that sector smoothly converges to its new long-run value l_B^f. Conversely, if the economy shifts from flexibility to rigidity, a mass $l_B^f - l_B^r$ of jobs are destroyed, while sector A only arises gradually along the transition path to the new equilibrium; therefore unemployment jumps from u^f to $u^f + l_B^f - l_B^r$.[5]

As we have ruled out any upward jump in employment, nobody finds a job instantaneously as the result of reform. The value of the jobs created by the reform, however, affects the outflow rate from unemployment in the post-reform world, which is reflected in the value of being unemployed.

We can compute the support for reform in the same way as in the previous section. The number of job losers is the same, but all the unemployed remain so after the reform. So the total number of people who do not change status is now $u^r + l_B^r + l_A^f = 1 - (l_A^r - l_A^f)$, and there are no job finders. Consequently, the total number of workers who support a shift from rigidity to flexibility is now

$$(1 - (l_A^r - l_A^f))(1 - H(0)) + (l_A^r - l_A^f)(1 - H(Q)).$$

Rearranging, we see that reform will pass if and only if

$$H(0) < \tfrac{1}{2} - (l_A^r - l_A^f)(H(Q) - H(0)). \qquad (6.1b)$$

This equation is the counterpart of (6.1) in the case where employment cannot jump upwards. Before showing the existence of status quo bias, let us discuss how the rent affects the support for reform.

Inequality (6.1b) is less likely to hold, the greater the rent Q. The constituency against the reform is larger, the larger the rent Q. This result tells us that in some sense, greater rigidity in wage formation makes reform more difficult. If $Q = 0$, the relationship becomes $H(0) < \tfrac{1}{2}$,

---

[5] In some cases, however, the rigid society may be associated with regulations that prevent layoffs in sector B, so that employment reduction in that sector will also take place gradually.

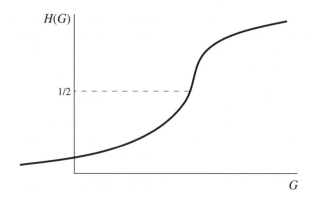

Figure 6.1. The median has a positive gain

which is equivalent to saying that the median in the distribution of G has a strictly positive gain, as illustrated in Figure 6.1. That is, we are in the familiar case where the decisive voter is the median of the distribution of $G(i)$. Note also that in this case the initial allocation of workers between employment in both sectors and unemployment is irrelevant: it does not enter the political viability condition, contrary to what happens in (6.1b).

In the presence of a rent, the balance of power is tilted toward rigidity. The decisive voter is somebody who likes reform less than the median of the distribution of G, because a mass of job losers that would have supported the reform in the absence of rents now side against it.

To measure the extent of status quo bias, we have to compare (6.1b) with what would happen if the economy were originally in the flexible regime. In that case a shift to rigidity implies a loss of jobs for a fraction of workers in sector B. For any worker of type i who is either unemployed or will keep his job, the gain from shifting to rigidity is $-G(i)$. Among those workers, the proportion who support flexibility—which is now the status quo—is still $1 - H(0)$, just as before. For those who lose their jobs, the gain is $-G(i) - Q$. There are $l_B^f - l_B^r$ workers in that situation. They will support flexibility if $-G(i) - Q < 0$, that is $G(i) > -Q$. The proportion of job losers who support flexibility is thus $1 - H(-Q)$. The condition for a majority of workers to prefer flexibility is therefore

$$(1 - (l_B^f + l_B^r))(1 - H(0)) + (l_B^f - l_B^r)(1 - H(-Q)) > \tfrac{1}{2}.$$

The first term represents the contribution of the unemployed and of workers in sector B who anticipate keeping their job—there are l_B^r such workers. The second term is the contribution of job losers. This condition is equivalent to

$$H(0) < \tfrac{1}{2} + (l_B^f - l_B^r)(H(0) - H(-Q)). \qquad (6.2)$$

Equation (6.2) is always more likely to be satisfied than (6.1b). That is, there exists a range of parameter values, for example, a range of values for the average gain of reform, where both the flexible society and the rigid society are a self-sustaining situation. When the rent Q increases, the likelihood that (6.1b) is satisfied falls, while the converse happens for (6.2). This confirms the point that the status quo bias is stronger—in the sense that the range of parameters where both societies are stable is wider—the larger the rent. At $Q = 0$ (6.2) and (6.1b) are identical; the status quo bias disappears in the absence of rents.

Therefore, we have just established that if job creation is sluggish, the constituency effect leads to status quo bias, and that the strength of that bias is increasing in the rent enjoyed by employed workers over their alternative option.

6.3 Is status quo bias a problem?

Now, status quo bias may not be *per se* something to worry about. In Chapter 4, we saw that, in the context of employment protection, the social planner values the initial stock of low productivity jobs more than private firms do, because the latter perceive a cost of labour which is too high relative to its true social level. This creates a bias in favour of the status quo from the point of view of the social planner. Indeed, the bias arises because sluggish job creation implies that there is a cost in moving from one steady state to another, since the new jobs are only created slowly. In other words, a shift to rigidity when society is in the flexible steady state is not the reverse experiment of a shift to flexibility when society is in the rigid steady state. The social planner naturally takes into account the time it takes to create jobs, which leads him to value existing jobs, thus having some preference for the status quo.

The above results tell us that the constituency effect tends to create a bias in favour of the status quo when decisions are made according to majority voting; but it does not tell us that there is too much status quo bias relative to what the social planner wants. In this section, we study the condition under which there will be excess status quo bias relative to the social planner's optimum.

The impact of job losers on the political decision making process depends on how many votes they represent or, more generally, how well they are organized. The greater their political weight, the greater the status quo bias. (In the above computations their political weight is simply proportional to their number, but it is easy to extend the analysis to allow for differences in political influence, as we do below.) By contrast, their impact on the social planner's preferences depends on their economic contribution to aggregate output. If it is very low, then the social planner will not value their jobs, and his status quo bias will be reduced accordingly.

Consequently, there will be too much status quo bias if job losers have a large political weight relative to their economic weight, and too little if the converse occurs.

Let us analyse how the social planner would choose between the two societies. Let $\bar{G}$ be the mean value of $G(i)$ in the population (formally $\bar{G} = \int G h(G) \, dG$). Then the social planner is simply aggregating the gains of everybody. Therefore, if society is originally rigid, the total social gain from becoming flexible is

$$(l_B^r + u^r + l_A^f)\bar{G} + (l_A^r - l_A^f)(\bar{G} - Q).$$

The first term is the gain to the unemployed and the employed who will keep their jobs, while the second term is the gain to those employed workers in sector A who will lose their rent Q. Note that the social planner, through that term, takes into account the social welfare loss associated with the fact that jobs are destroyed instantaneously but only created smoothly over time.

Thus, the social planner will opt for flexibility if the above quantity is positive, or equivalently

$$\bar{G} - (l_A^r - l_A^f)Q > 0. \tag{6.3}$$

To determine the political equilibrium in (6.1b) we had to add votes, computing how many people among non job losers gained more than zero and how many people among job losers gained more than Q. Now we simply add gains.

If society is originally flexible the gain from becoming rigid is

$$(l_A^f + l_B^r + u^f)(-\bar{G}) + (l_B^f - l_B^r)(-\bar{G} - Q).$$

Flexibility will prevail if that quantity is negative, or equivalently

$$\bar{G} + (l_B^f - l_B^r)Q > 0. \tag{6.4}$$

Just as in the case of voting, there exists a range of parameters for which (6.4) is satisfied while (6.3) is violated. Over that range, the social planner will choose not to change the initial situation, whether it be flexible or rigid.

Is there too much or too little status quo bias in the political decision making relative to the social optimum? Again, this depends on the political power of job losers. Consider the case where the economy is initially rigid. Intuitively, if $l_A^r - l_A^f$ is very small, then job losers command little political power and might be unable to block the reform even if they all vote against it. If it is large, then they may block it by massively voting against it, even though their individual losses from the reform are small, small enough for a social planner to decide to go ahead with reform when weighing them against other people's gain. This points to the following result: if $l_A^r - l_A^f$ is small—if there are few job losers—then reform will occur too often relative to the social optimum: there is too little status quo bias. If $l_A^r - l_A^f$ is larger than some critical mass, there is too much status quo bias.

Can we prove such a result? Yes, in some cases. Let us look at the case where the distribution of gains is hump-shaped and symmetrical around its mean, as illustrated in Figure 6.2. Because of this symmetry, there are as many people, among those whose labour market status does not change, who lose more than average as people who gain more than average: $H(\bar{G}) = \frac{1}{2}$. Assume that on average people gain, that is, $\bar{G} > 0$. Then it follows that $H(0) < \frac{1}{2}$ and that (6.4) and (6.2) are always satisfied. If society starts flexible, it will stay there, and a benevolent social planner would agree. Now, there will be excess status quo bias in the rigid society if reform does not take place while the social planner would undertake it, that is, if (6.3) holds but not (6.1b). If, on the other hand, (6.1b) holds but not (6.3), then there is too little status quo bias.

Using our assumptions on the shape of the distribution of G, we can draw the regions over which the status quo is preferred by the central planner and by voters; this is depicted in Figure 6.3. On the horizontal axis there is $l_A^R - l_A^f$, the number of job losers. On the vertical axis there is Q, the total rent. The PP line represents the reform frontier for the voting process. Reform toward flexibility is agreed by the majority of voters if the economy is below (and to the left of) PP; that is, if the rent

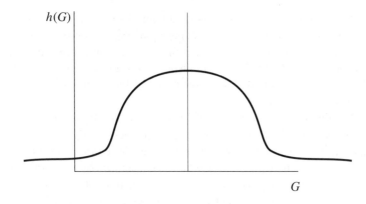

Figure 6.2. A symmetrical distribution

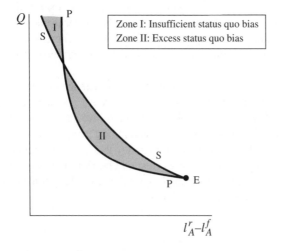

Figure 6.3. Excess and insufficient status quo bias

Q is not too high and/or the constituency of job losers $l_A^r - l_A^f$ not too numerous. The SS line represents the social planner's reform frontier. Just as PP, it is downward sloping. The social planner is less likely to undertake reforms, the greater the number of job losers and the greater their losses.

Note that the two curves intersect at point E where $l_A^r - l_A^f = 1$ and $Q = \bar{G}$. If everybody were to lose their job after the reform, then the social planner would value it only if the average gain exceeds the rent lost. A majority of people vote in favour of it if more than 50 per cent of voters have a gain $G(i)$ above their rent Q; that is, if $H(Q) < \frac{1}{2} = H(\bar{G})$ or, equivalently, $Q < \bar{G}$.[6]

But the most salient feature of Figure 6.3 is that PP is above SS at low values of $l_A^r - l_A^f$ and below it at high values of $l_A^r - l_A^f$. Thus, there exists a zone, zone I, where people vote for reform in spite of the fact that it is inefficient, and that zone is characterized by a low value of $l_A^r - l_A^f$. And, for higher values of $l_A^r - l_A^f$, there exists a zone—zone II—where there is excess status quo bias—reform is efficient but does not take place.

Indeed, SS has a vertical asymptote at $l_A^r - l_A^f = 0$, while PP has a vertical asymptote at a strictly positive value of $l_A^r - l_A^f$, given by $\tilde{l} = (\frac{1}{2} - H(0))/(1 - H(0))$. This simply means that even if there are very few losers, for very high rents their total loss is large enough to deter the social planner from implementing the reform; whereas as long as they are fewer than $\tilde{l}$, they cannot prevent the reform even if they *all* vote against it.

Therefore our conclusion is that the existence of status quo bias in political decision making is not necessarily a problem, because status quo bias may well be socially efficient. As we already noted in Chapter 4, however, this is only true in a 'second best' sense, because if the social planner could eliminate the inefficiency that generates rents, everybody would be employed in both worlds, and he would opt for reform whenever $\bar{G} > 0$. But, as long as it is not the case, the job losses caused by the reform entail some social loss.

6.4 Factors increasing the severity of the status quo bias

The case for excess status quo bias can be strengthened in the following circumstances.

First, when computing welfare we have simply added the utility of

___

[6] our assumptions of a symmetrical distribution around its mean, so that the median is equal to the mean. If the median were different from the mean, the two curves would not cross at point E.

all workers. This is only correct, as we already have seen, if the firms that employ them all make zero profit. But, in many cases, existing jobs will be associated with profits—reflecting the resources already spent on hiring—or losses—reflecting dismissal costs. In such a case, the social value of a job is no longer equal to the utility of the worker holding it. In principle, taking into account that effect may either reinforce or reduce the status quo bias. But in the case of a reduction in the degree of employment protection, the sector that disappears when the firm shifts to flexibility was making losses under the rigid institutions, and these losses have to be added to the gains from flexibility. The condition for the reform to takes place now becomes

$$\bar{G} - (l_A^r - l_A^f)(Q - L) > 0,$$

where L now represents the losses of unproductive firms. Thus the scope for status quo bias is reduced, although, as we have seen in Chapter 4, we typically expect L to be smaller than Q (we had established that unproductive jobs are socially productive at the margin), so that taking into account loss-making firms does not completely eliminate the social planner's status quo bias.

Note that we have assumed that firms have no impact on the political process. If they could influence that process, then they would also reduce the support for rigidity.

Second, the weight of job losers in the political process may be enhanced by several factors. In particular, it is reasonable to think that the unemployed have a lower political power than the employed; they are less organized and tend to participate less in elections, perhaps because it is more difficult economically to have a party representing their interests.

Suppose, for example, that only a fraction $\lambda < 1$ of the unemployed vote. Then the condition for a majority of voters to support flexibility becomes

$$(l_B^r + \lambda u^r + l_A^f)(1 - H(0)) + (l_A^r - l_A^f)(1 - H(Q)) > \tfrac{1}{2}(l_A^r + l_B^r + \lambda u^r).$$

The left-hand side is the total number of votes in favour of reform, which has to be greater than the right-hand side, equal to half the number of voters. This is equivalent to

$$H(0) < \frac{1}{2} - \frac{l_A^r - l_A^f}{1 + (\lambda - 1)u^r}(H(Q) - H(0)). \qquad (6.5)$$

This condition is less likely to be satisfied than (6.1b), because the last term, which represents the contribution of the losers, is now proportional to $\frac{l^r_A - l^f_A}{1+(\lambda-1)u^r}$, the share of job losers among voters, rather than l^r_A, their share in the total workforce. Therefore, the status quo bias is reinforced if the unemployed vote less. This is because the constituency against the reform is made of employed voters who do not want to lose their rent.

It is worth noting that a lower political power of the unemployed relative to the employed is in itself a *source* of status quo bias. That is, even if job creation is not sluggish, there will be status quo bias if the unemployed's weight is lower than the employed. The unemployed workers made happier by a shift from f to r because they find jobs are no longer as powerful as the employed workers made worse off by a shift from r to f because they lose jobs. Thus, the effective support for flexibility is lower if rigidity is originally in place.

Formally, if the unemployed have a weight $\lambda < 1$, condition (6.1) must be replaced by

$$
H(0) + \frac{l^r_A - l^f_A}{1 + (\lambda - 1)u^r}(H(Q) - H(0))
$$
$$
- \frac{\lambda}{1 + (\lambda - 1)u^r}(H(0) - H(-Q))\left(l^f_B - l^r_B\right) \qquad (6.6)
$$
$$
< \tfrac{1}{2}.
$$

Relative to (6.1), the number of job losers is multiplied by $1/(1 + (\lambda - 1)u^r)$, which is greater than one, while the number of job finders is multiplied by $\frac{\lambda}{1+(\lambda-1)u^r}$, which is less than one. These corrective terms reflect the differences in political power between the employed and the unemployed. Similarly, the condition for flexibility to be supported if the economy is originally flexible is

$$
H(0) + \frac{\lambda}{1 + (\lambda - 1)u^f}(l^r_A - l^f_A)(H(Q) - H(0))
$$
$$
- \frac{1}{1 + (\lambda - 1)u^f}(H(0) - H(-Q))\left(l^f_B - l^r_B\right) \qquad (6.7)
$$
$$
< \tfrac{1}{2}.
$$

The contributions from job losers and job finders are again multiplied by factors representing their relative political weight. Clearly, this equation is more likely to be satisfied than the previous one, meaning that there is status quo bias. The strength of that bias is greater, the lower the political participation of the unemployed. It is also increasing with the rent Q and disappears at $Q = 0$. In a no-rent society, job loss and job finding do not distort preferences, so that the lower political power of the unemployed is irrelevant since labour market status does not affect the net gain from reform.

Finally, the weight of the unemployed's income in the social planner's welfare function may be larger than that of the employed, which tends to reduce its status quo bias. If the social planner cares about inequality, then he will put a greater weight in his social welfare function to the value of the unemployed than to the value of the employed. For example, if $\lambda > 1$ is the weight of the unemployed workers, then the total social gain is given by

$$(l_B^r + \lambda u^r + l_A^f)\bar{G} + (l_A^r - l_A^f)(\bar{G} - Q).$$

It is positive if and only if

$$\bar{G} - \frac{l_A^r - l_A^f}{1 + (\lambda - 1)u^r} Q > 0. \tag{6.8}$$

To obtain equation (6.8), one has to correct equation (6.3) in the same way as (6.1b) was changed to get (6.3). In the contribution of losers to the social decision rule, we now have $\frac{l_A^r - l_A^f}{1+(\lambda-1)u^r}$, the share of job losers in the total population *weighted* by their contribution to social welfare, instead of $l_A^r - l_A^f$. The big difference, of course, is that now the unemployed have a *higher* weight than the employed, so that the last term is reduced, which makes reform more likely. Therefore if the social planner cares about inequality the reform is more likely to occur.

6.5 The case of employment protection

The clearest example of a status quo bias generated by a constituency effect is employment protection. As we showed in Chapter 4, employment protection maintains labour resources in inefficient firms, that would disappear should this regulation be removed. Workers in those sectors know that they would lose their jobs if the labour market were made flexible, and therefore oppose reform. In order for reform to be blocked they must have enough political power.

Assume, for example, that they are the majority. Let us recall our computations of Chapter 4. The welfare of an employed worker in the rigid economy was

$$V_{er} = \frac{\bar{m}}{r} - q\frac{\sigma}{r(r+\sigma)}.$$

The welfare of an unemployed in the flexible economy was given by

$$V_{uf} = \frac{m_H - q}{r}.$$

Incumbent workers in low productivity firms will only accept the reform if they end up better off unemployed in the flexible economy than employed in the rigid one. This is equivalent to $V_{uf} > V_{ef}$ or, equivalently,

$$m_H - m_L > q\frac{r}{r+\sigma}\frac{r+\sigma+\gamma}{\gamma}. \tag{6.9}$$

This condition is clearly more stringent than the one needed for employees in high productivity firms to accept the reform, which was

$$m_H - m_L > rq/(r+\sigma). \tag{6.10}$$

If the economy is originally flexible and decides whether to go rigid or not, nobody will lose their job as the result of the reform, since employment protection prevents it. It is true that in the long run, employment in high state firms ends up being lower. But that outcome is only gradually reached through lower job creation. Hence, in that case, there is no constituency of job losers against the reform, and, to the extent that the employed are politically decisive, they will decide to remain flexible if and only if equation (6.10) holds.

Both flexibility and rigidity are self-sustaining situations if (6.10) holds while (6.9) is violated. The region where this situation occurs is represented in Figure 6.4 in the $(q, m_H - m_L)$ plane. It lies between the two frontiers LL and HH that represent inequalities (6.9) and (6.10), respectively. Given the rent q, there exists an interval of values of the productivity loss $m_H - m_L$ such that both regimes are self-sustaining. This interval is wider, the larger the rent q, which captures the fact that the existence of rents lies at the root of the status quo bias mechanism.

It should also be noted that when γ, the likelihood of falling into the low productivity state, is smaller, the LL frontier shifts upwards, which widens the zone where the status quo prevails. When γ is small, low

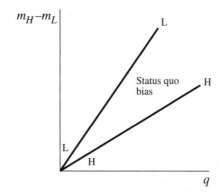

Figure 6.4. Status quo bias in employment protection legislation

productivity is a rare event, so that wages are almost as high as m_H, the wage that would prevail in the purely flexible economy. With larger wages, those who lose their jobs because of the reform are more likely to oppose it. At the same time, it should be pointed out that when γ is smaller there are fewer workers in low productivity firms in steady state, so that they are less likely to be politically decisive; but holding their political power constant, a fall in γ does increase the status quo bias.

6.6 Other examples

Most policy decisions have reallocative consequences. Therefore, the principles exposed in this chapter do not only apply to labour market reform, but to any policy change in general. High rents automatically create a constituency against policy change.

Take the example of trade protection. It typically increases the relative price of import-competing goods, thus moving resources from other sectors to these sectors. A removal of trade barriers would require job destruction in import competing goods, and job creation elsewhere. Those who have jobs in the import-competing sector will oppose the reform; more so, the greater the rent.

Many labour market reforms affect relative prices in a similar way. In Chapters 2, 3, and 5 we discussed how institutions such as minimum wages and unemployment benefits allowed some groups of workers to

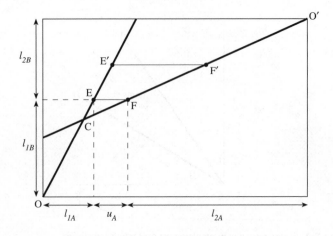

Figure 6.5. Wages and the intersector allocation of labour

increase their wages. In our framework there was only one sector, so that sectorial reallocation was precluded by assumption. But one can easily extend the analysis to deal with several sectors, and it is then unlikely that reform does not lead to sectorial reallocation.

Let us return, for example, to our analysis of Chapter 2, where rigidity arose because of the redistributive conflict between two groups of workers, groups A and B. It is interesting to consider the case where there exist two sectors, one which is intensive in skilled labour (B-labour), and the other which is intensive in unskilled labour (A-labour). An increase in the wage of A-labour shifts the allocation of that input away from the unskilled intensive sector toward the skilled intensive one. The skill-intensive sector is more able to pay high wages to type A workers than the other one, since in the former A-workers cooperate with a larger number of B-workers.

The argument is illustrated in Figure 6.5. We assume that the market for B-workers is perfectly competitive, so that they are always fully employed. By contrast, the market for A-workers is imperfectly competitive, in a way we have already analysed in previous chapters. The allocation of B-labour is represented on the vertical axis, while the allocation of A-labour is represented on the horizontal axis. The economy is represented by two points: a point E representing employment in sector 1, and a point F representing employment in sector 2. The slope of the line OE represents factor proportions in sector 1, while the slope of O′F represents factor proportions in sector 2. We assume these factor proportions are fixed, so that the points E and F can only move along their respective lines. Because sector 1 is more intensive in the use of skilled labour than sector 2, OE is steeper than O′F, meaning that a unit increase in output uses more type B labour and less type A labour in sector 1 than in sector 2. The horizontal distance between O and E measures the amount of type A labour used by sector 1, l_{1A}, and the vertical distance how much B-labour it utilizes, l_{1B}. The same holds for O′ and F in sector 2. Because type B labour is always fully employed, E and F must lie on the same horizontal line. If there was full employment for type A labour as well, E and F would coincide. The horizontal distance EF is equal to the unemployment level of type A labour, u_A.

An increase in wages for type A labour, which may be triggered by various policy changes, as we saw in previous chapters, increases unemployment for this type of labour. Given the relative steepness of the two curves, the only way that can happen is if employment increases in sector 1 and falls in sector 2, as illustrated in Figure 6.5, where the economy moves from (E,F) to (E′,F′) as the result of the increase in wages for A-workers. Consequently, an increase in type A's ability to get high wages always reallocates labour from the unskilled-intensive to the skill-intensive sector. The converse occurs when there is a reduction in type A's wages.

For those familiar with microeconomic theory, the argument can also be depicted using the 'factor-price frontier' (FPF), as represented in Figure 6.6. Here factor prices are simply the wages of each type of labour, w_A and w_B. The FPF is the set of combinations of w_A and w_B such that cost equals price (under fixed factor proportions, these curves should be straight lines). This frontier shifts upwards when the price of the good we consider increases. In sector 1, which uses more skilled labour, it takes a greater reduction in the wages of unskilled labour to offset a given increase in the wages of skilled labour. Consequently, FPF1 is flatter than FPF2. In any equilibrium the economy must be at the crossing point of the two curves, meaning that factor prices are the same in both sectors. An increase in the wage of type A labour would trigger an incipient shift of the economy toward points G and H. G, the corresponding point on FPF1, is above H. That is, costs increase more in the unskilled intensive sector, so that a greater reduction of the wages of skilled labour would be needed in that sector. To offset that, it must be that the price of good 2 rises relative to the price of good 1, so that demand is reallocated towards the skilled intensive sector; the

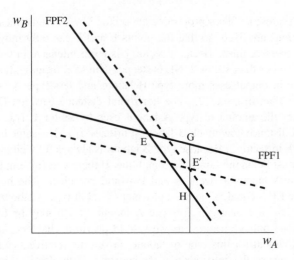

Figure 6.6. Impact of an increase in wages on the factor price frontiers

FPF of good 2 shifts upwards, while FPF1 shifts downwards, so that the economy moves from the original equilibrium E to E'.

Hence, in the case of reforms that reduce the insider's ability to set wages, the status quo bias will come from workers in industries intensive with highly skilled people, who are more likely to oppose it than those in low-skill intensive industries. The high-skill intensive industries are too large relative to the perfectly competitive equilibrium outcome (which would be represented by point C in Figure 6.5); some workers in those industries consequently expect to lose their jobs as the outcome of a wage liberalization, which gives them additional reasons to oppose the reform. The economic mechanism behind this job loss phenomenon is the reverse of what was illustrated in Figure 6.6: the drop in wages allows the unskilled-intensive sector to cut prices more aggressively than sector 1, which ends up suffering despite the fall in its labour costs.

6.7 The role of labour reallocation

The magnitude of the opposition to reform not only depends on the size of the rent, but also on the nature of the labour reallocation process following reform. In the above examples we assumed that jobs were only gradually created in the new sectors, and that the redundant lost their jobs on the day of reform, ending up unemployed in the new economy. But the labour market may function in such a way that their situation is not as bad as the originally unemployed. For example, if employers hire people on the basis of *ranking*, giving priority to those who have been unemployed for a shorter period, then it will be easier for those workers displaced at the time of reform to find new jobs relative to those who were previously unemployed. This ranking property has been found to negatively affect the performance of the labour market (see Blanchard and Diamond 1994), but from a political economy perspective it helps to overcome the incumbent constituency against the reform.

From there, it is not difficult to see that the reform itself can be designed so as to generate such ranking. If it specifies that displaced workers will have some degree of priority over the new jobs, for example by putting them into retraining programmes or job counselling, then their opposition will obviously be alleviated. One may object to this argument that the unemployed's support will be lowered, but as we have seen, status quo bias is a problem when the job loser's political weight is somewhat excessive relative to their economic weight, which is likely to be associated with the unemployed's political weight being low.

6.8 An application to reform design: preannouncement and mobility

Another strategy is to motivate job losers to move directly to the new sectors without going to unemployment by announcing the reform in advance, so as to give them the opportunity to look for a job in the other sector. The mere fact of announcing the reform will motivate them to look for jobs in the other sector, making it more likely that they are already in the new sector at the time of reform. In that way, it increases their gain from the reform relative to the no-announcement case.

Let us consider a simple example to illustrate how this strategy may work. Prior to reform the economy has two sectors, labelled 1 and 2, that each pay the same wage w. Employment in each sector is l_1 and l_2. We consider this as fixed and exogenous, so that the mere announcement of reform has no effect on the performance of the economy. That is, announcement of reform has no impact on its aggregate gains, only on the distribution of these gains between workers in both sectors and the unemployed.

A fraction s of jobs is destroyed per unit of time, their holders become unemployed, and to maintain l_1 and l_2 constant an equivalent number of unemployed must find jobs. The job finding probability a is therefore given by

$$a = s \frac{l_1 + l_2}{1 - (l_1 + l_2)}. \tag{6.11}$$

Reform increases the wage paid by sector 2 from w to $w' > w$, and at the same time eliminates sector 1. This is exactly as if productivity increased to w' in sector 2 but stayed equal to w in sector 1, so that the bidding up of wages in sector 2 makes sector 1 unprofitable. We also know from our previous analysis that such an increase in wages and productivity is typically associated with an increase in the job finding probability. Thus we assume that it jumps from a to $a' > a$.

We denote by V_e' the value of being employed (necessarily in sector 2) right after the reform, and by V_u' the value of being unemployed right after the reform.

In the absence of announcement, at the time of reform the economy finds itself in a steady state where all employed workers earn w, all unemployed workers earn 0, and where the former lose their jobs with probability s per unit of time, while the latter find jobs with probability a per unit of time. Using the equations we are already familiar with, it follows that the value of being employed satisfies

$$r V_e = w + s(V_u - V_e),$$

while the value of being unemployed is

$$r V_u = a(V_e - V_u).$$

Consequently, the value of being employed in the pre-reform world is

$$V_e = \frac{(r + a)w}{r(r + s + a)},$$

while the value of being unemployed is given by

$$V_u = \frac{aw}{r(r + s + a)}.$$

The unemployed will support the reform provided $V_u < V_u'$. Those who work in sector 2 keep their jobs after the reform; therefore, they will support the reform provided $V_e < V_e'$. Those most likely to oppose the reform are workers in sector 1, who lose their jobs. They will support it if they are better off unemployed in the post-reform world than employed in the pre-reform world, i.e. if $V_e < V_u'$.

Suppose now that the reform is announced in advance; that is, at time $t = 0$ it is publicly said that the reform will take place at time $t = t_1$. People now consider that it is better to hold a job in sector 2 than in sector 1, since the latter jobs will disappear with certainty at t_1. This creates incentives for workers to move from sector 1 to sector 2, if they can. Thus we are in a situation where unemployed workers are looking for jobs in both sectors, while workers employed in sector 1 are looking for jobs in sector 2.

The announcement makes it more likely that incumbent employees in sector 1 support the reform, for two reasons. First, they have a positive probability of being employed in sector 2 at the time of reform, so that it is less likely that they will lose their job at the time of reform. Second, because the reform is somewhat remote and because they might have lost their job between the date of the announcement and the date of the reform, they may be unemployed at the time of reform, in which case they will gain more from it. In other words, because of mobility between unemployment and employment, the more remote the reform, the more people's choice resemble what would obtain under a 'veil of ignorance', that is if they voted ignoring their current situation.

Given that announcement increases the support from employees in sector 1, and given that it does not affect aggregate gains, it must a priori reduce the support from some other groups. Indeed, both the unemployed and the employed of group 2 gain less from the reform than if it had not been preannounced. The reason is, interestingly, that competition from employees in sector 1 reduces the likelihood of finding a job in sector 2. In the absence of preannouncement, a worker unemployed at $t = 0$ would have a probability of being employed in sector 2 at the time of reform t_1 which is proportional to that sector's employment share, $l_2/(l_1 + l_2)$. Indeed, the probability per unit of time of finding a job in sector 2 is just $al_2/(l_1 + l_2)$. Under preannouncement, workers who move from sector 1 to sector 2 increase the hiring rate in sector 1 at the same time as they reduce the probability of finding a job in sector 2. Thus job seekers are more likely to end up in the 'wrong' sector than without announcement, which harms the unemployed and also employees in sector 2, who might end up unemployed prior to the implementation of the reform.

Thus preannouncement automatically redistributes the gains from reform from the unemployed and the employed in sector 2 to the employed in sector 1. This is good news for the reform, because the employed in sector 1 are actually those who gain the least. In fact, it can be shown that the redistribution of gains that is due to preannouncement can never be so strong as to invert the ranking of preferences for reform. That is, it can never be strong enough so that employees in sector 1 vote in favour of the reform while the unemployed (or employees in sector 2) oppose it. If employees in sector 1 gain from the reform, so do employees in sector 2 who are already in the good sector—they are strictly better off than sector 1's employees under reform, and exactly as well off without reform. The unemployed also always gain from it since wages and job finding probabilities are unaffected between 0 and t_1, while both increase after t_1.[7]

Under what circumstances will postponement be able to achieve political support for a reform that would otherwise be blocked? One can show (see the appendix) that if the aggregate welfare gains from reform are strictly positive, there always exists a remote enough date t_1 such that people will agree on the reform as of $t = 0$.

This result is very general. When there is mobility between the various states of the labour market, the probability of being in any given state at a future date t_1 becomes less and less dependent on the initial state as t_1 increases. As t_1 reaches infinity, that probability becomes equal to the unconditional probability, so that an individual's welfare becomes proportional (up to a discount factor) to the average welfare of a representative individual. When asked to vote over future decisions, people act more as though under a veil of ignorance, the more remote these decisions. They are, therefore, more likely to be unanimous in favour of the reform, if that reform increases aggregate welfare.

---

[7] One can actually prove more generally that if the employed in sector 1 support the reform, the unemployed will support it even though w' or a' might be lower than its pre-reform value. The argument runs as follows. First, the unemployed and the employed in sector 1 have the same exit rate to jobs in sector 2. Consequently, an individual has the same probability R of being employed in sector 2 at $t = t_1$ whether he is initially unemployed or working in sector 1. Second, the initially unemployed have a higher probability of being unemployed at $t = t_1$ than the initially employed. Call P_u that probability and P_e the corresponding probability for the initially employed: $P_u > P_e$. Third, the contribution to the value of being unemployed of expected income flows between $t = 0$ and $t = t_1$ does not depend on whether or not there is reform. Therefore, an individual initially unemployed will support reform if and only if $R(V'_e - V_e) + P_u(V'_u - V_u) + (1 - R - P_u)(V'_u - V_e) > 0$. An individual initially employed in sector 1 supports reform if and only if $R(V'_e - V_e) + P_e(V'_u - V_u) + (1 - R - P_e)(V'_u - V_e) > 0$. The difference between the first and the second expression is $(P_u - P_e)(V_e - V_u) > 0$. Therefore, if the second inequality holds, so does the first. This result simply reflects the fact that the unemployed are less likely to end up in the state where the gains from the reform are minimal than those initially employed in sector 1.

This result does not hinge on the possibility of job-to-job mobility, nor, strictly speaking, on the existence of a constituency effect. For this result to hold two —more general—conditions, are necessary.

First, the net gain from reform only depends on current labour market status, not on the individual. So, a welfare-improving reform that redistributes between skilled and unskilled, men and women, blacks and whites, etc., cannot be systematically implemented with postponement. People know that whatever the date of the reform they will still have the same skill levels, skin colour, and sex, so that postponing does not induce them to vote under a veil of ignorance. However, it is still true that postponing reduces the inequality in the distribution of gains from reform that is associated with labour market status. The above-mentioned constituency effect is a clear case of a loss associated with labour market status —namely, holding a job in the sector that will disappear. But there can be other examples.

Second, the process driving mobility between the various states of the labour market must be such that in the long run the probability of ending in any given state converges to the average one regardless of the initial one. In technical terms this process must be stationary and ergodic. Even without job-to-job mobility, postponement increases the likelihood of holding the right type of job at the time of reform for those originally employed in sector 1, and given that people move between the three states of the labour market with constant transition probabilities, the stationarity and ergodicity property is satisfied. If direct job-to-job mobility from sector 1 to sector 2 is possible, sector 1's workers' support for the reform is increased—equivalently, the minimum delay necessary to get their support is lower. If, on the other hand, there exists some labour market status unreachable from some initial situation, the result would not hold. For example, if sector 2 was a 'guild' only hiring from a certain subset of workers, then postponing the reform would be far less efficient in getting the support of employees in sector 1, since most of them expect to be excluded from the right jobs.

Postponement is more efficient, the more quickly incumbent employees in sector 1 expect to change status; that is, it is more likely to achieve reform, the greater labour market mobility, and, in particular, the greater the hiring rate in sector 2. Postponement achieves little in a situation where workers don't move and where the hiring rate is low. As shown in the appendix, an increase in labour mobility (as measured by the transition rates a and s) by, say, 10 per cent reduces the minimum delay of preannouncement for reform to be viable by the same order of magnitude.

It should be added that the announcement strategy is associated with an important credibility problem. When the critical date t_1 arrives there exists a new constituency of l_1 employees in sector 1 who are different from the original ones, but as numerous, and who are going to lose their jobs instantaneously. They have every incentive to overturn the reform that was already decided at date $t = 0$.

6.9 Another application: past events and initial conditions

An important implication of the constituency effect is that the prospect for reform will depend on the initial distribution of workers across sectors that oppose the reform and sectors that support it. This distribution itself reflects past economic events such as booms, crises, structural changes, etc. The timing of reform is therefore affected by business fluctuations through these initial conditions.

Let us return to our example of employment protection, where the constituency against reform came from workers in obsolete industries. From Chapter 4 we can recover the number of workers in productive and obsolete industries, respectively:

$$l_{Hr} = \frac{r+\sigma}{\sigma+\gamma} \frac{(\bar{m}-q)\sigma}{\bar{m}(r+\sigma)-rq} = \frac{\sigma}{\sigma+\gamma} l$$

$$l_{Lr} = \frac{r+\sigma}{\sigma+\gamma} \frac{(\bar{m}-q)\gamma}{\bar{m}(r+\sigma)-rq} = \frac{\gamma}{\sigma+\gamma} l.$$

We have expressed employment in both sectors as a function of the total employment level l, which itself can vary with the economy's parameters, such as q and m_H and m_L, which enter through their weighted average $\bar{m}$. These formulae imply that the constituency against flexibility, given by the size of the job losers group l_{Lr}, is smaller, the smaller the employment level l. At the end of a recession there are fewer employed workers, implying fewer workers in obsolete industries, which increases the scope for reform. This result depends on the assumption that the unemployed — who prefer flexibility—vote. If the unemployed do not vote then in steady state the ratio between the number of workers in obsolete industries and total employment is $\gamma/(\sigma + \gamma)$, which does not depend on l. A change in l then has no impact on the prospects for reform.

The most interesting effects, however, arise when we look at what happens out of steady state. Consider the impact of a boom, for example an increase in productivity which raises the feasible wage $\bar{m}$. At the time of the change, wages jump to the new value of $\bar{m}$, and labour market tightness a increases. In the long run, it has the same proportional impact on l_H and l_L. But, because new entrants are high productivity firms, the stock of low productivity jobs will lag the stock of high productivity jobs, that is, it will rise more slowly. The evolution of these two variables is given by the out-of-steady-state equivalents of (4.21) and (4.22):

$$\frac{dl_H}{dt} = -(\gamma + \sigma)l_H + a(1 - l_H - l_L) \tag{6.12}$$

$$\frac{dl_L}{dt} = \gamma l_H - \sigma l_L. \tag{6.13}$$

When a jumps, the net job creation rate in high productivity firms jumps instantaneously. By contrast, a does not appear in the second equation, and the net creation rate of low productivity jobs rises only gradually as the stock of high productivity jobs rises. The response of the two stocks to the boom is represented in Figure 6.7, while Figure 6.8 depicts the evolution of the ratio between l_H and l_L.[8] As we can see, l_H actually overshoots its long-run value in the short run. This is because job destruction lags job creation for high productivity firms.

If the unemployed have as much political power as the employed, the conclusion remains that the boom reduces the prospects for reform: the number of people working in obsolete firms is greater than initially, over the whole transition path. If the unemployed are less powerful than the employed, then the support for reform depends on the weight of workers in high productivity firms *relative* to workers in low productivity firms. In the extreme case where they have no political power at all, it will only depend on that ratio. If we think of the employed determining labour market institutions by majority voting among themselves, then flexibility will prevail if high productivity employees are more numerous than low productivity ones, i.e. if $l_H/l_L > 1$. This critical level will be lower if a fraction of the unemployed vote or if there exist some other groups ('capitalists', pensioners) who support flexibility and whose votes add up to those of workers in high productivity firms.

---

[8] This is a system of linear differential equations whose solution is given in the appendix.

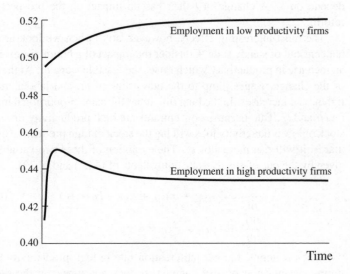

Figure 6.7. Employment response to a boom

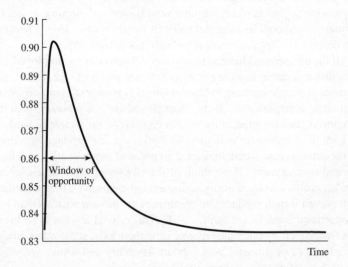

Figure 6.8. Evolution of l_H / l_L

Now, this ratio gradually rises and then falls back to its original value over the transition path. If it goes above the threshold above which obsolete workers can be overturned, the boom creates a 'window of opportunity' for reform (see Figure 6.8); the newly employed also gain in political influence relative to their previous situation, and given that they disproportionately work in high productivity firms, they support flexibility. The window of opportunity is wider, the stronger the boom, and the greater the lag between the rise in high productivity employment and the rise in low productivity employment, i.e. the lower the transition rate γ.

The window ends up disappearing because newly created firms eventually become obsolete, and their workers change their minds about the desirability of a removal of the employment protection legislation.

6.10 Summary

In this chapter, we have studied the constituency effect, namely the fact that reform creates job losses, and that job losers are more likely to suffer, the more imperfect the labour market—the greater the rent. The constituency effect explains why there may be status quo bias, i.e. why several labour market institutions may be stable. It implies that preannouncement of reform may make it more viable, because current labour market status, which is crucial to the constituency effect, then has a lower weight in voters' preferences. It also implies that initial conditions, which reflect past events, affect the viability of reform, through the size of the group of job losers.

We saw that the constituency effect was stronger, the stronger the rent. The above discussion is therefore most relevant for reforms such that the rent remains large after the reform. By contrast, reforms that eliminate most or all of the rent are unlikely to be affected by the constituency effect.

A6.1 Properties of SS and PP

Assume $H(0) < \frac{1}{2}$ and $\bar{G} > 0$. The SS curve is determined by equality in (6.3), i.e.

$$\bar{G} = (l_A^r - l_A^f)Q. \qquad (A6.1)$$

It is a decreasing hyperbola which clearly has the properties described in the text. The PP curve is defined by

$$(H(Q) - H(0))(l_A^r - l_A^f) = \frac{1}{2} - H(0). \qquad (A6.2)$$

Its slope is therefore

$$\frac{\mathrm{d}Q}{\mathrm{d}(l_A^r - l_A^f)} \mid_{PP} = \frac{-(H(Q) - H(0))}{h(Q)(l_A^r - l_A^f)}. \qquad (A6.3)$$

Because $h(Q)$ is hump-shaped, it is decreasing with Q for all $Q > \bar{G}$, and increasing for $Q < \bar{G}$. Therefore, $H(\bar{G}) - H(0) < h(\bar{G})\bar{G}$. The slope of PP at $l_A^r - l_A^f = 1$ is therefore larger, algebraically, than $-\bar{G}$, which is the slope of SS at that point. Consequently, PP is flatter than SS at their intersection point $(1, \bar{G})$, which proves the existence of zone II. The existence of PP's vertical asymptote at $l_A^r - l_A^f = \tilde{l}$ follows straightforwardly from (A6.2), which proves the existence of zone I.

A6.2 Computing gains and losses when reform is preannounced

In this part of the appendix, we illustrate how announcing the reform in advance affects the gains and losses of various labour market participants. Consider that at time 0 it is announced that the reform will take place at time t_1. People anticipate that at t_1 their utility will be:

V_e' if they are in sector 2, as these people keep their jobs,

V_u' if they work in sector 1, since these workers lose their jobs, and

V_u' if they are unemployed.

Let $V_{e2}(t)$, $V_{e1}(t)$, and $V_u(t)$ be the value of working in sector 2, sector 1, and being unemployed, respectively. As stated in the text, despite the fact that both types of job pay the same wage, we now have that $V_{e1}(t) < V_{e2}(t)$, as these values now reflect the expectation that jobs in sector 1, but not in sector 2, will disappear at t_1.

Between $t = 0$ and $t = t_1$ these quantities evolve according to the following equations:

$$rV_{e2}(t) = w - s\left[V_{e2}(t) - V_u(t)\right] + \frac{\mathrm{d}}{\mathrm{d}t}V_{e2}(t) \qquad (A6.4)$$

$$rV_{e1}(t) = w - s\left[V_{e1}(t) - V_u(t)\right] + a\theta\left[V_{e2}(t) - V_{e1}(t)\right] + \frac{\mathrm{d}}{\mathrm{d}t}V_{e1}(t) \qquad (A6.5)$$

$$rV_u(t) = a\theta \left[V_{e2}(t) - V_u(t)\right] + a(1 - \theta) \left[V_{e1}(t) - V_u(t)\right] + \frac{d}{dt}V_u(t).$$
$$(A6.6)$$

In the above equations, a is the probability of finding a job per unit of time. θ is the probability that this job is in sector 2 and $1 - \theta$ is the probability that it is in sector 1. While sector 2 employees can only move to unemployment (if they lose their job), sector 1 employees are looking for jobs in sector 2 and can move either to unemployment or to sector 2. This is reflected in the two terms in brackets in the right-hand side of (A6.5). Finally, one also has to distinguish between exits to sector 1 and exits to sector 2 for the unemployed, as these yield different values; this is reflected in the two terms in brackets in the right-hand side of (A6.6). Note that we have ruled out any 'ranking' or discrimination against unemployed job seekers, as a and θ are the same for both employed and unemployed job seekers.

It is easy to compute a and θ. While a is given by (6.11), θ can be computed by equating inflows into sector 2 with outflows. The inflow is given by $a\theta(1 - l_2)$, while the outflow is given by sl_2. Therefore, $\theta = sl_2/[a(1 - l_2)]$ or, equivalently,

$$\theta = \frac{l_2}{l_1 + l_2}\frac{1 - (l_1 + l_2)}{1 - l_2} < \frac{l_2}{l_1 + l_2}.$$

Note that θ is actually lower than the proportion of sector 2 employment in total employment. This is because sector 1 hires more than sector 2, as sector 1 has to replace exits to sector 2 in addition to job losses, while sector 2 only hires to replace job losses.

In order to compute whether people will oppose or support the reform one must compute the value functions V_{e2}, V_{e1}, and V_u at the time of the announcement, $t = 0$. To do so we must solve for (A6.4)–(A6.6) under the following terminal conditions:

$$V_{e2}(t_1) = V_e', \, V_{e1}(t_1) = V_u', \quad \text{and} \quad V_u(t_1) = V_u'.$$

One can check that the solution for $V_{e1}(t)$ is the following:

$$\begin{aligned}
V_{e1}(t) &= \left[\left(\frac{\theta a}{s + \theta a}\right)\left(1 - e^{-(s + \theta a)(t_1 - t)}\right)e^{-r(t_1 - t)}\right]V_e' \\
&+ \left[\left(\frac{s}{s + \theta a} + \frac{\theta a}{s + \theta a}e^{-(s + \theta a)(t_1 - t)}\right)e^{-r(t_1 - t)}\right]V_u' \\
&+ \frac{aw}{r(s + a)}(1 - e^{-r(t_1 - t)})
\end{aligned}$$
$$(A6.7)$$

$$+ \frac{sw}{(r+s+a)(s+a)}(1 - e^{-(r+s+a)(t_1-t)}).$$

Let us briefly discuss this formula. The first term is the contribution to my expected welfare of my future status at the time of reform, if that status is being employed in sector 2. It is the product of three factors: V_e' is the value of being employed right after the reform; $e^{-r(t_1-t)}$ is the discount factor between now and the date of reform; $\left(\frac{\theta a}{s+\theta a}\right)\left(1 - e^{-(s+\theta a)(t_1-t)}\right)$ is the probability of being employed in sector 2 at t_1, conditional on being employed in sector 1 at t. This probability is larger, the larger the job finding rate a, the larger the fraction of hires in sector 2, θ, and the lower the job loss rate s. It is also larger, the more remote the reform, i.e. the larger $t_1 - t$.

The second term is the contribution to my expected welfare of being either unemployed or in sector 1 at the time of reform. It is the product of V_u', the discount factor $e^{-r(t_1-t)}$, and the probability of not being employed in sector 2 at t_1.

The last terms are the contribution to my expected welfare of the wages I will earn between now and the date of reform, either in my current job or in other jobs.

The solution for $V_{e2}(t)$ gives a similar formula:

$$V_{e2}(t) = \left[\left(\frac{\theta a}{s+\theta a} + \frac{s}{s+\theta a}e^{-(s+\theta a)(t_1-t)}\right)e^{-r(t_1-t)}\right]V_e'$$
$$+ \left[\left(\frac{s}{s+\theta a}\right)(1 - e^{-(s+\theta a)(t_1-t)})e^{-r(t_1-t)}\right]V_u'$$
$$+ \frac{aw}{r(s+a)}(1 - e^{-r(t_1-t)})$$
$$+ \frac{sw}{(r+s+a)(s+a)}(1 - e^{-(r+s+a)(t_1-t)}).$$

The interpretation is the same. The probability of being employed in sector 2 at the time of reform is clearly greater for these workers than for workers in sector 1. The contribution of wages between t and t_1 is the same, as these workers have the same wages and the same transition rates between employment and unemployment as sector 1 workers. Given that $V_e' > V_u'$, it follows from this argument that

$$V_{e2}(t) > V_{e1}(t), \qquad \forall t. \tag{A6.8}$$

Those who are already in the right sector are, not surprisingly, better off than those who are not.

Finally, the unemployed's welfare is given by

$$
V_u(t) = \left[\left(\frac{\theta a}{s+\theta a}\right)\left(1 - e^{-(s+\theta a)(t_1-t)}\right)e^{-r(t_1-t)}\right]V_e'
$$
$$
+ \left[\left(\frac{s}{s+\theta a} + \frac{\theta a}{s+\theta a}e^{-(s+\theta a)(t_1-t)}\right)e^{-r(t_1-t)}\right]V_u'
$$
$$
+ \frac{aw}{r(s+a)}(1 - e^{-r(t_1-t)})
$$
$$
- \frac{aw}{(r+s+a)(s+a)}(1 - e^{-(r+s+a)(t_1-t)}). \tag{A6.9}
$$

The contribution of the status at the time of reform is now the same as for type 1 workers, as they compete for sector 2 jobs under the same terms. The contribution of wages expected to be earned between t and t_1 is clearly smaller. Consequently,

$$
V_u(t) < V_{e1}(t).
$$

In the absence of reform, the economy would remain in the original steady state. The value of being employed in either sector would then be

$$
\bar{V}_e = \frac{(r+a)w}{r(r+s+a)}.
$$

Workers in sector 1 therefore support the reform if $\bar{V}_e < V_{e1}(0)$. Using (A6.7) we see that this is equivalent to

$$
\left(\frac{\theta a}{s+\theta a}\right)\left(1 - e^{-(s+\theta a)t_1}\right)V_e'
$$
$$
+ \left(\frac{s}{s+\theta a} + \frac{\theta a}{s+\theta a}e^{-(s+\theta a)t_1}\right)V_u'
$$
$$
\geq \frac{aw}{r(s+a)} + \frac{sw}{(r+s+a)(s+a)}e^{-(s+a)t_1}. \tag{A6.10}
$$

An increase in t_1 increases the weight on V_e' while reducing it on V_u', thus increasing the left-hand side. This reflects the greater probability of being employed in the right sector at the time of reform. At the same time the right-hand side is reduced because of the last term. This reflects the greater likelihood of having lost one's job between now and the time of reform; that is, in addition to affecting an individual's initial conditions at the time of reform, postponement allows him to reap a greater part of his current employee rent, thus lowering opposition to the reform.

When t_1 goes to zero, this inequality becomes equivalent to $V'_u > \bar{V}_e$, the no-postponement condition. When t_1 goes to infinity, it becomes equivalent to

$$\frac{\theta a}{s + \theta a} V'_e + \frac{s}{s + \theta a} V'_u > \frac{aw}{r(s + a)}.$$

Replacing a and θ with their values, we see that this is equivalent to

$$l_2 V'_e + (1 - l_2) V'_u > (l_1 + l_2)\frac{w}{r}.$$

This condition is exactly the one for a social planner to support the reform. The left-hand side is equal to total social welfare after reform, since unemployment jumps to $1 - l_2$. The right-hand side is the present discounted value of wages paid by the pre-reform economy.

If this condition holds, by continuity there exists t_1 large enough such that (A6.10) holds. Thus, we have established that if the reform is welfare-improving, postponing it by enough will ensure support from workers in sector 1. The minimum delay is the value of t_1 such that (A6.10) holds with equality. The impact of labour market mobility on the minimum delay can be seen from that equation, at least in the case where $r = 0$. If a and s increase by the same factor, t_1 must shift so as to maintain $(s + \theta a)t_1$ constant, which then leaves both sides unaffected. Therefore, the minimum delay is reduced by exactly the same factor as the transition rates a and s increased.

If workers in sector 1 support the reform, then so do workers in sector 2. This is because they are always better off than workers in sector 1 under the reform (see (A6.8)), while they have the same welfare absent reform.

The condition for them to support the reform is

$$\left(\frac{\theta a}{s + \theta a} + \frac{s}{s + \theta a}e^{-(s+\theta a)(t_1 - t)}\right) V'_e$$

$$+ \left(\frac{s}{s + \theta a}\right)(1 - e^{-(s+\theta a)(t_1 - t)}) V'_u$$

$$> \frac{aw}{r(s + a)} + \frac{sw}{(r + s + a)(s + a)}e^{-(s+a)t_1}. \quad (A6.11)$$

Note that postponing is much less likely to increase their net gains from reform, as the left-hand side always falls with t_1. However, this is irrelevant as these workers always support the reform if workers in sector 1 do.

Turning finally to the unemployed, their welfare absent reform is given by

$$\overline{V}_u = \frac{aw}{r(r+s+a)}.$$

Comparing this with (A6.9), we see that the unemployed will support the reform provided

$$\left(\frac{\theta a}{s+\theta a}\right)\left(1 - e^{-(s+\theta a)t_1}\right)V_e' + V_u'\left(\frac{s}{s+\theta a} + \frac{\theta a}{s+\theta a}e^{-(s+\theta a)t_1}\right)$$

$$> \frac{aw}{r(s+a)} - \frac{aw}{(r+s+a)(s+a)}e^{-(s+a)t_1}. \qquad (A6.12)$$

Again, postponing the reform does not necessarily increase their net gains. The reason is now that the right-hand side is increasing with t_1. This reflects the fact that reform may well catch them in a situation where they have found a job in sector 1, in which case they will regret the former situation. But, again, this is irrelevant, since the right-hand side of (A6.12) is always strictly smaller than that of (A6.10). So, if workers employed in sector 1 support the reform, the unemployed also support it, since they compete on equal terms for sector 2 jobs and have less to lose from the removal of the previous arrangement.

A6.3 Solution to (6.12)–(6.13)

This is a standard linear system. The solution is obtained by computing the eigenvalues and eigenvectors of the matrix

$$\begin{pmatrix} -(a+\gamma+\sigma) & -a \\ \gamma & -\sigma \end{pmatrix}.$$

The solution is, between $t = 0$ and $t = \infty$:

$$l_H(t) = Ae^{-(\gamma+\sigma)t} + Be^{-(a+\sigma)t} + l_H^*$$

$$l_L(t) = -Ae^{-(\gamma+\sigma)t} - B\frac{\gamma}{a}e^{-(a+\sigma)t} + l_L^*.$$

l_H^* and l_L^* are the long-run values given by

$$l_H^* = \frac{a\sigma}{(a+\sigma)(\sigma+\gamma)}$$

$$l_L^* = \frac{a\gamma}{(a+\sigma)(\sigma+\gamma)}.$$

The integration constants A and B are given by

$$A = \frac{a(l_L^* - l_L(0)) + \gamma(l_H^* - l_H(0))}{a - \gamma}$$

$$B = -a\frac{l_H^* + l_L^* - l_L(0) - l_H(0)}{a - \gamma},$$

where $l_H(0)$ and $l_L(0)$ are the initial values of l_H and l_L.

7
The identifiability effect

Up to now we have been careful to assume that, when voting on policy, people know exactly the situation in which they end up right after the policy change. In reality, however, the reallocation of employment brought about by reform is associated with individual uncertainty about one's labour market status right after reform. If reform reduces employment in my sector by 20 per cent, I may or may not lose my job as the outcome of reform.

These considerations may again lead to status quo bias through a mechanism that we call the identifiability effect.

By identifiability effect we refer to the following phenomenon. Reform, by definition, takes place in the future, so people are always uncertain to some extent about the effect of reform on their welfare. Thus, when evaluating reform, their preferences will to some extent reflect a veil of ignorance. For example, if an employed believes that he has some probability of losing his job as the result of reform, he will evaluate his post-reform welfare as a weighted average of the utility of being employed and that of being unemployed after reform. As with the constituency effect, it is because of the reallocative effects of reform that this uncertainty arises.

By contrast, the status quo is already there, and people know for sure what their welfare is under the status quo. The degree of uncertainty about how reallocation will proceed at the time of reform therefore clearly affects its political support. The next question is: how, and under what conditions is that likely to lead to status quo bias? As for the constituency effect, we show that status quo bias will arise only under certain circumstances. More specifically, for uncertainty to lead to status quo bias, it is necessary that the decisive voter would expect to be better off than average without uncertainty. Or, equivalently, that losses are redistributed by uncertainty from less powerful to more powerful workers.

In the context of labour market institutions, these conditions are likely to be satisfied, because the decisive voter is likely to be employed and uncertainty is associated with his probability of losing his job. This implies that the support for an institution will be greater, the more one can identify those who lose from it. Because the losers from the status quo are perfectly identified, there will be a bias in its favour.

The identifiability effect is subsidiary to the constituency effect. Without a constituency effect uncertainty about the distribution of job losses associated with a given situation would not give rise to status quo bias, since people would not care about losing their jobs. However, given the constituency effect, the identifiability effect is likely to create or strengthen the status quo bias.

7.1 The basic arithmetics of identifiability

Let us consider two alternative institutions, A and B. Let V_A and V_B be the welfare of the decisive voter if institutions A and B prevail, respectively. Let W_A (resp. W_B) be the *expected* welfare of the decisive voter if the initial situation is B (resp. A), and one changes the institutions to A (resp. B). That is, W_A and W_B reflect the veil of ignorance of the decisive voter relative to his or her situation after reform.

Society will elect institution B if originally in situation A if and only if

$$V_A < W_B. \tag{7.1}$$

It will choose to stay in situation B if originally in that situation if and only if

$$W_A < V_B. \tag{7.2}$$

When can we say that there is status quo bias? Whenever (7.2) is more likely to hold than (7.1). Or, in mathematical language:

$$(V_A < W_B) \implies (W_A < V_B), \tag{7.3}$$

meaning that every time situation B is supported as a reform it will also be supported as the status quo.

Now, the mere existence of uncertainty about the distribution of gains from reform does not guarantee that (7.3) holds. It is a priori equally plausible that the converse holds, in which case uncertainty does not lead to status quo bias, but to instability and policy cycles. That is, a situation may arise where when in situation A society votes for B and vice versa.

But there is an assumption that guarantees that (7.3) holds, and that assumption is very relevant in the case of labour market reform. Assume that

$$V_A > W_A \quad \text{and} \quad V_B > W_B. \tag{7.4}$$

This assumption means that the decisive voter in situation A has a higher welfare than what the decisive voter of institution B expects to get if society shifts to A. Or, more loosely but more intuitively, that in both worlds *the decisive voter is better off than average*. In other words, uncertainty *redistributes losses from non-decisive to decisive voters, thus pushing W_B and W_A below V_A and V_B.*[1]

Clearly, if (7.4) holds, so does (7.3), since if $(V_A < W_B)$ then $W_A < V_A < W_B < V_B$. Therefore, if the decisive voter is better off than average, then uncertainty about the gains from reform leads to status quo bias. The reason is that uncertainty brings the decisive voter's welfare more in line with the average, thus reducing his or her expected gain from reform.

Equation (7.4) is likely to hold in the case of labour market reform, because the decisive voter is typically employed, so that V_A and V_B are the welfare of employed workers in worlds A and B, whereas W_A and W_B reflect the possibility of being unemployed. The basic arithmetic can be illustrated as follows. Assume, as before, that wage formation pins down the difference between the value of being employed and that of being unemployed:

$$V_e = V_u + Q,$$

where Q is the total rent. Consider any reform that does not affect the rent. If such reform did not affect anybody's employment status, there

---

[1] Fernandez and Rodrik (1991), in the context of trade reform, have showed how in certain circumstances uncertainty may lead to status quo bias. In particular, they give the following example. Assume that there is a reform such that 60 per cent of the people gain 1, while the remaining 40 per cent lose 1. If everybody knew exactly whether they gain or lose, the reform would clearly pass. Assume now that two-thirds of the winners, i.e. 40 per cent of the population, know that they gain, while the rest of the population is completely uncertain. These people know that one-third of them will gain 1, and that two-thirds will lose 1. Consequently, their expected gain is $\frac{1}{3} \times 1 + \frac{2}{3} \times -1 = -\frac{1}{3} < 0$. They all vote against the reform, which does not pass.

It is clear that in this example, the losses are redistributed from non-decisive voters (the 40 per cent of winners that are identified), to decisive ones (the 60 per cent remaining). If instead they were redistributed from decisive voters to non-decisive ones, uncertainty would create a bias against the status quo, not in favour of it.

would be unanimity between the employed and the unemployed over the reform. If superscript + denotes what prevails right after the reform, the employed and the unemployed will support it if and only if

$$V_u^+ > V_u. \tag{7.5}$$

Now, assume the reform has some reallocative effect, so that some of the employed will lose their job. An individual who loses his or her job with probability p as the outcome of the reform will support it only if his or her expected welfare is greater than prior to the reform, i.e.

$$pV_u^+ + (1 - p)V_e^+ > V_e,$$

or, equivalently, given that $V_e^+ = V_u^+ + Q$,

$$V_u^+ - V_u > pQ. \tag{7.6}$$

For these individuals the gains from the reform $V_u^+ - V_u$ must be large enough to compensate for the expected rents lost, pQ. Equation (7.6) is less likely to hold than (7.5), which reflects the fact that uncertainty about how the job reallocation effects of the reform will be distributed among the employed lowers the support for reform.

The right-hand side of (7.6) gives us a measure of how strong the status quo bias is. Depending on the reform p is allocated across the employed according to some distribution, and what matters is whether (7.6) holds for the 'decisive' voter. The status quo bias is smaller when the labour market is more competitive (Q smaller), but also when the decisive voter is less exposed to the job reallocation effects of the reform.

What would happen if, instead, policy were decided by the unemployed? From their point of view, the reallocative effects of reform are translated into a one-off opportunity to find a job. Let p' be the probability that they have found a job as the outcome of reform. The unemployed support the reform if

$$(1 - p')V_u^+ + p'V_e^+ > V_u,$$

or equivalently

$$V_u^+ - V_u > -p'Q. \tag{7.7}$$

This is now *more* likely to hold than (7.5) implying that, if it is the unemployed who are decisive, uncertainty leads to a bias against the status quo, not in favour of it. The key point is that (7.4) no longer holds:

the decisive voter is now poorer than average and is likely to gain, rather than to lose, from uncertainty.

In the case of labour market reform, (7.4) is quite plausible, so we expect the identifiability effect to lead to status quo bias. There exist other important instances, however, where it is far less plausible, so that we expect policy cycles and instability to be more likely than status quo bias. An example is that of redistributive taxation, which was discussed in Chapter 3. It is usually believed that as the distribution of income is skewed to the right, the decisive voter is likely to be poorer than average. He or she may then favour reform if that reform triggers mobility across income groups that may increase his or her expected income.

The interesting aspect of (7.6) is that the decisive p can to some extent be altered by the policymaker. The reform may be designed so as to lower the probability of job loss for the decisive voter, thus increasing its political viability. For example, one may specify that the required layoffs will take place according to some seniority rule, or introduce a two-tier system such as the one examined in Chapter 8, or introduce a mechanism that gives incumbent employees some priority over the newly created jobs in the post-reform economy.

7.2 Determination of the decisive voter

While it sounds plausible to assume that the decisive voter is employed, this will, in general, depend on the contents of the reform and on the structure of political decision making. If people vote over the reform, the decisive voter will be determined endogenously, being a member of a group whose voting decision is more sensitive than others to marginal changes in the alternatives.

When the gains from reform differ across individuals, it is not enough to claim that the employed are more numerous than the unemployed to conclude that they are politically decisive. It may well be that the unemployed have more intense views about the reform and end up being more likely to change their voting behaviour in response to a change in one of the alternatives. In that case the decisive voter may well be unemployed. More generally, there may be several decisive voters, i.e. several voters who are indifferent between the two alternatives. For example, there may be one employed decisive voter and one unemployed one, in which case it does not make sense to claim that the decisive voter is employed or that uncertainty redistributes losses to the decisive voter.

Nevertheless, the basic logic outlined above remains valid. To see how it applies when the decisive voter is determined endogenously, let us take the simple reallocation model used at the beginning of Chapter 6 and introduce uncertainty into it. For simplicity, we assume that there is a single sector, and that people vote between two alternatives, 1 and 2, such that employment in 2 is smaller than in 1: $l^1 > l^2$. We assume that there is a continuum of individuals indexed by (i), and that individual i gains $G(i)$ if the economy shifts from 1 to 2 and he keeps the same labour market status. G is distributed across the population with c.d.f. $H(G)$.

We allow for instantaneous job creation, and assume that the unemployed have the same voting weight as the employed. Therefore, we know from the previous chapter that without uncertainty, there would not be any status quo bias. We now assume, however, that at the time of a shift from 1 to 2, employed workers are randomly allocated to unemployment, while if the economy was to shift from 2 to 1, the unemployed would randomly be allocated to the new jobs.

The accounting of gainers and losers must be modified as follows. Consider first what happens if the economy shifts from 1 to 2. There is a mass $l^1 - l^2$ of employed workers who lose their jobs. Hence, each employed worker has a probability

$$p = \frac{l^1 - l^2}{l^1} \tag{7.8}$$

of losing his job at the time of the shift. The expected gain of an employed worker of type i is therefore equal to $(1 - p)G(i) + p(G(i) - Q) = G(i) - pQ$. Employed workers support the reform if and only if $G(i) > pQ$. Thus there are $l^1(1 - H(pQ))$ employed workers who support the reform. The unemployed workers remain so at the time of reform; therefore they support it if and only if $G(i) > 0$. Hence there are $(1 - l^1)(1 - H(0))$ unemployed workers who support the reform. The reform is politically viable if $l^1(1 - H(pQ)) + (1 - l^1)(1 - H(0)) > \frac{1}{2}$, or equivalently

$$H(0) + l^1(H(pQ) - H(0)) < \frac{1}{2}. \tag{7.9}$$

This equation has an interpretation similar to (6.1). The corrective term $l^1(H(pQ) - H(0))$ represents the mass of employed workers who would support the shift if their jobs were not threatened but oppose it because their job is threatened; their gain is positive but smaller than the expected rent lost.

What, now, if the economy was to consider a shift from 2 to 1? All employed workers would keep their jobs, while a mass $l^1 - l^2$ of unemployed workers find a job. Hence, each unemployed worker has a probability

$$p' = \frac{l^1 - l^2}{1 - l^2} \tag{7.10}$$

of finding a job. The employed oppose the shift if $G(i) > 0$, while the unemployed oppose it if $G(i) > p'Q$. Consequently, the support in favour of arrangement 2 if it is originally the status quo is given by $l^2(1 - H(0)) + (1 - l^2)(1 - H(p'Q))$. Rearranging, we see that it is greater than $\frac{1}{2}$ if and only if

$$H(0) + (1 - l^2)(H(p'Q) - H(0)) < \frac{1}{2}. \tag{7.11}$$

The corrective term $(1 - l^2)(H(p'Q) - H(0))$ represents the mass of unemployed workers who would favour the status quo if the shift to 1 did not increase their job finding opportunities, but who favour the shift because of such opportunities.

Contrary to what happened in Chapter 6, the two conditions are not equivalent: the status quo now matters. However, at face value status quo bias is not more likely than policy cycles. Status quo bias will prevail if (7.11) is more likely to hold than (7.9), i.e. if

$$l^1(H(pQ) - H(0)) > (1 - l^2)(H(p'Q) - H(0)). \tag{7.12}$$

That is, the prospect of job loss in situation 1 creates more opponents to situation 2 than the number of unemployed in situation 2 who support a shift to 1 because of the prospect of job finding. The political importance of the employed vs. the unemployed is now determined by their propensity to switch from support to opposition when taking into account the prospects of job loss or job finding. The above equation tells us that if there are more employed who are likely to switch than unemployed workers, then status quo bias prevails.

Using (7.8) and (7.10), we see that (7.12) is equivalent to

$$\frac{H(pQ) - H(0)}{pQ} > \frac{H(p'Q) - H(0)}{p'Q}. \tag{7.13}$$

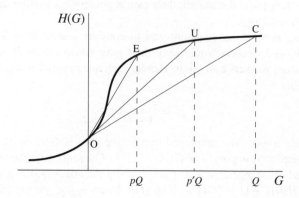

Figure 7.1. Determination of the average densities of switchers

That is, the average density of people whose gain is between 0 and pQ (the employed switchers) must be greater than the average density of people whose gain is between 0 and $p'Q$ (the unemployed switchers).

There is no a priori reason why this condition should hold. It does not follow from the employed being more numerous than the unemployed. However, we can show that if the distribution of gains is unimodal, it is likely to hold. To see this, first note that we expect that $1 - l^2 < l^1$, since $1 - l^2$ is unemployment in situation 2 and l^1 employment in situation 1. Consequently we expect that $p' > p$. If the density of gains is unimodal, then $H(.)$ will be S-shaped, as illustrated in Figure 7.1. If the mode of the distribution (the point where the cumulated density $H(.)$ is steepest) is not too far from zero, then it is likely that (7.13) will hold, as illustrated in Figure 7.1. The average density of employed switchers, given by the slope of OE, is greater than the average density of unemployed switchers, given by the slope of OU.

The interpretation is as follows. Because the unemployed are less numerous than the employed, a shift from 2 to 1 yields a greater job finding probability for the unemployed than the job loss probability imposed on the employed by a reverse shift. Because of that, the decisive unemployed worker in a shift from situation 2 to 1 is more 'extreme' (in the sense of having a greater gain from situation 2) than his employed counterpart in the reverse shift. But, if preferences are unimodal, being more extreme means being less numerous—further down along the tail of the distribution—and therefore less politically important, or equivalently less sensitive to a marginal change in one of the alternatives.

Note that the lower the number of unemployed workers in situation 2, the greater p', and the greater their support for a shift to situation 1. For that reason, the total number of unemployed switchers need not fall when unemployment falls. The political importance of the unemployed does not only depend on their total numbers, but on their sensitivity, which is greater, the greater p'.[2] However, if we are in the configuration of Figure 7.1, the gap between the two slopes increases when p' increases (point U moves to the right), so that the status quo bias is greater, the smaller the unemployment level in situation 2. But, if the distribution of gains were uniform, both sides of (7.13) would be equal to 1, and there would not be any status quo bias.

We conclude from this section that when we endogenize the decisive voter in a context where people are heterogeneous and the gains from reform differ across types of worker, it is still plausible that the identifiability effect will lead to status quo bias. However, the notion of the political importance of employed vs. unemployed workers must be redefined as the propensity to change one's mind when taking into account the reallocative consequences of reform, and it must be that that propensity is greater for the employed than for the unemployed.

If the unemployed have lower political power than the employed, then the scope for status quo bias is increased. As shown in the previous chapter, this would be true even if gainers and losers were perfectly identified. But it is likely that uncertainty will strengthen the status quo bias. To see this, let us consider the case where the unemployed do not vote at all ($\lambda = 0$ in the terminology of Chapter 6). Then, a shift from 1 to 2 is politically viable if less than half the employed oppose it, i.e.

$$H(pQ) < \frac{1}{2}. \qquad (7.14)$$

A shift from 2 to 1 is blocked by a majority of employed workers if

$$H(0) < \frac{1}{2}. \qquad (7.15)$$

As (7.15) is more likely to hold, there is status quo bias. The extent of status quo bias is measured by the difference between the left-hand

---

[2] It is for this reason that it is the differences in average densities that matter for the comparison between the political influence of the employed vs. the unemployed rather than simply their numbers.

side of (7.14) and that of (7.15), i.e.

$$SQB_U = H(pQ) - H(0).$$

To compute the status quo bias in the absence of uncertainty, we can simply use equations (6.6) and (6.7), assuming $\lambda = 0$, eliminating sector B and changing labels. We get that the condition for situation 2 to be supported when the economy is originally in 1 is

$$H(0) + \frac{l^1 - l^2}{l^1}(H(Q) - H(0)) < \frac{1}{2},$$

while the condition for a shift from 2 to 1 to be blocked remains $H(0) < \frac{1}{2}$. Consequently, the extent of status quo bias in that case is given by

$$SQB_C = \frac{l^1 - l^2}{l^1}(H(Q) - H(0)) = p(H(Q) - H(0)).$$

Uncertainty increases status quo bias provided $SQB_C < SQB_U$, or equivalently

$$\frac{H(Q) - H(0)}{Q} < \frac{H(pQ) - H(0)}{pQ}.$$

That is, the average density between 0 and Q is smaller than the average density between 0 and pQ. This condition is even more likely to hold than (7.13), as Figure 7.1 makes clear—the average density between 0 and Q is given by the slope of OC. The interpretation is similar as that of equation (7.13). Without uncertainty, job loss is concentrated on a subset of employed workers who are sure to lose their jobs if reform takes place. For that reason, they have extreme views about the reform; but this also means that they are insensitive to a change in one of the alternatives, i.e. politically unimportant. By contrast, uncertainty redistributes job losses to the bulk of the employed, who will be more sensitive and thus more decisive.

Therefore, if the employed do not vote, there is status quo bias without uncertainty, but uncertainty is likely to strengthen it.

7.3 Example: status quo bias in a simple wage–setting model

Let us now illustrate how status quo bias may play a role in the case of an institution that allows wages to be bid up, as we have discussed in

the case of the political insider model of Chapter 2. Again we assume
that the employed of group A choose between a flexible world where the
rent is equal to zero and a rigid one with a strictly positive rent Q. In
Chapter 2 we had assumed that people knew for sure whether they would
be employed or not after a policy change. Now, however, we assume that
whenever the policy change destroys jobs in a given sector, these losses
are uniformly distributed across that sector's employees.

If the economy is initially rigid and contemplates becoming flexible,
then employment of type-A workers will necessarily increase. For simplicity, although this is not the most realistic assumption, we allow it to
jump upwards instantaneously, as in the previous section, the economy
remaining in the new steady state thereafter. As in Chapter 2, let L_A be
the total supply of type-A workers and $w(l)$ the wage schedule for these
workers. Let $w^R > w(L_A)$ and $l^R < L_A$ be the wage and employment
levels in the rigid world. The value of being employed for a type-A
employee is then given by

$$V_e = \frac{w(L_A)}{r} = \frac{w^*}{r} = V_e^*,$$

meaning that under free markets the rent is equal to zero and people are
paid their marginal product w^*. Note that the job loss rate s does not
appear, as any job loser finds another job instantaneously at the same
going wage.

In the rigid world the employed earn $w = w(l) = w^R > w^*$, but
lose their rent with probability s per unit of time:

$$V_e = \frac{w^R - sQ}{r} = V_e^R.$$

The employed of group A will prefer the rigid world whenever $V_e^R >
V_e^*$, or equivalently

$$w^R - w^* > sQ. \tag{7.16}$$

That is, the wage gain must be greater than the average cost of losing
one's job. This condition is less likely, the smaller the exposure level s,
as we have already discussed.

What happens, next, if society is originally flexible? Then if it were
to move to rigidity some workers of group A would lose their jobs. Thus
they no longer consider that their welfare in the rigid world will be equal
to V_e^R. If the job loss probability is uniformly allocated, the value of

rigidity to an incumbent worker is

$$EV = \frac{l^R}{L_A} V_e^R + \left(1 - \frac{l^R}{L_A}\right) V_u^R.$$

That is, they consider that they will only keep their job with probability l/L_A, and be unemployed otherwise.

This may be rewritten as

$$EV = V_e^R - \left(1 - \frac{l^R}{L_A}\right) Q$$

$$= \frac{w^R - sQ}{r} - \left(1 - \frac{l^R}{L_A}\right) Q.$$

Rigidity is now preferred to flexibility if $EV > V_e^*$, i.e.

$$w^R - w^* > sQ + r\left(1 - \frac{l^R}{L_A}\right) Q. \tag{7.17}$$

This condition is more stringent than (7.16), meaning that rigidity is more likely to be supported if it is the status quo in the first place. The right-hand side is now the total expected rent lost, which is the sum of two terms. The first term sQ is the annuity equivalent of the rents lost due to regular job losses in the rigid world. The second term is the annuity equivalent of the expected rent lost due to the mass of dismissals that take place at the time of reform, as a response to the wage hike.

As long as the decisive voter does not know for sure whether he will keep his job, there is status quo bias; the losers from rigidity are well identified if society is rigid, but not if it contemplates becoming so.

The identifiability of the losers does not only depend on the nature of the status quo. It is also affected by other dimensions of the economic environment. It also depends on which institution we are dealing with. A uniform increase in the rent Q, as we have just analysed, implies much more uncertainty about who will lose one's job than an increase in the minimum wage. If we return to the minimum wage example developed in Chapter 2, we see that the losers were perfectly identified; they were the workers whose productivity was below the minimum wage. To the extent that the decisive voter's income is above the minimum wage, an increase in that wage will affect his exposure to unemployment by much less than a uniform increase in wages. In fact, as we saw in Chapter 2, an increase in the minimum wage actually *increased the demand* for skill levels paid more than that. Thus, we do not expect an institution like the minimum wage to be associated with as much status quo bias as institutions (such as work rules) that allow all workers to increase their rent.

7.4 Application: business cycles and labour market reform

Another important aspect of reform where identifiability effects come into play is its timing with respect to the business cycle. It affects the prospects of job loss and job finding after the reform.

Let us consider the case where business cycles generate fluctuations in the labour demand of individual firms and where these firms can only gradually adjust their workforce to its desired level (the detailed computations are worked out in the appendix). Furthermore, consider that in each firm there is an exogenous source of turnover, so that a constant fraction s of the workers quit their jobs per unit of time. Let l_{it} be firm i's employment level at date t. As long as the firm is not reducing its workforce by an amount greater than sl_{it}, it can use natural attrition to adjust its workforce downwards and does not need to lay off anybody. In such a situation, the firm's employees have a constant probability s per unit of time of losing their jobs. If, on the other hand, the firm is reducing its workforce by more than sl_{it}, then the firm's employees have a probability of losing their job equal to $-(dl_{it}/dt)/l_{it}$, which is greater than s and is larger, the larger the rate of reduction of the firm's workforce. Therefore, we can distinguish two regimes. One regime (regime I) where the firm does not reduce its workforce beyond natural attrition and where the probability of job loss does not depend on the firm's employment policy, and another one (regime II) where the firm reduces employment by more than sl_{it} and where the job loss rate is greater, the more the firm reduces its workforce.

Now, in a boom firms typically hire more and dismiss less, meaning that the fraction of firms in regime II is lower in a boom, and that those who remain in that regime reduce their workforce by less. The converse occurs in a recession.

How do these considerations interact with labour market reform? Consider the effect of a shift toward a 'rigid' society, i.e. a world where wages are higher. An increase in wages reduces the desired employment

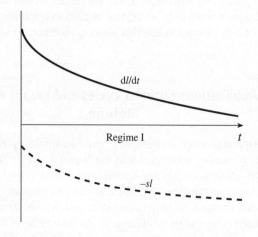

Figure 7.2. (a) Response of a hiring firm

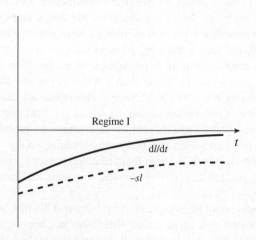

Figure 7.2. (b) Slow reduction in employment

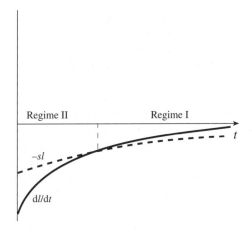

Figure 7.2. (c) Rapid reduction in employment

level of all firms. The response of individual firms to the increase in wages is depicted in Figure 7.2.

In panel (a) we have a firm which is expanding, despite the higher wages, because its initial employment level was (and still is) too low relative to its long-run target. The firm will go on hiring people and remains in regime I after the reform.

Panel (b) depicts a firm which reduces its desired employment level, but at a pace lower than the natural attrition of its workforce. The firm remains in regime I throughout the transition, and its employees' exposure to unemployment is not higher because it is reducing its workforce.

Finally, panel (c) describes a firm which is reducing its workforce at a fast enough rate to have to lay off people in excess of the natural attrition rate. It spends a fraction of the transition in regime II before reaching regime I. Because its target employment level is lower in the rigid case than in the flexible one, it would reduce employment at a faster rate if the economy became rigid and that would increase the fraction of time spent in regime II and its employees' unemployment risk.

To sum up, incumbent employees bear the adverse employment effects of the wage hike only to the extent that they have greater chances of losing their jobs. That is, only employees in firms that are in regime II after the reform will bear these adverse consequences. Therefore, *the support for rigidity is greater, the smaller the fraction of employees in regime II.* Conversely, the support for flexibility is greater, the larger the fraction of employees in regime II. This logic tells us that it is at the end of a recession (at the start of an expansion), when most firms are hiring, that the support for rigidity is greater. And, the appropriate time for increasing flexibility is the start of a recession.

Why? Because business cycles play a role in sorting out losers from winners. Identifiability of the losers from rigidity is maximum at the start of a boom because the previous recession has temporarily allocated a fraction of the employed to unemployment, and these are the natural candidates to bear the adverse effects of rigidity on employment. Conversely, identifiability is minimal at the start of a recession where the number of employed is at a peak.

Note, however, that this conclusion need not extend to any sort of 'rigidity'. In the case where the 'rigid' institution is employment protection, matters are more complex. We have seen that the status quo bias, in that case, comes from workers in low productivity firms, and that a boom generated a window of opportunity for reform, because the fraction of high productivity firms is higher in a boom. This tends to suggest that it is in the middle of a boom that the scope for reform is highest, which is not incompatible with the above considerations. On the other hand, a sharp recession, by eliminating many low productivity firms, may also increase the scope for reform.

7.5 Concluding comments

The basic message of this chapter is that in the presence of rents, uncertainty about how the job losses induced by a policy shift are distributed is likely to increase and/or create a status quo bias, because it is likely to redistribute job loss from less decisive to more decisive voters.

To conclude, we want to point out that the above persistence mechanism is essentially identical to an unemployment persistence mechanism already identified in the literature on labour unions, known as 'membership effects'. Finally, we argue that greater turnover is likely to reduce the scope for status quo bias.

7.5.1 Political hysteresis

The above considerations suggest that the identifiability effect may generate *political hysteresis*. The word hysteresis applies when temporary shocks have permanent effects. Macroeconomists have identified different channels that may increase unemployment persistence. These include loss of skill during unemployment and membership effect (see Blanchard and Summers 1986; Gottfries and Horn 1985; Pissarides 1992 and Layard *et al.* 1991). The latter refer to the fact that when employment is lower, so is the pool of unionized insiders who set wages, and the higher are the wages that they will want to set. It is fundamentally that same phenomenon which is at work here. The difference is that rather that negotiating wages at the firm level, people vote on political institutions that affect their ability to get high wages. Again, the political system acts as a coordination device to achieve monopoly power for insiders, even though such power is nonexistent at the firm level.

How can the identifiability effect lead to political hysteresis? Consider a temporary recession. When the recession ends the support for rigidity is maximal. People vote for a change in labour law that allows them to increase their wages. Because of status quo bias this change never goes away, and employment is permanently lower, even though the initial recession is temporary.

7.5.2 The role of turnover

We already know that labour turnover—captured by the parameter s—reduces the support for the high wage outcome by making the employed more sympathetic to the unemployed. How does it affect status quo bias and political hysteresis?

The above computation implies that the extent of status quo bias, as measured by the gap between the right-hand side of (7.16) and that of (7.17), is actually unaffected by s. It is simply equal to the annuity value of the expected rent lost because of reform, $r(1 - \frac{l}{L_A})Q$. However, this computation is somewhat spurious, because it assumes that all the job losses caused by the reform occur instantaneously. This assumption is convenient to establish the existence of status quo bias but hides the real effect of labour turnover. It implies that the exposure to unemployment generated by the reform is independent of the one associated with regular turnover, so that the two can be added.

Assume firms face costs in adjusting employment, as we did in our analysis of business cycles. Then if the economy shifts from flexibility to rigidity, the economy will again be split into firms that are in regime I, i.e. using only natural attrition to reduce their workforce, and firms in regime II, i.e. laying off people to reduce their workforce at a speed greater than s. The larger s, the larger the proportion of employees who work in type-I firms, and the lower the fraction of employees whose exposure to unemployment is increased because of the reform. Hence, the smaller the extent of the status quo bias.

Appendix. Determination and properties of the two regimes

We consider a firm i that starts with an initial employment level l_{i0}. At any date t its total output is $\theta_i l_{it} - b l_{it}^2/2$. It has to pay a wage cost equal to w and a quadratic labour adjustment cost equal to $c(sl_{it} + dl_{it}/dt)^2/2$, where s is the exogenous quit rate. It maximizes the present discounted value of its profits:

$$\max \int_0^{+\infty} \left[\theta_i l_{it} - b l_{it}^2/2 - w l_{it} - c(sl_{it} + dl_{it}/dt)^2/2 \right] e^{-rt} \, dt.$$

Applying variation calculus we see that the first-order condition is

$$\frac{d}{dt} \frac{\partial L}{\partial \dot{l}} = \frac{\partial L}{\partial l},$$

where the Lagrangian L is defined as

$$L = \left[\theta_i l_{it} - b l_{it}^2/2 - w l_{it} - c(sl_{it} + dl_{it}/dt)^2/2 \right] e^{-rt}.$$

The first-order condition may be rewritten as

$$\theta_i - b l_{it} - w - cs(sl_{it} + dl_{it}/dt) = rc(sl_{it} + dl_{it}/dt) - c(sdl_{it}/dt + d^2 l_{it}/dt^2).$$

Thus employment in firm i follows the linear differential equation

$$c\ddot{l}_{it} - rc\dot{l}_{it} - [cs(r + s) + b] l_{it} = w - \theta_i.$$

Clearly, one characteristic root is negative (call it $-\lambda$), and the other is positive. Any dependence of l_{it} on the positive root eigenvector will generate explosive dynamics, which we rule out. Thus the solution must be

$$l_{it} = (1 - e^{-\lambda t}) \frac{\theta_i - w}{cs(r + s) + b} + e^{-\lambda t} l_0.$$

Employment converges to its long-term level, which is $l^* = \frac{\theta_i - w}{cs(r+s)+b}$. A wage hike at date 0 reduces that target employment level but employment adjusts only gradually.

One has

$$\lambda = \frac{-rc + \sqrt{r^2c^2 + 4(cs(r+s)+b)c}}{2c},$$

implying $\lambda > s$.

At any point in time the probability of losing one's job is $\max(s, -\dot{l}_{it}/l_{it})$. It will be greater than s if and only if

$$\lambda e^{-\lambda t}\left(\frac{\theta_i - w}{cs(r+s)+b} - l_0\right)$$
$$< -s\left((1 - e^{-\lambda t})\frac{\theta_i - w}{cs(r+s)+b} + e^{-\lambda t}l_0\right). \qquad (A7.1)$$

This equation determines the boundary between regime I and regime II. If it holds then the firm is in regime II. Note that firms that are reducing their workforce in regime I are actually hiring some people to prevent their labour force from falling at a pace equal to s. The reason is that they will have to rehire fewer people later, when they have reached their steady state, which allows them to save money by smoothing labour adjustment costs over time.

Note also that as $\lambda > s$, the equation is less likely to hold when l_0 is smaller, meaning that the fraction of firms in regime I is greater at the time of a boom. A fall in θ_i clearly reduces the left-hand side while the right-hand side is increased, thus making it more likely that the firm is in regime II. Firms will be in regime I if and only if their demand shock θ_i exceeds $\tilde{\theta}$, which is given by

$$\tilde{\theta} = w + (cs(r+s)+b)\frac{e^{-\lambda t}l_0(\lambda - s)}{\lambda e^{-\lambda t} + s(1 - e^{-\lambda t})}.$$

How does turnover affect the threshold shock $\tilde{\theta}$? In order to deal with this question, one first has to note that turnover increases the average cost of labour. In steady state, firms have to rehire a fraction s of their workforce, paying an adjustment cost equal to $cs^2l^2/2$, which increases labour costs and reduces the target level of employment. In order to insulate the pure effect of turnover, we have to hold the target level of employment constant, that is reduce c so as to maintain $cs(r+s)$ unchanged. If this is so, it is clear that λ is also unchanged, and that the right-hand side of (A7.1) falls when s rises. Consequently, the fraction of firms in regime I increases when s increases.

8
Two-tier systems

In Chapters 6 and 7, we have studied the sources of status quo bias. Status quo bias is important because it tells us that both rigidity and flexibility may be self-sustaining equilibria. The question is then: how do we go from one equilibrium to another? We have already seen some strategies that may work, like announcing the reform in advance or taking advantage of external macroeconomic circumstances.

The strategy that we examine here is a two-tier system, which consists of buying the support of incumbent employees by granting that the new arrangements will only apply to new contracts, not to them.[1]

We illustrate this strategy in the context of the model of employment protection discussed in Chapter 4. In that world, the unemployed were always in favour of flexibility. The employed favoured flexibility if the rent was low but rigidity if it was high. Finally, workers in the least productive 'obsolete' firms were more likely to support rigidity than other workers, and this constituency effect led to status quo bias as such workers only existed if the economy was initially rigid enough to prevent these firms from closing.

8.1 A two-tier reform

Let us now consider what would happen if at date $t = 0$ the government tries to reform the labour market by leaving existing contracts unchanged but stipulating that all new contracts will have no firing restriction.

New firms entering the market know that nothing will prevent them from shedding labour when they fall into the low productivity state. Consequently they act as if they were in the flexible economy, and their

---

[1] This chapter elabourates and updates Saint-Paul (1993).

value is given by (4.15), which we rewrite here for convenience:

$$r J_H = m_H - w - \sigma J_H + \gamma(\hat{J}_L - J_H). \qquad (4.15)$$

Again, $\hat{J}_L$, their value in the bad state, cannot be negative, otherwise they would close. As long as there is free entry, we still have $J_H = 0$, from which $w \geq m_H$ must follow, implying $J_L < 0 = \hat{J}_L$. Thus, firms will close when falling into the bad state and they drive up wages to m_H, the level prevailing in the fully flexible economy.

What about labour market tightness? It is clear that no new entrant will want to offer a job under an old contract, since it would make zero profits when productive and negative ones when in the low state. So the unemployed anticipate that any future job that they might hold will necessarily be flexible. Thus labour market tightness, which adjusts so as to make wages (as determined by the worker's outside option) compatible with productivity, is simply determined by (1.16), after making the appropriate substitutions:

$$a = (w/q - 1)(r + s), \qquad (8.1)$$

with w and s corresponding to the new contracts, i.e. $w = m_H$ and $s = \sigma + \gamma$.

To sum up, as far as such key variables that characterize the economy such as wages and labour market tightness are concerned, the outcome is identical to a full reform of the labour market that would have eliminated all firing restrictions including the original contracts. Old contracts are simply a deadweight; their number is gradually reduced at a rate of σ per unit of time, and this shrinking deadweight does not interfere with the functioning of the rest of the economy. In the long run, the economy ends up being composed only of flexible contracts, exactly as if a full reform had taken place.

This result is useful to keep in mind but it is a bit too stylized. The increase in wages eliminates profits in incumbent high productivity firms and increases losses in incumbent low productivity firms. Here these firms are essentially passive; they just wait for an exogenous shock to occur and allow them to close. But in a more general setting, where firms' productivities could take a continuum of values and employment protection takes the form of a tax on dismissals, their closing point would be endogenous, and the rise in wages and labour market tightness brought about by the reform would actually generate a mass of job losses among low productivity firms. Therefore, the two-tier system is not completely efficient at sheltering incumbent employees from job loss, because its positive general equilibrium effect on wages makes it optimal for the least productive firms to close. One should also mention that the assumption of constant returns to scale plays a role in insulating the rest of the economy from the mass of old contracts. Under decreasing returns, for example, the mass of old contracts would reduce the marginal product of labour for new entrants. The two-tier system would then achieve, in the medium run, a lower wage and a lower exit rate from unemployment than if complete reform had taken place. Again, in the long run, nothing is changed.

It is also interesting to look at the response of employment to the reform. Under a complete reform employment falls brutally as a mass of low productivity firms closes. It then increases gradually to the long-term level that corresponds to the flexible economy, which, as we have seen, may be either larger or smaller than the rigid level. Under the two-tier system, the response is much smoother, as illustrated in Figure 8.1. Because old contracts are left unaltered, obsolete firms, whose employment is represented in the top panel, cannot close. The economy enjoys the boost in job creation but is spared the mass of job destruction.[2] Employment in productive firms (shown in the middle panel), however, rises more slowly than if the reform had been complete, as there are fewer job seekers. But total employment (shown in the bottom panel) unambiguously rises right after the reform. Depending on its long-term level, it may rise forever or eventually fall, thus overshooting its long-term target.[3] The bottom panel of Figure 8.1 has been drawn in the no-overshooting case, but there must be overshooting if flexibility has a lower steady state employment level than rigidity (see Figure 8.2).

Now, the interesting question is how does the use of a two-tier system affect political incentives? The answer is simple to obtain. For the unemployed, the situation is the same as if complete reform had taken place, and we know that they are better off. The incumbent employees earn a higher wage and on top of that their job loss probability has not increased. Furthermore, when they lose their job they will also benefit from the higher wages and job finding probabilities, as the unemployed do. Therefore, the incumbent employees are clearly made better off

---

[2] As was made clear in the preceding paragraph, this would not be the case in a more general setting, but it is still true that employment would fall by less than under a complete reform.

[3] See Bentolila and Saint-Paul (1992) for a discussion of employment overshooting following the introduction of a two-tier system.

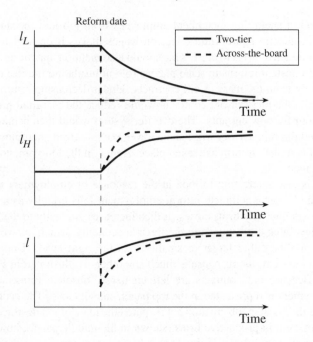

Figure 8.1. Employment responses to a two-tier reform and an across-the-board reform

by the reform, regardless of parameter values. To conclude, our model predicts that a reform engineered in this way is certain to succeed. The two-tier system is able to overcome the status quo bias and to shift the economy away from a rigid equilibrium into a flexible one.

Does this mean that there is a free lunch? Obviously, no. The hike in wages financially harms existing firms; and firms in the unproductive state continue making losses, whereas they could have closed instantaneously had a complete reform occurred. So it is incumbent firms, or 'capitalists', who finance the burden of preserving incumbent employees' favourable employment situation. This is not surprising as incumbent firms are competing on unequal terms with new entrants, who face fewer restrictions and end up exerting upward pressure on wages. It is as if a transfer was paid to incumbent employees in order to buy their support for reform and this transfer was paid by their employers.

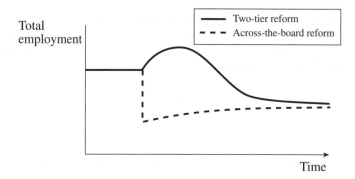

Figure 8.2. Employment overshooting when reform reduces steady state employment

As long as incumbent 'capitalists' are not too powerful, then, the reform is politically viable and approved by all workers.

8.2   Consensus in the case of a 'pure' two-tier system

The above example has the merit of highlighting the general equilibrium effects of a two-tier system. But it is a two-tier system in a limited way, since incumbent employees are insulated from new legislation but not from market forces. Here these market forces enhance their support for the reform as wages are increased. But in other cases this could be reversed. For example, if there were decreasing returns to scale, the increase in employment brought about by the reform might well lead to a reduction in wages.

Having incumbents *entirely* insulated from both market forces and new legislation is clearly an extreme case, and it is probably not feasible. But it is useful to consider this extreme case briefly, because we can then establish a simple analytical result which, in the context of labour market reform, makes the political virtues of two-tier systems more transparent.

This result tells us that if a reform is implemented in a perfect two-tier way, there is *consensus* between the employed and the unemployed about the reform. That is, the employed support it if and only if the unemployed do. The two-tier system therefore overcomes conflicts of interests between the employed and the unemployed.

To prove this is very simple. Consider an incumbent employee who earns a wage w and loses his job with a probability s per unit of time. If V_u denotes the utility of being unemployed, we have seen that the welfare of such an incumbent employee is given by

$$V_e = \frac{w + sV_u}{r + s}. \qquad (8.2)$$

Now, under a perfect two-tier system, the incumbent's job characteristics s and w are left *unchanged* at the time of reform: neither wages nor job loss are affected by the reform. What are, then, the gains from reform to the incumbent? If we denote them by ΔV_e we must have

$$\Delta V_e = \frac{s}{r + s} \Delta V_u, \qquad (8.3)$$

where ΔV_u is the gain to the unemployed. Consequently, ΔV_e has always the same sign as ΔV_u. Incumbent employees gain from the reform if and only if the unemployed do. The two-tier system generates consensus between the two.

Why? Since the characteristics of my current job are left unaffected, the new state of affairs will only affect me if I lose my job. But, in that case, I will be unemployed. So it is only through the value of being unemployed that the reform affects my welfare. If that value increases, so does my utility.

In (8.2) and (8.3) we have implicitly assumed that the value of being unemployed V_u jumped to its new steady state level at the time of reform and stayed constant forever thereafter. This consensus result could in principle be overturned if one considers a reform such that V_u is not constant after reform. What matters for incumbent employees is the *future* value of V_u (i.e. the one that will prevail at the time when they lose their job), whereas the unemployed will decide whether or not to support the reform by looking at V_u at the time of reform. In principle, then, one could think of a reform such that the currently unemployed gain but future unemployed workers lose, and incumbent employees could be against it while the unemployed would support it. However, in the more plausible cases where ΔV_u has the same sign in all future periods, the consensus result holds.

8.3 Low exposure and lock-in

Since the gains to incumbent employees of the two-tier reform are intimately associated with the fact that they might lose their job, these gains are smaller, the lower their exposure to unemployment. Equation (8.3) tells us that they always gain as long as $\Delta V_u > 0$, but the lower s, the lower the gain. If one introduces any cost of the reform to incumbent employees, say an administrative cost or some uncertainty about whether their existing contract will indeed be protected, then for low enough values of exposure the gains will not exceed the losses and the reform will be blocked.

This result tells us that while two-tier systems are generally efficient in generating support for the reform, this does not occur if the incumbent's exposure to unemployment is very low, i.e. if employment protection is very strong to begin with. The economy is then locked in a situation of highly rigid institutions, where it is precisely this rigidity that makes it difficult for incumbent employees to share the gains from job creation, since they already have a job and do not expect to lose it.

However, this is only true of a 'total' two-tier system where incumbent employees are insulated from market forces as well as the legal environment. In the example we consider above and below, it is not true that their gains from the reform become negligible as their exposure to unemployment diminishes toward zero. Part of their gain is in the form of higher wages, and that part does not go down with exposure. It is only the part of their gain associated with higher job finding rates that goes down with exposure.

8.4 Political dynamics

One important aspect of the two-tier system is that after the reform the employed are split into two groups: those who have a new type of contract and those who are still under old contracts. This fact has important implications if we consider that voting may take place again.

First of all, for reform not to be reversed it must be that flexibility is an equilibrium, that is that condition (4.25) is violated:

$$m_H - m_L > rq/(r + \sigma). \tag{8.4}$$

Otherwise, once a sufficient fraction of the workforce is under flexible contracts, they will vote for a return to the old ways. That is, while the two-tier system is politically viable regardless of parameter values, if (8.4) fails to hold we are merely engineering a *temporarily* to be more flexible, but these 'others' want employment protection and as their number is growing, they end up being able to impose it. It is actually conceivable that the economy be subjected to policy cycles, which move it back and forth between complete rigidity and the emergence of a flexible tier.

On the other hand, if all the employed, including those in low productivity firms, support flexibility, the two-tier system is unnecessary: workers would even prefer a complete reform of the labour market. In Chapter 6 we saw that this will occur if

$$m_H - m_L > q \frac{r}{r+\sigma} \frac{r+\sigma+\gamma}{\gamma}.$$

Thus, it is in the status quo bias zone, where $rq/(r+\sigma) < m_H - m_L < q \frac{r}{r+\sigma} \frac{r+\sigma+\gamma}{\gamma}$ and where workers in unproductive firms can block a reform, that two-tier systems can make a difference. By compensating these workers from their losses by maintaining their employment conditions unchanged, two-tier systems manage to implement a transition from one political equilibrium (rigidity) to another (flexibility), that would be impossible with a complete reform. The incentives for policy reversal are no longer there, because they would have to come from workers employed in low productivity firms *and* not having employment protection. But, precisely, such workers do not exist.

On the other hand, the mass of workers in low productivity firms— those who block a complete reform—is gradually shrinking. Therefore one will reach a critical time when they are no longer powerful enough to block the reform. At that critical time a full reform of the labour market is now feasible. Hence, in the status quo bias zone the post-reform political dynamics tend to *accelerate* the transition to flexibility. After the critical time the government could successfully pass another reform stipulating that all existing contracts are converted into new ones. How is this critical time determined? Here one has to be careful. It is true that if the choice is only between rigidity and complete flexibility, then under our assumptions only workers in low productivity firms support rigidity. But, if the choice is between an existing two-tier system and flexibility, workers in high productivity firms will also support the status quo. They already enjoy the high wage and job finding rates of the flexible world, and a complete reform would now harm them as they would only get the bad side of it. So, the complete reform can only occur at a time where *both* the initially employed who work in high productivity firms and those who work in low productivity firms are unimportant enough.

But, if incumbent employees in low productivity firms realize that the complete reform will take place after a finite delay, it will reduce their support for the initial reform as they anticipate retaining their employment protection level only for a limited time. This is not the case for incumbent employees in high productivity firms, whose welfare will always be above their initial 'rigid' one, even though it falls at the time of complete reform. But workers in low productivity firms will oppose the reform if complete reform occurs too early, as they lose their jobs.

So, it is possible to use holders of flexible contracts as a constituency in favour of a complete reform. But that possibility is a double-edged weapon: while it allows an accelerated transition, it may also make the initial reform impossible. In some cases the government would like to commit on not proposing any other reform before some date $\hat{t}$. If that commitment is impossible, there is a time consistency problem. In order to ensure that the reform is passed one needs to promise that no other reform will take place. But that promise is not credible, because after a critical date a policymaker interested in increasing labour market flexibility would have an interest in reneging on that promise.

How does the critical date affect the welfare of incumbent workers in low productivity firms? It is possible to show—and this is done in the appendix— that if the two-tier system is introduced at date $t = 0$ and if all contracts are made flexible at date $t = t^*$, it is given by

$$V_{eL}(0) = e^{-(r+\sigma)t^*} V_{uf} + (1 - e^{-(r+\sigma)t^*}) V_{ef}^T, \qquad (8.5)$$

where V_{uf} is the same as in Chapter 4, i.e. it is the utility of an unemployed worker in the flexible economy, while V_{ef}^T is the utility of a worker who would hold forever[4] a *rigid* job in the *flexible* economy. This utility is greater than that of a worker holding a flexible job in the flexible economy: $V_{ef}^T > V_{ef}$.

Equation (8.5) simply tells us that the utility of this group of workers is a weighted average of the utility of an unemployed and that of a worker holding a rigid contract in the flexible world, with a weight on the first component equal to $e^{-(r+\sigma)t^*}$, the appropriate discount factor between

---

[4] By 'forever' we mean until the job is hit by the exogenous job destruction shock, which occurs with flow probability σ. That is, this is the value of holding a rigid job in the flexible economy if no legislative change occurs that turns the job into a flexible one.

now and the date of the second reform. This weight is smaller, the more remote the second reform.

When will these people support the two-tier system at $t = 0$? This will be the case if $V_{eL}(0) > V_{er}$, which is equivalent to (see the appendix):

$$m_H - m_L > \frac{r + \sigma + \gamma}{\gamma} \frac{r}{r + \sigma} q e^{-(r+\sigma)t^*}. \tag{8.6}$$

As t^* goes from zero to infinity, the right-hand side monotonically goes from $\frac{r+\sigma+\gamma}{\gamma} \frac{r}{r+\sigma} q$, which by (6.9) is greater than $m_H - m_L$, to zero. Therefore, (8.6) defines the minimum delay to elapse between the introduction of the two-tier system and the complete reform so as to get the support for the two-tier system from incumbent workers in low productivity firms. This minimum delay is defined as the value of t^* such that (8.6) holds with equality. The reform is harder to implement, the longer this minimum delay.

The credibility problem arises whenever the critical time $\hat{t}$ after which complete reform is feasible does not satisfy (8.6). If this is so incumbent employees in low productivity firms will oppose the two-tier system, because they anticipate that it will not last long enough and that they are too likely to still hold their jobs, and therefore to lose them, at the time of the complete reform.

How is $\hat{t}$ determined? Remember that while rigid workers in high productivity jobs always support the two-tier system when it is introduced, they will always oppose the complete reform. Therefore, for the complete reform to be viable it must take place at a date when holders of rigid contracts in both high and low productivity firms have lost enough political power. Assume that this occurs when their number is reduced to a fraction $\theta < 1$ of its initial level. Since the exit rate from protected contracts is σ, the stock of original contracts (call it $l_r(t)$) dies out at rate σ. At any date t it is therefore given by $l_r(t) = l_r(0)e^{-\sigma t}$. The critical time is such that $l_r(\hat{t}) = \theta l_r(0)$, or equivalently

$$\hat{t} = \frac{-\ln \theta}{\sigma}.$$

Substituting into (8.6) we get a condition which is necessary and sufficient for the two-tier system to be politically viable *ex ante*, if incumbent employees correctly anticipate that it will only last until $\hat{t}$.

Hence when there is a credibility problem, it is no longer the case that the two-tier system is always supported by incumbent voters. Furthermore, the way the underlying characteristics of the economy affect the support for reform is substantially different from what we concluded in other circumstances.

Consider, for example, how σ, the job loss rate, affects the support for the two-tier system.

When σ goes to zero, $\hat{t}$ goes to infinity, so that (8.6) ends up being satisfied. For low values of σ, the two-tier system is always supported: incumbent employees know that their number will erode very slowly, so that the complete reform is very remote. Hence the lock-in result of the previous section is somewhat reversed. In the absence of a credibility problem, low exposure is likely to lead to lock-in. This is captured by the fact that *controlling* for t^*, the right-hand side of (8.6) is falling when σ increases, thus making reform more likely at high σ's. Whenever there is a credibility problem, however, a low exposure of incumbent employees enhances the credibility of the two-tier system because it guarantees that this group of workers will erode slowly enough so as to preserve their political influence over most of the transition path toward the fully flexible economy. At $\sigma = 0$, the complete reform never occurs, and the two-tier system is unambiguously supported. However, this is again an extreme result, because even if incumbent employees are fully protected their share in population will eventually go down because of retirements and new entrants.

How, then, does the political viability of reform vary with the turnover rate σ? When σ becomes large, the right-hand side of (8.6) ends up being monotonous. It can be shown that it is increasing if and only if

$$|\ln \theta| > \frac{\gamma}{r}. \tag{8.7}$$

If this condition holds, then the right-hand side of (8.6) is typically increasing. As illustrated in Figure 8.3, which plots the right-hand side of (8.6) as a function of σ, the reform is politically viable if and only if σ is low enough. So it is when incumbent employees are very sheltered that the reform is politically viable, contrary to what happened in the previous section. In this situation credibility effects are dominating. This situation is more likely to happen, the lower is θ, i.e. the greater the political power of incumbent employees—because the critical date is then more sensitive to σ; also the higher is r, the rate of time preference; and the lower is γ, the probability of falling into the low state.

If condition (8.7) does not hold, then we have a hump-shaped pattern as illustrated in Figure 8.4. At very low exposure rates, the credibility of the two-tier system is very high, so incumbent employees support it. At

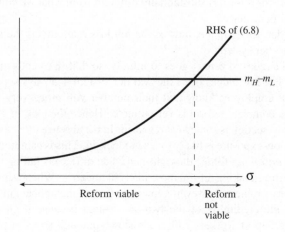

Figure 8.3. Impact of turnover on political viability of reform when credibility effects dominate

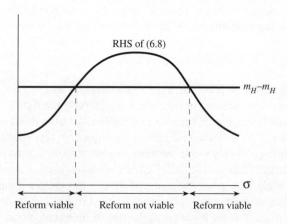

Figure 8.4. Impact of turnover on political viability of reform when credibility effects are not so strong

high exposure rates, they feel they benefit a lot from the increased job creation, as they fear to lose their jobs rather quickly. Therefore, they also support the two-tier system. At intermediate levels of exposure, however, the losses due to the relative lack of credibility of the system outweigh the gains associated with exposure; they end up opposing the two-tier system.

8.5 Impact of restrictions on the use of flexible contracts

In this section we examine a version of the two-tier system where a fraction μ of flexible contracts per unit of time must be converted into rigid contracts (we call this a 'conversion clause'). This resembles some real world arrangements where, for example, temporary contracts cannot be renewed as such for more than a limited period.

We want to make two points about the role of such restrictions. First, they may help to overcome the credibility problem that arises from the incentives to impose complete reform after a critical time. Second, they may naturally arise as an equilibrium outcome in situations where the two-tier system is unstable because holders of flexible contracts would prefer employment protection to be restored.

8.5.1 Conversion and credibility

If employees on flexible contracts must eventually be given a rigid one, the stock of rigid contracts no longer falls to zero as time passes. There is now, in addition to an outflow of rigid contracts due to the attrition of that stock, an inflow due to conversion of existing flexible contracts. This inflow slows the rate at which the stock of rigid contracts will decay, thus postponing the critical date $\hat{t}$ beyond which they do not hold political power.

Is it still the case that holders of flexible contracts support the complete reform? In the above case, they were actually indifferent, since they were already experiencing the wage and exposure levels of the flexible economy; full reform was only eliminating the deadweight mass of rigid workers in low productivity firms, while not affecting the rest of the economy. Now, however, things are different as the full reform also eliminates the flexible worker's prospects that their jobs will be converted into rigid ones. So it is no longer obvious whether flexible workers will support the full reform. The reform not only eliminates a deadweight but also genuinely increases the flexibility of all existing employment relationships.

In the appendix, we compute the gains and losses from a two-tier system with conversion clauses and we show that if it is true, as assumed in the previous section, that the flexible economy is a political equilibrium, then indeed flexible workers will support the complete reform of the labour market at $\hat{t}$.

Next, how will incumbent employees determine the conversion rate at the time of reform? Here they face a trade-off. On the one hand, a greater conversion rate postpones the time of complete reform, which allows them to enjoy their privileges over a longer period. On the other hand, the conversion rate affects wages and labour market tightness. A greater conversion rate makes it more likely that an entering firm will end up being forced to operate in the low productivity state, because the contract was converted into a rigid one when it was operating in the high productivity state. Thus, the greater the conversion rate, the lower the expected productivity of a firm over its lifetime, the lower the wage and the lower the job creation rate. Indeed, one can show (see the appendix) that the equilibrium wage is now given by

$$w = P(\mu)m_H + (1 - P(\mu))m_L.$$

That is, it is a weighted average of the high and low productivity levels. One can show that $P(\mu)$, the weight on the high productivity level, is a decreasing function of the conversion rate μ. As it increases from zero to infinity, w moves monotonically from m_H, the wage level prevailing in a fully flexible economy (or in the no-conversion two-tier system considered above), to $\bar{m}$, the wage level associated with the fully rigid economy. This is not surprising. A value of μ equal to zero means that flexible contracts remain so forever, so we are back to the case we have already analysed, while $\mu = \infty$ means that they become rigid the instant they are signed, which is equivalent to the no reform case.

Similarly, the rate of job creation a falls when μ increases, which reflects two effects. First, there is the usual positive effect of labour market tightness on wages that is implied by wage formation behaviour, and that we have already seen. Second, a higher value of μ means more employment security, meaning that unemployed workers can achieve the same utility level with a lower job finding rate. Formally, a can be written as an increasing function of w and a decreasing function of μ.

Therefore, conversion generates losses for incumbent employees, because it reduces the flexibility of new contracts, which harms their future job prospects and reduces their outside option in bargaining. The conversion clause will not be used if there is some way to write down in the law a minimum date before which complete reform cannot take place; in the appendix we formally show that in the absence of a credibility problem the incumbent employees' preferred value of μ is $\mu = 0$. But if this is impossible they may prefer a conversion clause to a quick erosion of their political influence.

It is actually possible to compute how the conversion clause affects the time of complete reform t^*, as well as the welfare of incumbent employed workers in low productivity firms; this, however, involves tedious numerical computations, that are described in the appendix. The numerical results suggest that in the zone of status quo bias, it is indeed likely that these workers would want to impose a conversion clause, which will substantially postpone the date of the complete reform. For example, with a given set of parameters,[5] in the absence of conversion clauses, complete reform occurs about five years after the introduction of the two-tier system. But if able to impose a conversion clause, initial insiders will write down into the law that about 11 per cent of flexible contracts must be converted into rigid ones each year, which postpones the critical date to more than twelve years after the reform. Because of this conversion clause, initial wages are about 5 per cent lower than in its absence (i.e. the flexible level m_H). This is moderate; but the job creation rate a, in turn, is substantially lower as a result of a conversion clause. The exit rate from unemployment jumps from its rigid level of 0.28 to 0.55, but this is much lower than the flexible level, 0.985, to which the economy would jump if μ were equal to zero instead of 11 per cent. A reduction of γ, the rate at which firms fall into the low state, from 0.2 to 0.1, induces them to elect a slightly higher value of μ (around 13 per cent) which in effect postpones the complete reform for ever. This is because a lower value of γ reduces the fraction of time spent by firms in the low productivity state, which mitigates the adverse effect of the conversion clause on wages, thus reducing its cost to incumbent workers. A higher rent, which increases their bias against flexibility, also induces them to choose a more stringent conversion clause ($\mu = 0.12$ instead of $\mu = 0.11$) which, despite being only marginally higher, is enough to postpone complete reform by more than sixteen years. Finally, an increase in σ, the exogenous rate of job loss, drastically increases the attrition rate of the original pool of rigid workers, thus considerably

[5] $\gamma = 0.2, \sigma = 0.05, \theta = 0.75, q = 0.7, r = 0.05, m_H = 3, m_L = 2.5$.

reducing the critical time t^* for any given value of μ. But, at the same time, a faster firm death reduces the likelihood that they will fall in the low productivity state, which mitigates the negative effect of the conversion clause on wages. So, workers can afford a more stringent conversion clause. They now want 22 per cent of flexible contracts to be converted into rigid ones. This leads to an initial wage loss of 4 per cent compared with $\mu = 0$, and postpones complete reform by eight years, whereas it would occur in three years in the absence of a conversion clause.

8.5.2 Conversion and instability

We now return to the case where the flexible economy is *not* a political equilibrium, that is if (8.4) does not hold. We have seen that, in such circumstances, incumbent employees gain from liberalizing new contracts, but flexible employees will eventually restore the original status quo. The economy is subjected to policy cycles, which result from the existence of conflicts of interests between flexible workers and rigid workers, as all want rigidity for themselves, but flexibility for others. The policy cycle arises from the fact that each group benefits from a measure that ends up reducing its size and thus its political influence.

One can show that a two-tier system with a conversion clause may end up emerging as a stable equilibrium, thus eliminating that instability. As shown in the appendix, the rigid workers' utility is decreasing with the conversion rate μ, while if (8.4) is violated by a sufficient margin,[6] the flexible workers' utility is increasing with μ. If the political power of one group exactly balances that of the other, then any value of μ can emerge as an equilibrium, since when people vote between two values, the flexible workers will always favour the high μ and the rigid ones will always prefer the low μ. Which one is stable? The one which yields subsequent dynamics which exactly preserve that balance of power. Consider, for example, the very simple case where the unemployed do not vote. Equilibrium is reached if flexible workers are exactly as numerous as rigid ones. Let l_f and l_r be the stock of flexible and rigid contracts, respectively. The evolution equation for the stock of rigid contracts is

$$\dot{l}_r = \mu l_f - \sigma l_r.$$

---

[6] More specifically, equation (A8.7b) must hold.

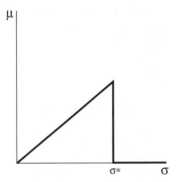

Figure 8.5. Impact of the turnover on the equilibrium conversion clause

The first term μl_f is the inflow of flexible contracts being turned into rigid ones. The last term σl_r is the outflow of rigid contracts being destroyed. In a steady state, l_r must be constant. In order for that to be compatible with the balance of power condition, $l_f = l_r$, it must be that

$$\mu = \sigma.$$

This defines a stable political equilibrium where the rate of conversion of flexible contracts is exactly equal to the job destruction rate. Contrary to some earlier results, this condition tells us that in some sense, the economy will be more rigid, the greater the exposure of rigid employees to unemployment. This is because the logic at work is quite different from earlier instances. Here the conversion rate is defined so as to compensate the erosion of the stock of rigid employees. An increase in σ increases rigidity because in a world where new hirees have flexible contracts, it boosts the stock of flexible workers, who support rigidity. Note, however, that when σ gets too large, flexible workers no longer support rigidity, since equation (4.25), which defined the condition for an employed worker to prefer rigidity to flexibility, no longer holds; past this threshold, which is given by the value of σ such that (4.25) holds exactly, i.e.

$$\sigma^* = \frac{rq}{m_H - m_L} - r,$$

the conversion rate μ will brutally drop to zero, at least as long as we ignore credibility problems.

Thus the response of the conversion rate μ to exposure σ is non-monotonic, as illustrated in Figure 8.5. Over the zone where flexible employees prefer rigidity, μ increases with σ; past this zone, it is equal to zero.

8.6 Summary

It is useful to summarize our findings regarding two-tier systems. Our key insight is that the availability of two-tier systems widens the scope for reform, because the contract conditions of the initial employees are preserved.

The least interesting case is a situation where rigidity is not a political equilibrium, either because all the employed support flexibility or because the employed in obsolete firms are not powerful enough. In such a case, a once-and-for-all complete reform is politically viable in the sense that it defeats the status quo. Even in that case, however, a two-tier system may arise, since, as we have seen, incumbent employees enjoy the best of both worlds: high wages, high job finding rates, and high employment security in their current job.

In the case where both rigidity and flexibility are political equilibria, the two-tier system allows the status quo bias to be overcome. The economy converges to a fully flexible one, and there is no incentive to revert to the original one. The gradual erosion of the initial stock of rigid workers may allow the policymaker to use flexible workers—who all work in high productivity firms—as a constituency to impose a further reform. But the prospect of this further reform may reduce the gains of the initial reform to incumbent employees, and even lead to their rejection of it. The use of conversion clauses allows one to build credibility into the design of the reform, but at the cost of a lower degree of flexibility, and therefore lower wages, productivity, and job creation, during the transition period to the complete reform.

In the case where only rigidity is a political equilibrium, the two-tier system is supported by incumbent employees, but is self-defeating. When employees with flexible contracts are sufficiently numerous to seize political power, they impose a return to the rigid economy. The economy may experience policy cycles, moving back and forth between liberalization at the margin and increases in employment protection. A conversion clause may lead the economy to a stable equilibrium instead of these cycles. At this stable equilibrium the conversion rate is such that it maintains a balance of power between rigid workers, who want flexibility for others, and flexible workers, who want rigidity for themselves.

Finally, the analysis leads to a reassessment of the role of exposure. Up to now the typical result was that low exposure of the employed to unemployment favours rigidity, as is implied by condition (4.25) or by the above discussion of policy lock-in in the case of low exposure. However, we have highlighted another effect, namely that at higher exposure levels the political power of employees in rigid contracts is eroded more quickly. This may lead, under various mechanisms, to a more rigid outcome, as a compensation. For example, when there is a credibility problem, high exposure may take the economy to a zone where the two-tier system is no longer politically viable, or may increase the conversion rate necessary to achieve political viability. Or, in the policy cycle case, higher job loss shifts the balance of power in favour of flexible workers, who favour rigidity, so that in equilibrium the conversion rate must increase in order to compensate for that.

A8.1 Computation of the employed's welfare under a critical time

Consider a worker in a low productivity firm. The evolution equation of his welfare is given by

$$r V_{eL}(t) = w + \sigma(V_u - V_{eL}(t)) + \mathrm{d}V_{eL}(t)/\mathrm{d}t, \qquad (A8.1)$$

where $w = m_H$ is the wage prevailing in the two-tier world, and V_u is the corresponding value of being unemployed, given by

$$V_u = V_{uf} = \frac{m_H - q}{r}.$$

In steady state, (A8.1) gives us the value V_{eL} by simply replacing $\mathrm{d}V_{eL}(t)/\mathrm{d}t$ with zero. However, if these workers anticipate that at a critical time t^* there will be a full reform of the labour market, in which case they lose their job and their utility falls to V_{uf}, their present discounted welfare will gradually fall to that level as t approaches t^*. The corresponding dynamics of $V_{eL}(t)$ are obtained by solving (A8.1) under the terminal condition that $V_{eL}(t^*) = V_{uf}$. This is a standard linear equation and its solution is

$$V_{eL}(t) = \mathrm{e}^{(r+\sigma)(t-t^*)} \frac{r V_u - w}{r + \sigma} + \frac{w + \sigma V_u}{r + \sigma}.$$

This may be rewritten as

$$V_{eL}(t) = e^{(r+\sigma)(t-t^*)} V_u + (1 - e^{(r+\sigma)(t-t^*)}) \frac{w + \sigma V_u}{r + \sigma},$$

which proves (8.5). The term $V_{ef}^T = \frac{w+\sigma V_u}{r+\sigma}$ is the present discounted utility of a worker who holds a job paying w until it gets destroyed, which happens with an instantaneous probability equal to σ. It is therefore equal to the utility of somebody who holds a rigid job in the flexible economy if complete reform never occurs. Given that $w = m_H$ and $V_u = V_{uf} = \frac{m_H - q}{r}$, we can compute V_{ef}^T as

$$V_{ef}^T = \frac{m_H}{r} - \frac{\sigma q}{r(r + \sigma)}.$$

These people will support the introduction of the two-tier system at date $t = 0$ if and only if $V_{eL}(0) > V_{er}$, or equivalently

$$e^{-(r+\sigma)t^*} \frac{m_H - q}{r} + (1 - e^{-(r+\sigma)t^*}) \left(\frac{m_H}{r} - \frac{\sigma q}{r(r + \sigma)} \right)$$
$$> \frac{\bar{m}}{r} - q \frac{\sigma}{r(r + \sigma)}.$$

This may be rewritten as (8.6).

A8.2 Computation of equilibrium under a conversion clause

We now consider what happens when a flexible contract must be converted to a rigid one with probability μ per unit of time. This implies that during any interval dt a fraction μdt of all flexible contracts become rigid. At $\mu = 0$ we have the above system, while at $\mu = \infty$ flexible contracts must become rigid the day they are signed, so it is as if they did not exist.

How is the analysis modified? Firms can now be in one of three states. First, they can have a flexible contract and be in the high productivity state. Second, they can have a rigid contract and be in the high productivity state. Third, they can have a rigid contract and be in the low productivity state. A firm in the low productivity state that has a flexible contract will never want to continue, as competition drives wages at a level $w > m_L$.

The value of a rigid firm in the low state is clearly given by

$$J_{rL} = \frac{m_L - w}{r + \sigma}, \tag{4.14}$$

as in Chapter 4. The value of a rigid firm in the high state still obeys equation (4.15):

$$r J_{rH} = m_H - w - \sigma J_{rH} + \gamma (J_{rL} - J_{rH}). \tag{4.15}$$

Finally, the value of a flexible firm in the high state is given by

$$r J_{fH} = m_H - w + \mu \left[J_{rH} - J_{fH} \right] + \sigma \left[-J_{fH} \right]. \tag{A8.2}$$

The term $\mu \left[J_{rH} - J_{fH} \right]$ represents the capital loss being made when the firm is forced to convert its contract into a rigid one, which occurs with a probability μ per unit of time. Eliminating the firm's values between (4.14), (4.15), and (A8.2) and using the free entry condition $J_{fH} = 0$ we can compute the equilibrium wage:

$$
\begin{aligned}
w = \bar{w}(\mu) = {} & \frac{(r + \gamma + \sigma + \mu)(r + \sigma)}{(r + \gamma + \sigma)(r + \sigma + \mu)} m_H \\
& + \frac{\gamma \mu}{(r + \gamma + \sigma)(r + \sigma + \mu)} m_L.
\end{aligned} \tag{A8.3}
$$

Just as in Chapter 4, wages are a weighted average of the high and low productivity levels, with weights reflecting the appropriately discounted fraction of time that a new entrant expects to spend in each state. These weights now depend on μ, the conversion rate. An increase in μ reduces the weight on the high productivity state and increases the weight on the low productivity one, as the firm expects to have a rigid contract more quickly, which increases the likelihood that it will be forced to operate in the low productivity state. At $\mu = 0$ this equation is equivalent to $w = m_H$, the fully flexible wage, while as μ goes to infinity it converges to $w = \bar{m}$, the rigid one.

We can now compute the utility of workers. The employed now differ according to whether they hold a flexible or a rigid contract. The welfare of a worker who has a flexible contract is given by

$$r V_{ef} = w + \mu \left[V_{er} - V_{ef} \right] + (\sigma + \gamma) \left[V_u - V_{ef} \right],$$

where V_{er} denotes the utility of a worker who has a rigid contract. The term $\mu \left[V_{er} - V_{ef} \right]$ is the contribution of the capital gain made when the contract is made rigid, which again happens with probability μ per unit of time. V_{er} and V_u, the value of being unemployed, follow the same evolution equations as in Chapter 4:

$$r V_{er} = w + \sigma \left[V_u - V_{er} \right],$$

and

$$r V_u = a \left[V_{ef} - V_u \right].$$

Using the wage formation equation $w = r V_u + q$ we are now able to solve for the welfare of the three types of worker:

$$V_u = \frac{w - q}{r}$$

$$V_{er} = \frac{w}{r} - \frac{\sigma q}{r(r + \sigma)} \tag{A8.4}$$

$$V_{ef} = \frac{w}{r} - \frac{q}{r(r + \sigma)} \frac{\sigma \mu + (r + \sigma)(\sigma + \gamma)}{r + \mu + \sigma + \gamma}. \tag{A8.5}$$

Finally, we can also compute the equilibrium value of labour market tightness a

$$a = \left(\frac{w}{q} - 1 \right)(r + \sigma) \frac{r + \mu + \sigma + \gamma}{r + \mu + \sigma}.$$

Equation (A8.4) implies that given the wage, the frequency with which holders of rigid contracts lose their rent is unaffected by μ. Holders of rigid contracts want the wage to be as high as possible, just as the unemployed. This is achieved by having μ as low as possible, i.e. $\mu = 0$. Hence, if you already have a rigid contract, you want flexible contracts to be as flexible as possible.

By contrast, holders of flexible contracts may support the conversion clause, since it increases their employment security at the cost of lower wages. They face the same wage–exposure trade-off as analysed in Chapter 4. When μ increases the first term in (A8.5) falls but so does the last, negative term.

To know what is the preferred value of μ for workers with flexible contracts, we need to compute $\partial V_{ef} / \partial \mu$. We get

$$\partial V_{ef} / \partial \mu = \frac{-\gamma(r + \sigma)(r + \sigma + \gamma)(m_H - m_L)}{r[(r + \gamma + \sigma)(r + \sigma + \mu)]^2}$$

$$+ q \frac{\gamma}{(r + \sigma)(r + \mu + \sigma + \gamma)^2}.$$

This expression has the same sign as the following quadratic function of μ:

$$qr(r+\sigma+\mu)^2(r+\sigma+\gamma)-(r+\sigma)^2(m_H-m_L)(r+\mu+\sigma+\gamma)^2. \quad \text{(A8.6)}$$

One has to distinguish two cases.

Case 1. If the coefficient on μ^2 is positive, then this expression is convex. It is then either always positive, in which case $\partial V_{ef}/\partial\mu > 0$ for all μ and the flexible worker's preferred value of μ is $\mu = +\infty$; or first positive, then negative, then positive again. Note then that for $\mu = -(r+\sigma)$ it is negative, so that the first zone only contains negative values of μ. Consequently, in this case $\partial V_{ef}/\partial\mu$ is either always positive or first negative then positive as μ varies from zero to infinity, implying that the optimal value of μ is either $\mu = 0$ or $\mu = \infty$.

By gathering all terms in μ^2 we see that this regime will prevail if and only if $qr(r+\sigma+\gamma)-(r+\sigma)^2(m_H-m_L) > 0$, or equivalently

$$m_H - m_L < \frac{rq(r+\sigma+\gamma)}{(r+\sigma)^2}. \quad \text{(A8.7)}$$

Case 2. If condition (A8.7) does not hold, then the above expression is concave. It is then either always negative, in which case $\partial V_{ef}/\partial\mu < 0$ for all μ and the flexible worker's preferred value of μ is $\mu = 0$; or first negative, then positive, then negative again. In this case, however, substituting the contrary of (A8.7) into (A8.6) is enough to prove that $\partial V_{ef}/\partial\mu < 0$ for all μ. Thus in that case flexible workers unambiguously prefer $\mu = 0$.

To conclude, for any set of parameters the flexible worker's preferred level of μ is either $\mu = 0$ or $\mu = \infty$, that is no conversion at all or no flexible contracts at all. To determine which one is their preferred level, they just make the same computations as in Chapter 4. Thus, given that they are working in high productivity firms, they will prefer $\mu = \infty$ if and only if

$$m_H - m_L < rq/(r+\sigma). \quad \text{(4.25)}$$

If their preferred level is $\mu = 0$ then they will vote in favour of the complete elimination of rigid contracts after the relevant critical date $\hat{t}$. If they prefer $\mu = \infty$, then we are in the case of policy cycles: rigid workers want new contracts to be flexible, but flexible workers eventually impose employment protection for themselves.

Finally, note that if

$$m_H - m_L < rq/(r+\sigma+\gamma), \quad \text{(A8.7b)}$$

then (A8.7) holds and (A8.6) is positive at $\mu = 0$. In that case $\partial V_e / \partial \mu > 0$ for any value of μ.

A8.3 Critical times and conversion clause

In this section we describe how the numerical simulations discussed in the text were obtained. In order to compute the incumbent employee's utility if there is a critical time after which complete reform prevails and if there is a conversion clause, we have to take the following steps.

First, one has to note that between $t = 0$ and $t = t^*$, the value of a firm evolves according to the following equations:

$$r J_{fH}(t) = m_H - w(t) + \mu(J_{rH}(t) - J_{fH}(t)) + (\sigma + \gamma)(-J_{fH}(t))$$
$$+ \frac{dJ_{rH}(t)}{dt}$$

$$r J_{rH}(t) = m_H - w(t) + \gamma(J_{rL}(t) - J_{rH}(t)) - \sigma J_{rH}(t) + \frac{dJ_{rH}(t)}{dt}$$

$$r J_{rL}(t) = m_L - w(t) + \sigma(-J_{rL}(t)) + \frac{dJ_{rL}(t)}{dt},$$

where J_{fH} is the value of a flexible firm in the high state, J_{rH} the value of a rigid firm in the high state, and J_{rL} the value of a rigid firm in the low state. A flexible firm in the high state can either become rigid, because of conversion, which happens with probability μ per unit of time, or simply disappear, which happens with probability γ per unit of time. Note that it will never elect to continue if it falls into the low state, as being flexible allows it to close.

The free entry condition implies $J_{fH}(t) = 0$ at all times, so that the first equation is equivalent to

$$w(t) = m_H + \mu J_{rH}(t).$$

Substituting this into the other two equations, and noting that at $t = t^*$ both J_{rH} and J_{rL} must satisfy the boundary condition $J_{rH}(t^*) = J_{rL}(t^*) = 0$, one is able to solve for the time path of $J_{rL}(t)$, $J_{rH}(t)$, and therefore $w(t)$. We get

$$w(t) = \bar{w}(\mu) + \frac{m_H - m_L}{r + \sigma + \gamma} \frac{\mu\gamma}{\mu - \gamma} e^{-(r+\sigma+\gamma)(t^*-t)}$$
$$+ \frac{m_H - m_L}{r + \sigma + \mu} \frac{\gamma\mu}{\gamma - \mu} e^{-(r+\sigma+\mu)(t^*-t)}, \tag{A8.8}$$

where $\bar{w}(\mu)$ is the wage that would prevail if the two-tier system prevailed for ever; that is, it is the wage defined by equation (A8.3).

Turning now to workers, the evolution equations for their welfare are given by, between $t = 0$ and $t = t^*$:

$$r V_{ef}(t) = w(t) + \mu \left(V_{erH}(t) - V_{ef}(t) \right)$$
$$+ (\sigma + \gamma)(V_u(t) - V_{ef}(t)) + \frac{dV_{ef}(t)}{dt}; \quad (A8.9)$$

$$r V_u(t) = a(t) \left(V_{ef}(t) - V_u(t) \right) + \frac{dV_u(t)}{dt}; \quad (A8.10)$$

$$r V_{erH}(t) = w(t) + \gamma(V_{erL}(t) - V_{erH}(t))$$
$$+ \sigma(V_u(t) - V_{erH}(t)) + \frac{dV_{erH}(t)}{dt}; \quad (A8.11)$$

$$r V_{erL}(t) = w(t) + \sigma(V_u(t) - V_{erL}(t)) + \frac{dV_{erL}(t)}{dt}. \quad (A8.12)$$

In the above equations, $V_{ef}(t)$ is the value of having flexible contracts, which necessarily occurs in a high productivity firm; $V_u(t)$ is the value of being unemployed; $V_{erH}(t)$ the value of holding a rigid contract in a high productivity firm; and $V_{erL}(t)$ the value of holding a rigid contract in a low productivity firm. The corresponding terminal conditions are

$$V_u(t^*) = V_{erL}(t^*) = V_{uf} = \frac{m_H - q}{r} \quad (A8.13)$$

$$V_{erH}(t^*) = V_{ef}(t^*) = V_{ef} = \frac{m_H}{r} - \frac{q(\sigma + \gamma)}{r(r + \sigma + \gamma)}. \quad (A8.14)$$

It should be noted that $V_{erH}(t) \neq V_{erL}(t)$. Workers in low productivity firms, who hold a rigid contract, expect to be laid off when the complete reform occurs. This is not the case for their counterparts in high productivity firms.

Finally, the wage formation equation implies that at any point in time:

$$V_u(t) = \frac{w(t) - q}{r}. \quad (A8.15)$$

The above differential equations are linear and allow us to solve for the time path of all the value functions and of $a(t)$ between 0 and t^*. Using (A8.15),(A8.9),(A8.11),(A8.12), and (A8.8), as well as the boundary conditions (A8.13)–(A8.14), yields

$$V_{erL}(t) = \left(\frac{\bar{w}(\mu)}{r} - \frac{\sigma q}{r(r + \sigma)} \right) + \left(\frac{m_H - m_L}{r} - \frac{q}{r + \sigma} \right) e^{-(r + \sigma)(t^* - t)}$$

$$+\frac{m_H - m_L}{r + \sigma + \gamma} \frac{\mu(r + \sigma)}{r(\gamma - \mu)} \mathrm{e}^{-(r+\sigma+\gamma)(t^*-t)}$$

$$+\frac{m_H - m_L}{r + \sigma + \mu} \frac{\gamma(r + \sigma)}{r(\mu - \gamma)} \mathrm{e}^{-(r+\sigma+\mu)(t^*-t)}$$

$$V_{erH}(t) = \left(\frac{\bar{w}(\mu)}{r} - \frac{\sigma q}{r(r + \sigma)}\right)$$

$$+ \left(\frac{m_H - m_L}{r} - \frac{q}{r + \sigma}\right) \mathrm{e}^{-(r+\sigma)(t^*-t)}$$

$$+ \left[\frac{m_H - m_L}{r + \sigma + \gamma} \frac{\mu(r + \sigma)}{r(\gamma - \mu)} + \frac{q}{r + \sigma + \gamma}\right] \mathrm{e}^{-(r+\sigma+\gamma)(t^*-t)}$$

$$+ \frac{m_H - m_L}{r + \sigma + \mu} \frac{\gamma(r + \sigma)}{r(\mu - \gamma)} \mathrm{e}^{-(r+\sigma+\mu)(t^*-t)}$$

$$V_{ef}(t) = \left(\frac{\bar{w}(\mu)}{r} - \frac{\sigma q}{r(r + \sigma)} - \frac{\gamma q}{(r + \sigma)(r + \sigma + \gamma + \mu)}\right)$$

$$+ \left(\frac{\mu(m_H - m_L)}{r(\gamma + \mu)} - \frac{\mu q}{(r + \sigma)(\gamma + \mu)}\right) \mathrm{e}^{-(r+\sigma)(t^*-t)}$$

$$+ \left[\frac{(m_H - m_L)\left[\gamma(r + \sigma + \gamma) - \mu(r + \sigma)\right]}{r(r + \sigma + \gamma)(\mu - \gamma)}\right.$$

$$\left. + \frac{q}{r + \sigma + \gamma}\right] \mathrm{e}^{-(r+\sigma+\gamma)(t^*-t)}$$

$$+ \frac{m_H - m_L}{r + \sigma + \mu} \frac{\mu\gamma}{r(\gamma - \mu)} \mathrm{e}^{-(r+\sigma+\mu)(t^*-t)}$$

$$+ \left[\frac{(m_H - m_L)\gamma}{r(\gamma + \mu)} - \frac{\gamma q}{(\gamma + \mu)(r + \sigma + \gamma + \mu)}\right] \mathrm{e}^{-(r+\sigma+\gamma+\mu)(t^*}$$

$$V_u(t) = \frac{\bar{w}(\mu) - q}{r}$$

$$+ \frac{m_H - m_L}{r(r + \sigma + \gamma)} \frac{\mu\gamma}{\mu - \gamma} \mathrm{e}^{-(r+\sigma+\gamma)(t^*-t)}$$

$$+ \frac{m_H - m_L}{r(r + \sigma + \mu)} \frac{\gamma\mu}{\gamma - \mu} \mathrm{e}^{-(r+\sigma+\mu)(t^*-t)}.$$

With these formulas, it is straightforward to derive the time path for labour market tightness $a(t)$ by using (A8.10). Once this is done, a time path for employment in each state is computed by using the evolution equations of the employment levels, given by

$$\frac{\mathrm{d}l_f(t)}{\mathrm{d}t} = a(t)(1 - l_f(t) - l_{rH}(t) - l_{rL}(t)) - (\mu + \sigma + \gamma)l_f(t)$$

$$\frac{\mathrm{d}l_{rH}(t)}{\mathrm{d}t} = \mu l_f(t) - (\sigma + \gamma)l_{rH}(t)$$

$$\frac{\mathrm{d}l_{rL}(t)}{\mathrm{d}t} = \gamma l_{rH}(t) - \sigma l_{rL}(t).$$

This procedure allows us to compute total employment in rigid contracts at $t = t^*$, $l_{rL}(t^*) + l_{rH}(t^*)$. For an equilibrium to obtain it must be that this yields a value exactly equal to $\theta l_r(0)$. If this is not so, one has to iterate the procedure to find the right value of t^*. The procedure is iterated by dichotomy, with the new t^* being greater (smaller) whenever $l_{rL}(t^*) + l_{rH}(t^*) > (<)\theta l_r(0)$. This procedure has converged in all our simulations.

9

Politico-economic complementarities

The previous chapters have analysed the conditions under which various labour market institutions would arise. The present one asks whether we expect them to work together or not. For example, do we expect to see employment protection in places where the minimum wage is high or in places where it is low? Are active labour market policies more likely to prevail when unemployment benefits are more generous or not?...and so on.

To get an answer to such questions, we have to study the extent to which labour market institutions are *complements*.[1] Two institutions are complements, in the politico-economic sense, if the existence of one of them increases the political support for the other, and vice versa. When there is such complementarity, we expect institutions to work together, implying that different societies or countries will adopt different social models, (for example the 'American model', or the 'Scandinavian model', or the 'Japanese model', etc.), where by 'model' we mean a whole, coherent set of institutions.

An important message is that it is important for the policymaker to recognize the existence of such complementarities, because a comprehensive reform of the labour market where all institutions are changed at the same time will then be more viable than a piecemeal reform, since part of the support for a given institution comes from the existence of the other ones.

The main, broad conclusion of this chapter is that there are good reasons to believe that there exist complementarities across institutions that are 'rigid'—in the sense of reducing the incentives for job creation—although this does not apply uniformly to all institutions. In some cases,

---

[1] Coe and Snower (1997) have analysed the role of complementarities, in a somewhat different context.

the theoretical case in favour of complementarities is much weaker than in others.

9.1 The exposure–rents–protection nexus

One important source of complementarities across labour market rigidities involves the interactions between rents, exposure to unemployment, and employment protection. In Chapter 2 we have seen that rents will be higher when insiders are less exposed to unemployment. In Chapter 4 we have seen that a higher rent increases the political support for employment protection, and that employment protection reduces exposure to unemployment. Consequently, employment protection and rent-creating institutions mutually reinforce each other.

To illustrate this, let us return to the model of employment protection introduced in Chapter 4 and ask what would happen if the employed also set the rent, as is the case in Chapter 2. As long as the marginal product of labour does not depend on employment, the result of Chapter 1 still holds: the employed want to set the lowest possible value of the rent, $q = 0$. This is clear from formula (4.1). So, to get some support for the rent, we again need to assume a negative relationship between the marginal product and employment, which was done in Chapters 2 and 3 by assuming the existence of another group of people, group B.

Here we take a shortcut to simplify matters and directly postulate a positive relationship between the marginal product of labour and the rent q, although such a relationship is a reduced form of the general equilibrium effects of q on employment and wages.

More specifically, we assume that productivity in the high state is given by $m_H(q)$, where m_H is increasing and concave. Productivity in the low state is $m_L(q) = m_H(q) - \delta$, where δ is a positive constant. Therefore, the productivity differential between the two states is unaffected by the rent. The wage level of the rigid society is then given by equation (4.19), which is equivalent to

$$\bar{m} = m_H - \frac{\gamma \delta}{r + \sigma + \gamma}.$$

The optimal rent, from the employed's point of view, is simply obtained by maximizing the employed's utility, given by (4.20b) and (4.18b) in the rigid and flexible economies, respectively. The first-order condition is

$$m'(q) = \frac{s}{r+s},$$

where s is the relevant separation rate, equal to σ in the rigid economy and to $\sigma + \gamma$ in the flexible one. Clearly, $s/(r+s)$, the marginal cost of rents, is higher in the flexible economy, which will end up with a higher value of $m'(q)$ and therefore a lower value of q. This is just a special case of the result in Chapter 2 which told us that higher exposure reduced the optimal rent.

So, in the flexible economy the insiders will choose a rent q_f which is strictly lower than the one, q_r, that they would pick in the rigid economy:

$$q_f < q_r.$$

Now, recall that for a given value of the rent, and assuming that workers in high productivity firms are politically decisive, the rigid economy is a political equilibrium if and only if equation (4.25) holds, which we can rewrite as

$$\delta < \frac{rq}{r+\sigma}.$$

If the following inequality holds:

$$\frac{rq_f}{r+\sigma} < \delta < \frac{rq_r}{r+\sigma}, \tag{9.1}$$

then in each society (rigid or flexible), the rent elected by incumbent workers is consistent with their preferred level of employment protection, in the sense that given that rent, they do not want to change the employment protection level.

Does that imply that the complementarity between rents and employment protection might lead to the coexistence of a high rent/high protection equilibrium and a low rent/low protection one? So far, the answer is no. When evaluating the gains and losses of flexibility and rigidity, the decisive voter will fully take into account the fact that if employment protection changes, so will the rent, so that one should compare the utility of being employed in the rigid society, given by (4.20b), or equivalently

$$r V_{er}(q_r) = m_H(q_r) - q_r \frac{\sigma}{r+\sigma} - \frac{\gamma \delta}{r+\sigma+\gamma},$$

with that of the flexible society, given by (4.18b), or

$$r V_{ef}(q_f) = m_H(q_f) - q_f \frac{\sigma + \gamma}{r+\sigma+\gamma}.$$

Computing these two formulas one gets a threshold value of δ, δ^*, below which rigidity is preferred, and above which flexibility is preferred.[2] So there is only one equilibrium. Complementarities do not generate multiple equilibria; they simply tell us that we expect a high level of employment protection to be associated with a high rent. One prediction is that if one could plot employment protection against rents in a cross section of countries, one would find a positive association.

A formula like (9.1) is only relevant when it is considered that the rent, which is optimal given the initial status quo, will not change after the reform. While this is an extreme case, multiple equilibria may still arise whenever there is a problem in coordinating the change in the rent and the change in the employment protection level. For example, once employment protection has been removed, it may take a while to adjust other labour market institutions, so that the rent will remain equal to q_r for some time. The longer this time, the more incumbent employees will use a formula like (9.1) rather than a comparison between δ and δ^* in order to figure out which is their most preferred arrangement.

Labour market reform may therefore be blocked if the policymaker fails to put both issues at the same time on the political agenda. Complementarities imply that a comprehensive reform is more likely to be successful than a partial one. But the above model is not explicit about what obstacles such a comprehensive reform might encounter. If $\delta > \delta^*$ and the economy is initially rigid, there will be support for such a comprehensive reform. Again, so far, complementarities are not an obstacle to reform; they are a property of some subset of institutions that tell us that they will be observed together and must be changed in a coordinated fashion.

For completeness, we shall also mention another source of complementarity between rents and employment protection, which is more well known; namely the fact that by increasing turnover costs, employment protection increases the total surplus of existing firm/worker matches— the difference between their value and the alternative value of splitting the match and forming another one with an outsider. Higher turnover costs implies that there is more 'specificity' involved in the firm/worker relationship, because closing it is more costly. Because the surplus over which to bargain is larger, so is the rent that the worker is able to grab. This is clear from the 'insider' models of wage formation outlined in the appendix to Chapter 1.

---

[2] The formula is $\delta^* = \frac{r+\sigma+\gamma}{\gamma}(m_H(q_r) - m_H(q_f) + q_f \frac{\sigma+\gamma}{r+\gamma+\sigma} - q_r \frac{\sigma}{r+\sigma})$.

This complementarity mechanism is more 'automatic' than the previous one. It is not politico-economic in nature; indeed we are not dealing with a complementarity between two institutions on which people vote, rather with the fact that employment protection also increases the rent. In this book, we have not considered this fact, because we wanted to have a clear analytical distinction between institutions that lower turnover and institutions that increase rents. But in practice, the distinction is not so clear cut, and any tax on job separations automatically improves the worker's bargaining position.

9.2 A counterexample: unemployment benefits

Now, there is no general result that tells us that there exists a complementarity across all 'rigidities'—across all institutions that reduce job creation. Indeed, in Chapter 5, we saw that if insurance effects dominate, the logic driving unemployment benefits is the opposite of that driving other rigidities. One can similarly show that, in similar circumstances, a rise in other rigidities may reduce the support for unemployment benefits.

Take, for example, employment protection. It reduces exposure to unemployment, and therefore the employed's support for unemployment benefits, as we saw in Chapter 5.

Consider now an institution that allows wages to be set to their optimal level. As we saw in Chapter 5, if such an institution is set optimally, the first-order condition for unemployment benefits is the same as in the pure insurance case:

$$\frac{u'(w(1-\tau))}{u'(b)} = \frac{a}{r+p+a}\frac{s}{s+p} < 1. \tag{5.4}$$

Let $\rho = b/(w(1-\tau))$. ρ is the replacement ratio, i.e. the ratio between the income of an unemployed and the net income of an employed. If u is isoelastic, that is $u(c) = c^{\alpha}/\alpha$, then this formula is equivalent to

$$\rho = \left(\frac{a}{r+p+a}\frac{s}{s+p}\right)^{1/(1-\alpha)}. \tag{9.2}$$

This defines a positive relationship between ρ, the replacement ratio, and a, the job finding rate. This relationship must hold across all economies that have the same values of s and p, provided wage-setting institutions are set optimally in all these economies. Let us compare, for example, two economies, economy 1 and economy 2. Assume that economy 1 has a higher wage, say because labour demand is less responsive to wages. Then the job finding rate a is smaller in economy 1, and (9.2) tells us that the employed will like to set the unemployment benefit replacement ratio ρ at a lower level than in economy 2—which partly offsets the negative effect of wages on job finding.

The inference is clear: because unemployment is higher in economy 1, the tax cost of financing a given level of unemployment benefits is larger, so that people end up voting for a lower replacement ratio.

This suggests that there is a substitutability between rents—or any institutions creating real wage rigidity—and unemployment benefits. This may appear problematic in the light of the observation that countries with rigid real wages and powerful insiders also tend to have a high level of unemployment benefits.[3]

This raises the question: can we identify some mechanisms that would allow for a complementarity between rents and unemployment benefits?

One might think that higher unemployment increases the demand for unemployment benefits, which would provide a natural complementarity between these and real wage rigidity. But this is in fact a fallacy. Unemployment increases the demand for benefits only if it is associated with a rise in exposure s, not if it is associated with a fall in job finding a.

It is true that increased wages reduce a while leaving s unaffected only because we have assumed an exogenous job separation rate. If s was endogenous, one would also find that it typically increases when labour costs are higher—jobs are destroyed more often because they are more likely to become unprofitable. This is indeed what is implied by the model depicted in the appendix to Chapter 4. At best, this gives us an ambiguous result relative to the net effect of increased wages on ρ. While the associated fall in a reduces the demand for unemployment insurance, the increase in s increases it. But, because of the complementarity between rents and employment protection, an increase in the rent will trigger an increase in employment protection, so that on balance s is more likely to decrease. This argument is therefore unlikely to overturn the basic substitutability result.

More progress can be made if one reintroduces wage and employ-

---

[3] Compare Europe with the USA, although within Europe there appears to be some substitutability between employment protection and unemployment benefits.

ment effects, and assumes that the rent cannot be set at its optimal level. Complementarities between rents and benefits may arise if a higher rent boosts the wage-bidding power of benefits, that is if dw/db is greater, and/or da/db smaller, when the rent increases. To check that, we have run numerical simulations using the model of Chapter 5. We have assumed a fixed total rent Q, an isoelastic utility function $u(c) = c^\alpha/\alpha$, and an isoelastic dependence of wages on employment, $w(l) = m_0 l^{-\eta}$. These simulations suggest that, if labour demand is not too inelastic, over most of the relevant range for Q, an exogenous increase in the rent is associated with a higher optimal replacement ratio for the employed. Interestingly, this is less likely to happen when risk aversion is larger, suggesting that such complementarity is not due to a greater desire for insurance.

Another case for complementarity between unemployment benefits and rents could be made when the unemployed's search intensity is endogenized. This argument holds in a situation where the rent is no longer fixed, but depends positively on the degree of labour market tightness a, as is the case in the matching/bargaining models described in the appendix to Chapter 1, where a tighter labour market increases the hiring cost (because it is a search cost), and therefore the total surplus appropriable by workers in bargaining. In such a world, reducing the unemployed's search intensity reduces competition for jobs. It makes it more likely that a job searcher of a given intensity finds a job, and less likely that a firm finds a worker. That is, it makes the labour market tighter. Now, if unemployment benefits reduce search intensity, then the insiders will want to use them in order to increase tightness, hiring costs, and consequently the rent they earn. Higher benefits also mean higher rents. This effect is stronger, the greater the share going to workers in the bargaining process, that is, the greater their ability to grab rents. If that share was equal to zero they would just be paid their outside option and increasing benefits would have no effects on the rent.

This logic is illustrated in Figure 9.1. On the horizontal axis is a, the labour market tightness parameter. It is no longer defined as the probability of finding a job, but as the probability of finding a job for an unemployed worker who would put a *fixed*, unit level of effort into the search process. On the vertical axis there is x, the search intensity of the unemployed. The upward sloping locus UU describes the unemployed's optimal choice for their search intensity x. This locus is upward sloping, because a higher value of a increases the employed's rent, i.e. the capital gain made when finding a job, and therefore the incentives

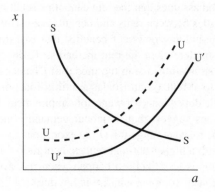

Figure 9.1. Impact of an increase in benefits on search intensity and tightness

to search. The downward sloping curve SS tells us that there is a trade-off between search intensity and labour market tightness. An increase in search intensity given tightness increases total employment, which, under decreasing returns, must reduce wages. But insiders can only be induced to accept lower wages if the labour market is less tight.

An increase in unemployment benefits typically reduces the unemployed's incentives to search, given the rent.[4] If we are willing to assume this, then, as Figure 9.1 makes clear, an increase in benefits shifts UU downwards to U'U', increasing tightness a. This is a standard argument, but the key point from a political economy point of view is that the increase in tightness may then benefit incumbent employees, because it allows them to obtain a higher rent.

---

[4] While this may sound obvious, this is only true if marginal search costs increase with consumption. The standard, partial equilibrium argument that benefits reduce search intensity assumes that the rent actually goes down, because wages do not increase while benefits do increase. In general equilibrium models where wage formation is taken into account, the rent may or may not go down. But to make an argument that search intensity increases given the rent, we clearly need to use another mechanism. That mechanism simply assumes that the opportunity cost of search increases when benefits are higher, because it depends positively on consumption.

9.3 Complementarities across institutions set by competing groups: the epidemics of rigidity

While, again, we should be cautious about assuming that complementarities are enough to generate multiple equilibria, this may indeed occur if institutions are set by several competing interest groups that do not coordinate among themselves. This is relevant as in many cases labour market institutions are not set by law but determined by bargaining between employees' and employers' representatives at the sector level.

It is known that bargaining at such a level typically leads to too high real wages and unemployment, relative to either more centralized and/or more decentralized bargaining, because workers do not take into account the negative externality exerted by their sector's higher price level on other sectors' workers, see Calmfors and Driffill (1988).

In this section we analyse what happens when employment protection is set by incumbent insiders at the sector level, in a fashion uncoordinated with other sectors. We show that the desired level of rigidity is greater, the more rigid the rest of the economy; there is a complementarity between rigidity in one sector and rigidity in other sectors. Consequently, lack of coordination in setting employment protection is likely to lead to multiple equilibria. An equilibrium where protection is high because job creation is low because protection is high may exist, but people could coordinate on a 'better' equilibrium with low employment protection but high job creation.

In Chapter 4 employment protection was set at the central level by majority voting among workers. They were fully taking into account the general equilibrium effects of their decisions on wages and job prospects; multiple steady states could arise because of the status quo bias generated by the constituency effect. But, given the status quo, a single equilibrium outcome prevailed. And, if workers in low productivity firms were not politically decisive, then the stationary political equilibrium was also unique.

The story might be quite different if employment protection legislation is not set at the central level. Under many circumstances, incumbent employees in a given sector will want more employment protection if it is more difficult to find a job elsewhere. But a greater level of employment protection in their sector reduces hirings and therefore the job finding rate of workers who are currently employed in other sectors. It therefore reinforces other workers' incentives to choose a high employment protection level, thus further reducing the job finding rate, and so on. In the process just described, employment protection spreads from one sector to another like an epidemy: my employment protection reduces your job prospects, and makes such an institution more attractive to you.

To make the argument more formal, let us use the model of Chapter 4 and assume that there is a large number of sectors, and that within each sector the employed decide on the level of employment protection that will prevail, taking as given institutions in other sectors. As in Chapter 4, firms fall into a low productivity state with probability γ per unit of time; they are then allowed to close if the economy is flexible but cannot do so if it is rigid. The job loss rate is again $\gamma + \sigma$ in the rigid society and just σ in the flexible one. Again as in Chapter 4, free entry by firms determine the wages paid by each sector. Therefore, the wage will be $w = m_H$ if the sector becomes rigid and $w = \bar{m}$ if it becomes flexible.

The key difference between the decision problem faced by the employed here and the one they faced in Chapter 4 is that institutions in a given sector have little impact on aggregate economic performance. For simplicity, we assume that each sector is small enough so that its workers do not take into account the impact of the employment protection level they choose on economywide labour market conditions. In particular, they consider that the value of being unemployed—which is relevant to them as they might lose their jobs—is unaffected by their sector's employment protection level. This would not be true if workers who lose their jobs have a large probability of finding a job in the sector where they were originally employed. But to make our point most clearly and simply it is best to assume that such probability is negligible.

Equation (1.4) in Chapter 1 allows us to compute the welfare of an employed worker as a function of his wage, his job loss probability, and the value of being unemployed. In steady state, we get

$$V_e = \frac{w + s V_u}{r + s}.$$ (9.3)

Therefore, if the sector opts for rigidity, the employed's welfare is

$$V_e^r = \frac{\bar{m} + \sigma V_u}{r + \sigma},$$ (9.4)

whereas if it decides not to have employment protection the employed's welfare will be

$$V_e^f = \frac{m_H + (\sigma + \gamma) V_u}{r + \sigma + \gamma}.$$ (9.5)

When deciding on their preferred level of employment protection, the insiders compare (9.4) and (9.5), *taking V_u as given,* instead of (4.18b) and (4.20b). In Chapter 4, people were considering that their decision had general equilibrium effects on V_u, i.e. they were not using the same value of V_u in both computations, thus using (4.18b) and (4.20b). Here these effects are neglected.

At this stage it is necessary to clarify the notation. A superscript r or f refers to the arrangement elected by an individual *sector,* while a subscript r or f refers to the arrangement prevailing in the economy as a whole. For example, if the sector decides to become rigid while the rest of the economy is flexible, we can write (9.4) as $V_e^r = \frac{\bar{m} + \sigma V_{uf}}{r + \sigma}$.

Using equations (9.4) and (9.5), we see that the rigid arrangement will be preferred if

$$(r + \sigma + \gamma)\bar{m} - (r + \sigma)m_H > r\gamma V_u.$$

Substituting in the definition of $\bar{m}$, which is given by (4.19), we finally get

$$m_L > rV_u. \tag{9.6}$$

This is a remarkably simple formula which tells us that employment protection will be preferred if the productivity of low state firms is strictly greater than the alternative wage rV_u. It calls for two comments.

First, the lower the unemployed's job prospects, i.e. the lower V_u, the more likely it is that this inequality is satisfied. A more depressed economy increases the support for employment protection if it is set by individual, uncoordinated sectors. Consequently, if V_u is smaller when the rest of the economy is rigid, the incentives for individual sectors to engage in employment protection are greater, which opens the scope for multiple equilibria. If sectors were coordinating or if voting took place at the economy wide level as in Chapter 4, people would take into account that employment protection reduces V_u and multiplicity would disappear.

Second, as we saw at the end of Chapter 4, this condition is exactly the same for the discretionary social planner to want to protect that particular job. In both cases, protection occurs whenever the job's output is greater than the social value of labour. This makes sense as both the discretionary social planner and the individual sector's incumbent employees ignore the depressing impact of their decision on job creation and on V_u.

Now, the intelligent reader has already noticed that the model is incomplete, and actually needs to be changed in order to remain sensible. The missing piece is the wage formation mechanism, and it is no longer possible to assume that it is determined by (4.10), since wages must fall in an individual sector that decides to become rigid rather than flexible even though rV_u is unchanged, which cannot happen if the intratemporal rent q remains fixed. In other words, we must allow for wages to potentially differ across sectors, which is ruled out by (4.10), since the economy may end up finding itself in a situation where some sectors are rigid and others flexible. This will not occur in political equilibrium, since condition (4.6) is the same for all sectors, but since to compute that equilibrium one must know what happens if one sector changes its mind we have to allow for that.

To allow for different wages we assume that the rent q depends positively on some sector-specific labour market tightness index, a_i, which is the probability per unit of time that an unemployed worker finds a job in sector i. That is, (4.10) must be replaced by

$$w_i = rV_u + q(a_i), \qquad (9.7)$$

where subscript i refers to a sector and $q(.)$ is an increasing function. The greater a_i, the more the sector is hiring, and the higher wages in that sector. In Chapter 1 and its appendix we have discussed some models of wage formation where the rent was greater in tighter markets.

This assumption implies that in order to pay higher wages, the less protected/most productive sectors must hire more in equilibrium: the distribution of employment is biased in favour of the less protected sectors. The mechanism is simple: firms are willing to pay more for employees in these less protected sectors; they recruit more heavily up to the point where their tightness allows their workers to ask for wages exactly equal to their willingness to pay m_H. Consequently, the job finding rate will be a^r in rigid sectors, and a^f in flexible ones. We must have that $q(a^f) = m_H - rV_u > \bar{m} - rV_u = q(a^r)$, implying $a^f > a^r$. This confirms that flexible sectors hire more than rigid ones, but it also implies that the rent actually tends to be *higher* in the flexible economy, because of the feedback effects of job creation on the rent.

It follows that it is not necessarily true that V_u is greater in the flexible economy than in the rigid one, since a higher rent, given wages, reduces V_u. Intuitively, there may be multiple equilibria only if V_u is indeed smaller in the rigid economy, which will happen if the rent is not too

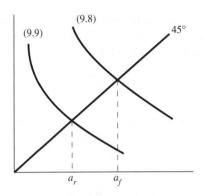

Figure 9.2. Determination of equilibrium

different across the two arrangements, i.e. if $q(.)$ is not too sensitive to a.

How do we close the model? Equations (4.20c) and (4.16b) still hold, but q has to be replaced by $q(a)$, so that they now give us an implict determination of labour market tightness in the flexible and the rigid economy. Thus we have

$$a_f = \left(\frac{m_H}{q(a_f)} - 1 \right) (r + \sigma + \gamma) \tag{9.8}$$

and

$$a_r = \left(\frac{\bar{m}}{q(a_r)} - 1 \right) (r + \sigma). \tag{9.9}$$

Determination of equilibrium is depicted in Figure 9.2. The right-hand side of (9.8) and (9.9) is decreasing in a. Hence there is a unique value of a that solves the equilibrium. As the right-hand side of (9.9) is smaller than that of (9.8), a and therefore q are larger in the flexible economy than in the flexible one.

From there one can compute V_u which is still defined by (4.18) and (4.20) which must now be rewritten as

$$V_{ur} = \frac{\bar{m} - q(a_r)}{r}$$

$$V_{uf} = \frac{m_H - q(a_f)}{r}.$$

Using these two equations and the definition of $\bar{m}$ we can get a condition for the unemployed to be worse off in the rigid economy, which implies that there may be multiple equilibria,

$$q(a_f) - q(a_r) < \frac{\gamma}{r + \sigma + \gamma}(m_H - m_L).$$

This condition is not necessarily satisfied as $q(a_f)$ is greater than $q(a_r)$. However it is the most relevant case as otherwise the unemployed would be better off in the rigid society.

9.4 Conclusion

While the rest of the book has analysed the support for rigid institutions taken separately, this chapter has examined how the existence of an institution may increase the support for another one. The case for such complementarities is reasonable, although not universal. They contribute to explaining why we observe the co-existence of different social models, where a 'model' is defined as a coherent set of mutually reinforcing institutions, whereas, at the same time, borrowing various elements from different models is unstable and politically painful. One consequence is that a comprehensive reform of the labour market will generate more political support than a piecemeal approach.

Bibliography

Acemoglu, Daron (1996), 'Technology, unemployment, and efficiency', mimeo, MIT.

Acemoglu, Daron and James Robinson (1998), 'Inefficient redistribution', mimeo, MIT.

Agell, Jonas (1999), 'On the benefits from rigid labour markets: norms, market failures, and social insurance', *Economic Journal,* 109, 143–164.

Agell, Jonas and Karl Lommerund (1992), 'Union egalitarianism as income insurance', *Economica,* 59, 295–310.

Akerlof, George 'The market for lemons: Quality uncertainty and the market mechanism', *Quarterly Journal of Economics,* 84(3), 488–500.

Alesina, Alberto (1994), 'Political models of macroeconomic policy and fiscal reforms' in Stephan Haggard *et al.,* eds. *Voting for reform: Democracy, political liberalization, and economic adjustment,* Oxford: Oxford University Press, 37–60.

Alogoskoufis, George, Charles Bean, Giuseppe Bertola, Daniel Cohen, Juan Dolado, and Gilles Saint-Paul (1995), *Unemployment: Choices for Europe,* London: CEPR.

Bean, Charles (1994a), 'European unemployment: A survey', *Journal of Economic Literature,* 32(2), 573–619.

—— (1994b), 'European unemployment: A retrospective', *European Economic Review,* 38(3–4), 532–534.

Becker, Gary (1983), 'A theory of competition among interest groups for political influence', *Quarterly Journal of Economics,* 98(3), 371–400.

—— (1985), 'Public policies, pressure groups, and dead weight costs', *Journal of Public Economics,* 28(3), 329–347.

Bentolila, Samuel and Gilles Saint-Paul (1992), 'The macroeconomic impact of flexible labor contracts' *European Economic Review*, 1013–1053.

Bernheim, Douglas and Michael Whinston (1986), 'Menu auctions, resource allocation, and economic influence', *Quarterly Journal of Economics*, 101(1), 1–31.

Bertola, Giuseppe, 'Microeconomic perspectives on aggregate labor markets', mimeo, forthcoming *Handbook of Labor Economics*.

Bertola, Giuseppe and Andrea Ichino (1995), 'Crossing the river: A comparative perspective on Italian employment dynamics', *Economic Policy*, 21, 359–415.

Blais, A., J.-M. Cousineau, and K. McRoberts (1989), 'The determinants of minimum wage rates', *Public Choice*.

Blanchard, Olivier (1996), 'How to decrease unemployment' in Mario Baldassari *et al.*, eds. *The 1990s slump: Causes and cures*, London: MacMillan, and Rome: Universita Tor Vergata, 281–291.

Blanchard, Olivier and Peter Diamond (1994), 'Ranking, unemployment duration, and wages', *Review of Economic Studies*, 61(3), 417–434.

Blanchard, Olivier and Stanley Fischer (1989), *Lectures on macroeconomics*, Cambridge, MA: MIT Press.

Blanchard, Olivier and Lawrence Summers (1986), 'Hysteresis and the European unemployment problem', *NBER Macroeconomics Annual*.

Burda, Michael 'Corporatism, labour unions and the safety net', *European Economic Review*, 41(3–5), 635–646.

Cahuc, Pierre and Philippe Michel (1996), 'Minimum wage unemployment and growth', *European Economic Review*, 40(7), 1463–1482.

Calmfors, Lars and Henrik Horn (1985), 'Classical unemployment, accomodation policies and adjustment of real wages', *Scandinavian Journal of Economics*, 87(2), 234–261.

Calmfors, Lars and John Driffill (1988), 'Centralization of wage bargaining and macroeconomic performance', *Economic Policy*, 11, 397–448.

Calmfors, Lars (1994), 'Active labour market policy and unemployment', *OECD Economic Studies*, 0(22), 7–47.

Card, David, Francis Kramarz, and Thomas Lemieux (1995), 'Changes in the relative structure of wages and employment: a comparison of the United States, Canada, and France', Princeton University Industrial Relations Section Working Paper # 355.

Coe, David and Dennis Snower (1997), 'Policy complementarities: The case for fundamental labor market reform', *IMF Staff Papers*, 44(1), 1–35.

Cukierman, Alex (1995), *Central bank strategy, credibility and independence: Theory and evidence*, Cambridge, MA: MIT Press.

Davis, Steven, John Haltiwanger, and Scott Schuh (1996), *Job Creation and Job Destruction*, Cambridge, MA: MIT Press.

de la Dehesa, Guillermo and Dennis Snower, eds. (1997), *Unemployment policy: Government options for the labour market?*, Cambridge: Cambridge University Press, 54–82.

Di Tella, Rafael and Robert MacCulloch,(1995), 'An empirical study of unemployment benefit preferences', Oxford Applied Economics Discussion Paper Series #179.

Driffill, John and Frederick van der Ploeg (1993), 'Monopoly unions and the liberalization of international trade', *Economic Journal*, 103(417), 379–385.

Fernandez, Raquel and Dani Rodrik (1991), 'Resistance to reform: Status quo bias in the presence of uncertainty', *American Economic Review*, 81(5), 1146–1155.

Frederiksson, Peter (1997), 'The political economy of public employment programmes', mimeo, Uppsala University.

Gottfries, Nils and Henrik Horn (1987), 'Wage formation and the persistence of unemployment', *Economic Journal*, 97(388), 877–884.

Gray, David M. (1995), 'All displaced workers are not created equal: The political economy of worker adjustment assistance in France', *Public Choice*, 85(3–4), 313–333.

—— (1998), 'When might a distressed firm share work? Evidence from the short-time compensation programme in France', *British Journal of Industrial Relations*, 36(1), 43–72.

Grossman, Gene and Elhanan Helpman (1994), 'Protection for sale', *American Economic Review*, 84(4), 833–850.

Grüner, H.P. (1999), 'Unemployment and labor market reform: A contract theoretic approach', IZA Discussion Paper # 49.

Guesnerie, Roger and Kevin Roberts (1987), 'Minimum wage legislation as a second best policy', *European Economic Review*, 31(1/2), 490–498.

Hassler, John and José Vicente Rodriguez Mora (1996), 'Labor market turnover and unemployment insurance', mimeo, Universitat Pompeu Fabra, Barcelona and Institute for International Economic Studies, Stockholm.

Hassler, John, José Vicente Rodriguez Mora, Kjetil Storesletten, and Fabrizio Zilibotti (1999), 'Equilibrium unemployment insurance', mimeo, Institute for International Economic Studies, Stockholm.

Kreps, David (1990), *A course in microeconomic theory*, Princeton: Princeton University Press.

Krueger, Anne (1974), 'The political economy of the rent-seeking society', *American Economic Review*, 64(3), 291–303.

Krugman, Paul (1994), 'Past and prospective causes of high unemployment', *Federal Reserve Bank of Kansas City Economic Review*, 79(4), 23–43.

Krusell, Per and Victor Rios-Rull (1996), 'Vested interests in a positive theory of stagnation and growth', *Review of Economic Studies*, 63(2), 301–329.

Layard, Richard, Stephen Nickell, and Richard Jackman (1991), *Unemployment: Macroeconomic performance and the labour market*, Oxford: Oxford University Press.

Lindbeck, Assar and Dennis Snower (1988), *The insider outsider theory of employment and unemployment*, Cambridge, MA: MIT Press.

Lipford, J. and B. Yandle (1987), 'Political dominance and state unemployment benefits', *Public Choice.*

Manning, Alan (1995), 'How do we know that real wages are too high', *Quarterly Journal of Economics,* 110(4), 1111–1125.

Meltzer, Allan and Scott Richard (1981), 'A rational theory of the size of government', *Journal of Political Economy,* 89(5), 914–927.

Mortensen, Dale and Christopher Pissaries (1994), 'Job creation and job destruction in the theory of unemployment', *Review of Economic Studies,* 61(3), 397–415.

Newell, A. and J.S.V. Symons (1987), 'Corporatism, Laissez-faire, and the rise in unemployment', *European Economic Review,* 31(3), 567–601.

OECD (1995), *Jobs study,* Paris: OECD.

Olson, Mancur (1982), *The rise and decline of nations,* New Haven, CT: Yale University Press.

Persson, Torsten, Gérard Roland, and Guido Tabellini (1997), 'Comparative politics and public finance', CEPR Discussion Paper # 1737.

Phelps, Edmund (1994), *Equilibrium unemployment theory.*

Pissarides, Christopher (1990), *Equilibrium unemployment theory,* Oxford: Blackwell.

—— (1992), 'Loss of skill during unemployment and the persistence of employment shocks', *Quarterly Journal of Economics,* 107(4), 1371–1391.

Rawls, John (1971), *Theory of justice.*

Robinson, James (1998), 'The dynamics of labor market institutions', mimeo, University of South Carolina.

Rodrik, Dani (1999), 'Democracies pay higher wages', *Quarterly Journal of Economics,* CXIV(3), 707–738.

Romer, David (1996), *Advanced macro-economics,* New York: McGraw-Hill.

Saint-Paul, Gilles (1993), 'On the political economy of labor market flexibility', *NBER Macroeconomics Annual*, 151–195.

—— (1994a), 'Unemployment, wage rigidity, and the returns to education', *European Economic Review*, 38(3/4), 535–544.

—— (1994b), 'Do labor rigidities fulfill redistributive roles? Searching for the virtues of the European model', *IMF Staff Papers*, 41(4), 624–642.

—— (1995), 'The high unemployment trap', *Quarterly Journal of Economics*, May CX(2), 527–5501.

—— (1996a), 'Unemployment and increasing returns to human capital', *Journal of public economics*, 61, 1–20.

—— (1996b), 'Labour market rigidities and the cohesion of the middle class', *International Tax and Public Finance*, 3, 385–395.

—— (1996c), 'Exploring the political economy of labour market institutions', *Economic Policy*, 23, 265–300.

—— (1996d), *Dual labor markets: A macroeconomic perspective*, Cambridge, MA: MIT Press.

—— (1997a), 'The rise and persistence of rigidities', *American Economic Review*, 87(2), 290–294.

—— (1997b), 'High unemployment from a political economy perspective', in G. de la Dehesa and D. Snower, eds. *Unemployment policy: Government options for the labour market?*, Cambridge : Cambridge University Press, 54–82.

—— (1997c), 'Economic integration, factor mobility, and wage convergence', *International Tax and Public Finance*, 4, 291–306.

—— (1997d), 'Is reforming Europe's labor markets politically feasible?', *Business in the Contemporary World*, IX(3), 593–606.

—— (1997e), 'Inégalités, rigidité salariale et pressions redistributives: vers une remise en cause du 'modèle Européen'?', *Revue Economique*, 48(5), 1165–1176.

—— (1998a), 'The political consequences of unemployment', *Swedish Economic Policy Review*, 5(2), 259–296.

—— (1998b), 'A framework for analyzing the political support for active labour market policy', *Journal of Public Economics*, 67, 151–165.

—— (1999a), 'Assessing the political viability of labor market reform: The case of employment protection', *Federal Reserve Bank of Saint-Louis Quarterly Review*, May–June, 73–88.

—— (1999b), 'The political economy of employment protection', Universitat Pompeu Fabra, mimeo.

Shapiro, Carl and Joseph E. Stiglitz (1984), 'Equilibrium unemployment as a worker discipline device', *American Economic Review,* 74(3), 433–444.

Siebert, Horst (1997), 'Labor market rigidities: At the root of unemployment in Europe', *Journal of Economic Perspectives,* 11(3), 37–54.

Silbermann, J. and G. Durden (1976), 'Determining legislative preferences on the minimum wage: An economic approach', *Journal of Political Economy.*

Teulings, Coen (1997), 'A new theory of corporatism and wage setting', *European Economic Review,* 41(3–5), 659–669.

Uri, N. and J. Mixon (1980), 'An economic analysis of the determinants of minimum wage voting behavior', *Journal of Law and Economics,* 23(1), 167–177.

Wright, Randall (1986), 'The redistributive roles of unemployment insurance and the dynamics of voting', *Journal of Public Economics,* 31(3), 377–399.

Index